CW00919836

Tennyson and the Fabrication of Englishness

Tennyson and the Fabrication of Englishness

Marion Sherwood

palgrave
macmillan

First published 2013 by
PALGRAVE MACMILLAN

Palgrave Macmillan in the UK is an imprint of Macmillan Publishers Limited,
registered in England, company number 785998, of Houndmills, Basingstoke,
Hampshire RG21 6XS.

Palgrave Macmillan in the US is a division of St Martin's Press LLC,
175 Fifth Avenue, New York, NY 10010.

Palgrave Macmillan is the global academic imprint of the above companies
and has companies and representatives throughout the world.

Palgrave® and Macmillan® are registered trademarks in the United States,
the United Kingdom, Europe and other countries.

ISBN 978–1–137–28889–9

This book is printed on paper suitable for recycling and made from fully
managed and sustained forest sources. Logging, pulping and manufacturing
processes are expected to conform to the environmental regulations of the
country of origin.

A catalogue record for this book is available from the British Library.

A catalog record for this book is available from the Library of Congress.

10   9   8   7   6   5   4   3   2   1
22 21 20 19 18 17 16 15 14 13

Printed and bound in Great Britain by
CPI Antony Rowe, Chippenham and Eastbourne

Contents

Acknowledgements

I would like to thank Paula Kennedy, Ben Doyle and Christine Ranft at Palgrave Macmillan for guiding my Tennyson project towards publication, and Rebecca Stott for continuing support and encouragement. I first encountered Englishness as a subject for study in the final presentation year of an Open University course on 'Arts and Society in 1930s Britain', then in a thought-provoking course on 'Literature in the Modern World'. But my interest in Englishness had its origins closer to home, in the life story of my late husband, who came to England at the age of sixteen as a refugee from Naziism and had to create a new – English – identity. This book is therefore dedicated to the memory of Heinz Sherwood, né Schapira (Vienna 1923–London 1985).

A Note on the Text

The following works are referred to frequently; the titles are therefore abbreviated:

Hallam Tennyson, *Alfred Lord Tennyson: A Memoir, By His Son*, 2 vols (London: Macmillan, 1897) – abbreviated to *Memoir, 1897*

The Letters of Alfred Lord Tennyson, ed. Cecil Y. Lang and Edgar F. Shannon, Jr, 3 vols (Oxford: Clarendon Press, 1982–90) – abbreviated to *AT Letters*

The Poems of Tennyson, ed. Christopher Ricks, 2nd edn, 3 vols (London: Longman, 1987) – abbreviated to *Poems*

Tennyson: A Selected Edition, ed. Christopher Ricks, 2nd edn (London: Longman, 1989) – abbreviated to *Selected Edition*

For references and bibliography I have followed the guidelines of the *MHRA Style Guide* (2002). When referring to nineteenth-century reviews of Tennyson's poems, I have modernized book titles and capitalization. When the author of an unsigned review is known, the name is placed in square brackets. The titles of long poems are italicized; the titles of short poems are in single quotation marks. I am grateful to Dr Valerie Purton, editor of the *Tennyson Research Bulletin*, for permission to reprint part of Chapter 2, which was published as an article on 'The Reception of *Poems* (1832)' in 2005, and to Dr Mike Rogers, of Lincolnshire County Council's Lincolnshire Archives, for the jacket image of Somersby Rectory, the 'cradle' of Tennyson's Englishness.

Introduction: The Enigma of Englishness

Critics and reviewers identified Tennyson as an English poet from the first reviews of his published poems. Early critics discerned in his work a 'desire to imitate the old English lyrical poets',[1] hailed him as successor to 'the great generation of poets which is now passing away',[2] and considered the poet's influence on 'national feelings and character'.[3] A kindly review of *Poems by Two Brothers* (1827) welcomed 'a graceful addition to our domestic poetry'.[4] In this study I examine Tennyson's 'domestic poetry' – his portrayals of English nature and landscape, the monarchy, medievalism and the 'English Empire',[5] written throughout his career and in their changing nineteenth-century context – to consider whether Tennyson's representations of England and the English were idealized portrayals, hence fabrications, and to consider whether and in what ways his representations reflected, shaped or subverted, established or emerging ideas of Englishness in the nineteenth century.

Tennyson's life and work spanned much of the nineteenth century; accordingly his poetry provides a unique insight into many evolving ideas and preoccupations of the Victorian age. He was first published as Reform Bill agitation raised questions of national identity, and critics of the early volumes sought to define Tennyson's role and responsibilities as a national poet. As Poet Laureate he became the public voice of English poetry – and one of the 'thinking men of England'[6] – and remained popular and influential for many years. His final poems, addressing the monarchy and the 'English Empire', were written only months before his death in 1892. Tennyson responded to and reacted against many of the nineteenth century's events, movements and figures and his ideas about England and the English changed with time. His portrayals were both descriptive and subtly or more overtly prescriptive, at times

1

attempting to 'raise the people and chastise the times'.[7] However, as T.S. Eliot observed – and later critics concurred – Tennyson was 'the most instinctive rebel against the society in which he was the most perfect conformist'[8] and the poems and their publication history betray doubts and ambivalences which suggest that the poet was willing to question not only his own conservatism but also 'the Victorian status quo he had come to represent'.[9]

A study of Tennyson and Englishness is timely. All enduring poetry is reread and reinterpreted and the twenty-first century is recovering Tennyson, a rediscovery aided by the 2009 bicentenary of the poet's birth, the publication of bicentennial essays and a recent biography[10] – and the choice of 'Ulysses' to provide the 2012 Olympic motto: 'To strive, to seek, to find, and not to yield'. The bicentenary of the birth of Tennyson's friend and inspiration, Arthur Henry Hallam, was celebrated in 2011. The 2012 Diamond Jubilee renewed interest in the monarchy. With a planned Scottish referendum, the question of Englishness/Britishness is the subject of continuing debate, and London 2012 raised the question of 'plastic' Britishness for naturalized British athletes born outside the United Kingdom. Recently published histories of England and the Empire by Simon Jenkins, Peter Ackroyd and Jeremy Paxman, and Roy Strong's Arcadian *Visions of England*,[11] confirm that themes which preoccupied Tennyson – including English landscape and identity, Empire and monarchy – are of lasting interest.

Texts exist in contexts.[12] Tennyson's poems are inseparable from his times: even in medieval disguise, Tennyson's protagonists are nineteenth-century English men and women. My approach to Tennyson is therefore historically sensitive, and although not overtly theoretical is indebted to gender theory for discussion of his idealized women and chivalric gentlemen and to postcolonial criticism for consideration of his 'English Empire'. As well as a historical approach I follow a generally chronological path – and cover the whole life's work – which reveals the changes and continuities obscured by studies with a narrower focus and illuminates with greater clarity developing ideas of Englishness in the nineteenth century. Examining in context Tennyson's poems of monarchy from accession to jubilee, for example, makes apparent not only the transformation in poetic form and tone between 'The Queen of the Isles' (1837) and *Carmen Saeculare* (1887) but also the differing forms of radical and republican dissent which continued to coexist with public reverence for royalty throughout Victoria's long reign. Each chapter is therefore chronological in structure and the study as a whole has an overarching chronology which spans the decades from the publication of *Poems by Two Brothers* (1827) to the final poem of monarchy – 'The Death of the Duke of Clarence and Avondale' (1892) – published eight months before the poet's death.

I have chosen the term *fabrication* in preference to the more usual *construction* for several reasons. The association of *fabrication* and weaving is particularly appropriate to the multiple strands of Tennyson's poetry and the poet's belief that 'Poetry is like shot-silk with many glancing colours',[13] open to the interpretation of individual readers. It is pertinent to this study, in which I interweave poems, letters and context with contemporary and more recent critical views. It also suggests the complexity of textuality and elements of fantasy or falsehood. Such definitions may be applied to Tennyson's often unsuccessful attempts to attribute Victoria and Albert's admired chivalric virtues to their descendants, or to the poet's domestic idyl/ls – with idealized women placed in 'genial'[14] English landscapes from which the rural poor are largely absent – that represent in microcosm Tennyson's ideally ordered world. Above all, I use the term *fabrication* as a reminder that ideas of national character are not given, but are fabricated for particular ideological reasons in particular cultural conditions.

The term *Englishness* predates Tennyson by only five years. Defined as 'the quality or state of being English or of embodying English characteristics',[15] *Englishness* was first used in a letter dated 6 July 1804 to Robert Southey from William Taylor, author and translator, who 'vouche[d] for the Englishness of several fairy-tales supposed to be French.'[16] Taylor appears to recast the late-twelfth-century Anglo-Norman legal term *Englishry*, used from 1439 to refer to 'that part of the population in Ireland that is of English descent', from 1603 to define English-speaking areas of Wales, and only from 1856 as a collective noun for English people.[17] *Englishness* was next used in the *New Monthly Magazine and Humorist* in 1838, when the anonymous author of a drily humorous essay on 'The Decencies' refers to 'the Englishness of everything about man, woman, and child born in the island, as embracing in one epithet a monopoly of all kinds of merit'.[18] The author notes universal praise for 'the courage of Englishmen' and 'the chastity of Englishwomen', perceived national characteristics which recur in Tennyson's poems throughout his career. By 1884 – the last recorded nineteenth-century use of the term – a reviewer regards *Englishness* as instantly recognizable, commenting that the 'attraction' of an exhibited portrait of 'Lord George Seymour . . . lies in its Englishness'.[19] Tennyson's writings give us a unique perspective on this period of history and demonstrate the role of poetry in producing and embedding such ideologies.

Tennyson left no theoretical writings on poetics or nationhood. The poet's views on England and the English must therefore be interpreted from his poems and letters, and from selected primary and secondary sources. In this study I also refer to the letters, writings and reviews of the poet's contemporaries, and examine the work of twentieth- and twenty-first-century critics, biographers and historians who clarify aspects of nineteenth-century Englishness, including history and character, language and landscape, monarchy, chivalry, class and gender, empire and race. The most valuable primary source is, of course, Tennyson's poetry. Tennyson's Englishness is not only exemplified by his overtly patriotic verse – or by poetic protagonists who embody the 'lofty examples' Gladstone considered necessary for the English 'race'[20] – but also subtly enhanced by poetic form and diction. He used the English popular ballad form to 'raise the people', and blank verse, with its subliminal Shakespearean echoes, for the 'English Idyls' and *Idylls of the King*. Additional insight can be gained from the poet's correspondence: a rare reference to 'we Englanders' in December 1846 regrets that 'our manners are as cold as the walls of our churches'.[21] The enduring interest in etymology Tennyson shared with Richard Chenevix Trench[22] and their fellow Cambridge 'Apostles' is encapsulated in his use of the seventeenth-century term *Englanders*. As Hallam Tennyson later confirmed, if Tennyson 'differentiated his style from that of any other poet, he would remark on his use of English – in preference to words derived from French and Latin', adding that he 'revived many fine old words which had fallen into disuse'.[23]

Englishness was a nineteenth-century term and a continuing nineteenth-century concern. Important primary sources are the writings of contemporary commentators on *England and the English*,[24] many of whom emulate Nassau Senior by 'using the word England as a concise appellation for the nation inhabiting the British islands'.[25] English and visiting observers reflected on national institutions and character – finding in each, as the *New Monthly Magazine* suggested, 'all kinds of merit'. *The Sketch Book*, written and published in England by the American author Washington Irving in 1819–20, included *vignettes* of English life and landscape;[26] his compatriot Ralph Waldo Emerson's observations on *English Traits* followed in 1856.[27] Emerson was drawn to England by 'the moral peculiarity of the Saxon race [and] its commanding sense of right and wrong',[28] while the anonymous author of 'The Decencies' emphasized 'that most English of all English virtues – English decency'.[29] Feminine virtues occupied a separate domestic sphere which exemplified Englishness for Sarah Stickney Ellis, who praised 'the domestic character of England – the home comforts, and fireside virtues for which she is so justly celebrated'.[30] Walter Bagehot analysed *The English Constitution* (1867), the functioning of parliament and the monarchy, noting approvingly that the 'mass of the English people' are both 'politically contented' and 'politically deferential', as a 'deferential community . . . is more suited to political excellence'.[31]

The history and nature of England and the English are enduring concerns which intensify at particular times. The current debate on Englishness perhaps began, Norman Davies suggests, with George Orwell's essays on the English, written during and soon after World War II.[32] Discussion intensified in the 1980s and 1990s – responding, Peter Mandler argues, to 'apparently relentless globalizing, Americanizing or Europeanizing forces'[33] – and in recent years there has been an outpouring of new publications in the field of national history and identity. Some historians take the long view. Robert Colls, for example, looks back to 'the origins of the English nation in the laws and territories and language of the Anglo-Saxon kingdoms';[34] Norman Davies's epic history of *The Isles* surveys the centuries from 600 BC to 1999. Countering claims that 'English national consciousness' flourished as early as the eighth century, Krishan Kumar argues that 'a clear concern with questions of "Englishness" and English national identity' is not found until 'the late nineteenth century'.[35] Of particular interest to this study are critiques and histories which focus on significant 'moment[s] of Englishness'[36] in the nineteenth century and thus illuminate the changing context of Tennyson's 'domestic poetry'. While observing that nations 'are always being made', Catherine Hall shares Kumar's view that particular defining 'moments' can be used to consider 'the state of the nation'.[37] With the 1832 Reform Act – a key moment of legislative change – the parliamentary franchise was extended and the political citizen 'formally named as masculine'. The 'masculine' franchise was extended again in 1867 and 1884, but 'the first organised petition to Parliament for the enfranchisement of women' (excluded from Walter Bagehot's 'politically contented' community) was not presented until 1866.[38] In 1837 'Victoria' was welcomed as 'Queen of England'[39] for her supposedly reforming tendencies and in the hope of restoring the monarchy's reputation. During her reign – and despite her self-imposed seclusion following the death of Albert in 1861 – Victoria 'became identified as an embodiment of England' and England became 'a royalist nation'.[40] The public writings and occasions which both contributed to and challenged this emblematic Englishness are examined by Richard Williams.[41]

To unravel 'the enigma of Englishness' it is necessary, Krishan Kumar believes, to explore England's historic engagement with its near and distant neighbours.[42] In the 1820s and early 1830s, awareness of national identity – both English and Other – was enhanced by movements for parliamentary reform and the abolition of slavery. In the mid-nineteenth century, perceptions of the 'English Empire' were shaken by the uprising known to contemporaries as the 'Indian Mutiny' (1857–59) and the Morant Bay Rebellion in Jamaica (1865), events which were sensationally and often inaccurately reported in the press and divided the 'thinking men of England'. Kumar discerns a significant 'moment of Englishness' in the late nineteenth century, responding to 'a sense of the possible decline of empire'. During the decades, Tennyson's early ambivalent view of the Empire had changed: he responded to 'the possible decline of empire' with an impassioned defence of 'ever-broadening England, and her throne | In our vast Orient'.[43] Ultimately, therefore, the poems of empire confirm that Laureate Tennyson was willing to question, but not to condemn, the Victorian status quo he had come to represent.

This is an 'ever-broadening' study. It begins with two brief reviews of *Poems by Two Brothers* and concludes with an extended exploration of 'Tennyson and Empire'. A study of Tennyson as an English poet should begin with contemporary critics' response – the reviews printed in newspapers, magazines and journals – as they encountered the poems for the first time. Chapter 1 places in context the publication and reception of Tennyson's earliest volumes and poems. His contributions to *Poems by Two Brothers* (1827) draw on the English literary past. As the reviewers recognize, Tennyson is a 'domestic' poet but not yet an original English poet. With *Timbuctoo* (1829), Tennyson won the Cambridge Chancellor's Gold Medal for English Verse. The poem links Establishment England with nineteenth-century colonial expansion; the reviewer hails Tennyson as heir to the passing generation of great English poets and anticipates later critics' concern with the nature and role of poetry and the poet. *Poems, Chiefly Lyrical* (1830), published in turbulent times, brought Tennyson early recognition as a true poet and influential critiques in which William Johnson Fox, Arthur Henry Hallam and John Wilson ('Christopher North') define their differing views of the poet's responsible national role. Chapter 2 examines the critical reception, context and contents of *Poems* (1832). Reviewers' growing concern with poetic language mirrors contemporary interest in etymology, increasingly inseparable from interest in national character. The content and effect of three influential and contrasting critiques are discussed. John Wilson attacks Tennyson as a radical and 'Cockney' poet of humble origin; William Johnson Fox and John Stuart Mill argue that Tennyson should use his powerful gifts to raise society to its potential perfection. The poems selected – and rejected – by reviewers foreshadow the idealized and exemplary portrayals of England and the English to be considered in the following, theme-based chapters of the study.

In Chapter 3 I trace the troubled progress towards publication of the two-volume *Poems* (1842), which established Tennyson as the foremost poet of his generation. The volumes were favourably reviewed in a wide range of periodicals, intended for all levels of society, and critics comment approvingly on the poet's 'keen eye for the beauties of nature'.[44] The poems declare and demonstrate Tennyson's 'manifesto' – that future inspiration will be drawn from 'Memory' of the English landscape. I consider Tennyson's creation of a uniquely English idyl/l and his differing depictions of English nature and landscape to conclude that in *Poems*, published in the Hungry Forties, Tennyson fabricates a myth of rural Englishness which ignores the contemporary reality of rural deprivation and depopulation. His exemplary figures, set in an idealized pre-industrial landscape, represent an England that is more imaginary than real. However, Tennyson's representations of Englishness are complex and often conflicting fabrications, betraying ideological and personal faultlines. Poetic imagery and the volumes' delayed publication suggest that Tennyson was neither wholly committed to republishing nor to a rural ideology. In Chapter 4 I examine in context the poems of monarchy, written to mark or mourn royal events during more than five decades of Victoria's reign. The contrast in content and form between the rapidly written accession ballad (1837) and the consciously classical jubilee ode (1887) exemplifies the linear progression of Tennyson's allegiance to the institution of monarchy, and to Victoria herself as she progressed from young royal motherhood to imperial matriarchy. The poems of monarchy influence contemporary perceptions of gender, enhance domestic ideology, and both mirror and perpetuate the veneration of monarchy which increased during Victoria's long reign. The coexisting, often intense criticism of the monarchy, which had been apparent since the accession, is not reflected in the poems. The unified England Tennyson portrays is thus a fabrication – an invented and exemplary realm – to be encouraged at times of depression, division or debate.

Chapter 5 studies Tennyson's response to England's Medieval Revival, defined as a powerful imaginative force inseparable from nineteenth-century thought and touching all levels of society. Tennyson's preoccupation with aspects of medievalism changed with time. Through fabrications – imaginative and often idealized representations – of the medieval past, the poet explores contemporary concern with religion and monarchical authority; he examines gender roles, relations and conduct, and celebrates the chivalric 'Godlike men'[45] of past and present distinguished by their courage and Englishness. Medievalist poems reflect the poet's public role, and his personal loss, and are inseparable from the upper classes. In *Idylls of the King*, written and published from the 1830s to the 1880s, Tennyson re-imagines Arthurian literature and medieval ideals to create a not wholly exemplary 'model for the mighty world'.[46] Chapter 6 explores Tennyson's poetic representations of and written and verbal references to empire, predominantly 'our English Empire', its peoples and critical historic moments such as the uprisings in India (1857–59) and Jamaica (1865). I trace Tennyson's changing attitude to the Empire from the ambivalence of the early 1830s to the Laureate's defence of 'ever-broadening England' (1873). The expanding Empire increased awareness of national identity and I examine Tennyson's representations of – and contemporary responses to – Otherness, including the development of 'race science'. Poetic portrayals range from the sympathetic, ballad-like 'Anacaona' (1830) to the complex, conflicted but ultimately discriminatory depictions of Indian soldiers within and without the 'Lucknow' garrison (1879), an uprising which demonstrates that imperial unity is a fabrication or fantasy inseparable from Laureate Tennyson's imperial vision. 'Akbar's Dream' (1892), published only months before the poet's death, reveals a new appreciation of Moghul religion and culture, but Christianity and the Raj finally prevail. The poems of empire also confirm that by 1892 the ennobled Poet Laureate had come to occupy – in both senses of the term – an 'imperial position in Poetry'.[47] However, Tennyson's pro-imperial position was attained at the end of a long career. The first question to be considered is how the young poet was received by contemporary reviewers when *Poems by Two Brothers* was published in April 1827.

1
'A Poet in the Truest and Highest Sense': The Early Poems and their Reception

Alfred Tennyson became a published poet at the age of seventeen, when *Poems by Two Brothers* was issued by the booksellers J. and J. Jackson, of Louth in Lincolnshire, in April 1827. From his first published volume Tennyson was reviewed in the periodical press and by January 1833 he was 'admitted on all hands to be a true poet'.[1] Tennyson's early poetry – *Poems by Two Brothers* (1827), *Timbuctoo* (1829), *Poems, Chiefly Lyrical* (1830) and *Poems* (1832) – appeared in turbulent times. Revolutions were taking place in many Continental countries and states; in England, transformed by industry, there were 'Swing' uprisings and agitation for electoral reform, concerns for the royal succession and for the future of poetry. In Chapters 1 and 2 I examine how critics of the early poems attempted to define and shape Tennyson as an English poet in the context of contemporary concerns, and consider the ways in which poems selected or rejected by reviewers reflect changing notions of nineteenth-century Englishness. Twentieth-century critics argue that *Poems, Chiefly Lyrical* 'immediately raised nearly all the problems which were to preoccupy critics during the next four decades'.[2] However, contemporary critics' concerns are foreshadowed in the earlier reviews of *Poems by Two Brothers* and *Timbuctoo*, which are also considered in this chapter. The reception of *Poems* (1832) is examined in Chapter 2.

Poems by Two Brothers

The 1827 volume was published anonymously, at the Tennyson brothers' request.[3] It was distributed by Simpkin and Marshall, a London wholesale distributing agent with Lincolnshire connections, and offered for sale at five shillings, with large paper copies seven shillings. It is not

9

known how many copies were printed, or sold, but in 1870 'a considerable stock of remainders, both bound and unbound' was discovered in the printer's warehouse.[4] Publication was therefore perhaps an act of friendship rather than practical business sense: Elizabeth Tennyson, the poet's mother, was the daughter of a Louth vicar, and while a reluctant pupil at Louth Grammar School Tennyson 'wrote an English poem . . . for one of the Jacksons'.[5] *Poems by Two Brothers* – which despite its title contained poems by three brothers, with Frederick contributing three and Alfred and Charles about fifty each – was advertised in two local newspapers and a French literary journal.[6] The volume brought the brothers twenty pounds in cash and books from J. and J. Jackson[7] and two anonymous reviews in London periodicals.

The reception of *Poems by Two Brothers* is mentioned only in passing by twentieth-century critics and biographers,[8] but the reviewers' remarks anticipate aspects of later criticism of Tennyson's work and are thus worthy of examination. The *Literary Chronicle and Weekly Review* published on 19 May 1827 (which gives the volume's publication date as 1820) selects for 'Review . . . All New Publications of Value and Interest', perhaps not wholly impartially as one of the *Chronicle*'s London distributors was Simpkin and Marshall. In a brief notice the reviewer declares: 'This little volume exhibits a pleasing union of kindred tastes, and contains several little pieces of considerable merit'. 'Stanzas' and 'God's Denunciations Against Pharaoh-Hophra, or Apries', by Charles and Alfred respectively, are thought 'deserving of extract'.[9]

A longer and more significant notice appeared in the *Gentleman's Magazine* for June 1827, among the 'Review[s] of New Publications'. Like many publications which printed reviews of Tennyson's poems, the *Gentleman's Magazine*, founded in January 1731 by Edward Cave, a London printer and publisher, and published continuously until September 1907, was a literary miscellany or 'monthly collection', designed 'to treasure up, as in a magazine' – in the sense of an arsenal or storehouse – 'the most remarkable pieces'.[10] Edited by 'Sylvanus Urban, Gent', the pseudonym adopted by Cave and used by editors throughout the publication's life,[11] the *Magazine* began by reprinting material collected from journals and newspapers throughout the country, but after 1739 increasingly commissioned its own essays, articles and reviews. Late-eighteenth- and early-nineteenth-century periodicals were priced beyond the reach of most buyers (the *Literary Chronicle* cost one shilling and the *Gentleman's Magazine* one shilling and sixpence) and the *Gentleman's Magazine* – its title reflecting a socially divided, patriarchal society – was, as the editorial pseudonym suggests, 'distinctly intended for the drawing-room in town and country'.[12] However, the *Magazine*, published in an unusual, pocket-sized format, was an instant success; in 1746, when the population of England was between six and seven million, it had a circulation of 3000 and by 1797 this had increased to 4550.[13] A wider readership was reached through the periodical's presence in eighteenth-century coffee houses – a masculine domain – and later in subscription reading rooms and libraries.

The *Gentleman's Magazine* review of *Poems by Two Brothers* anticipates the language, methods and concerns of Tennyson's later critics. Nineteenth-century reviewers were well-educated and well-read men, but not exclusively literary critics. Poetry was discussed in its social and cultural context and discussion could be wide-ranging. As Isobel Armstrong observes, reviewers' vocabulary, whether approving or condemnatory, was evaluative rather than specialized, emphasizing poetry's *'effect on the reader'*.[14] The *Magazine* reviewer begins by rejecting Dr Johnson's remark that 'no book was ever spared in tenderness to its Author'.[15] He believes 'occasion and circumstances' have often mitigated or reversed 'the censure of criticism', and praises the poems for their 'amiable feelings' – a frequently used term of critical approval – 'expressed for the most part with elegance and correctness'. Comparison was a popular nineteenth-century critical approach and the Tennyson brothers are associated by comparison with Byron, Crabbe and Moore, regarded as 'the only true poets among the moderns'.[16] The brothers are also seen by the reviewer as set apart from 'the larger class of mankind', who 'have barely reached the elements of thought', a view which anticipates Arthur Henry Hallam's belief in the immovably strong barrier between poets and 'the large majority of readers' unable to understand the poet's mind.[17] Rather than complain that the poems lack Byron's 'deep feelings', Moore's 'polished grace', or 'the perfect mastery of human passions which distinguishes Crabbe', the *Magazine* critic prefers to express surprise and admiration that, despite their youth, the Tennyson brothers share 'so much of good feeling', so poetically expressed.

The reviewer's benign conclusion – that 'the volume is a graceful addition to our domestic poetry, and does credit to the juvenile Adelphi' – suggests that *Poems by Two Brothers*, like the *Gentleman's Magazine*, is destined for the urban and rural drawing-room. However, if the term *domestic* is considered in its broader dictionary definition – 'pertaining to one's home country or nation' – the comment appears remarkably prescient. As the later chapters of this study demonstrate, Tennyson became increasingly preoccupied with the contemporary condition of England, its people and landscape, the monarchy and 'our English Empire' ('Hands All Round', 1882, 14).

Despite a lifelong hypersensitivity to hostile criticism, already apparent in poems and letters,[18] Tennyson's first submission 'to the microscopic eye of periodical criticism' ('Advertisement' or Preface) was well received, with the *Gentleman's Magazine* fortuitously suggesting, rather than shaping, his future role. However, nothing from *Poems by Two Brothers* was ever reprinted by Tennyson, who in later years 'could hardly tolerate what he called his "early rot"'.[19] His contributions to the published volume, later described as 'almost all exercises in the fashionable styles of the day',[20] are certainly less original than much of his early work. 'I dare not write an Ode', for example, a mock ode written in 1827 but not printed until 1965,[21] explores with wry – and rare – humour the lack of originality he believed inevitable because 'all the big things had been done'.[22] The 'Ode' and other early poems were deliberately omitted from the volume, probably by the Jacksons, as 'being too much out of the common for the public taste'.[23]

Poems by Two Brothers nevertheless remains, with the early reviews, 'of Value and Interest' as the *Literary Chronicle* suggests. The volume reflects the Englishness of class and gender suggested by the title *Gentleman's Magazine*, while Tennyson's contributions to the volume introduce themes which become lifelong concerns and reveal his youthful admiration for English poets, particularly Byron. At Louth and Somersby Tennyson received the classical education which 'in England . . . was the sign of a gentleman'[24] and the influence of Dr Tennyson's teaching, and the Rectory's extensive library, is immediately apparent from the volume. The Englishness of the nineteenth-century gentleman is exemplified by the practice of classical allusion – and embodied by the pseudonymous editor, 'Sylvanus Urban'. A Latin epigram on the title page states, with classically conventional poetic humility, 'we know these works of ours are worthless'[25] and, following the fashion of the day, literary epigraphs from classical and 'domestic' poetry and prose preface many poems. An apologetic 'Advertisement', or Preface, acknowledges the poets' youth and the lack of originality intimated by the Byronic declaration, 'we have passed the Rubicon'.[26] The 'Advertisement' warns that 'investigation' of the poems would reveal 'a long list of . . . imitations', and epigraphs and imagery reveal the influence of poets from Virgil to Byron. Later prose inspirations include contemporary fiction, of which all the Tennysons were avid readers, and eighteenth-century aesthetics. The speaker of 'On Sublimity' yearns for 'the wild cascade, the rugged scene, | The loud surge bursting o'er the purple sea', rejecting the 'vales in tenderest green,| The poplar's shade' (1–4) reminiscent of Tennyson's native Lincolnshire landscape, whose images recur throughout his later work. Ancient and eighteenth-century histories and travel narratives provide exotic, Other locations for 'Persia', 'Hindostan', and the Peruvians' 'Lamentation' for the destruction of their 'state' and 'strength' (2), which reveals a hostility to the depredations of Catholic Spanish imperial 'conquest' (7) still apparent in 'Columbus' published in 1880.

Tennyson draws constantly on the English literary past. Despite earlier denials, his published 'effusions' contain a great deal of what he described as 'Miltonic, Byronic . . . , Moorish, Crabbick, Coleridgick etc. fire'.[27] A Byronic sense of physical and emotional desolation pervades the poems, although this may reflect Tennyson's own emotional state at the time. (The domestic situation at Somersby Rectory was far from tranquil.[28]) Destroying hordes descend, like Byron's Assyrians, 'with wheels like a whirlwind, and chariots of fire!' ('God's Denunciations', 20) and – foreshadowing his enduring concern with English political freedom – Tennyson echoes Byron and Felicia Hemans's 'Exhortation to the Greeks' to rise and reclaim their ancient liberty.[29] Outcast speakers 'wander in darkness and sorrow' throughout the poems, but overpunctuated and relentless rhyme often results in bathos:

> In this waste of existence, for solace,
> On whom shall my lone spirit call?
> Shall I fly to the friends of my bosom?
> My God! I have buried them all!

> (25–9)

Tennyson's 'passion for the past' was noted as early as July 1831 by Arthur Henry Hallam,[30] the friend he buried in 1833 but whose influence endured until Tennyson's own death in 1892. The importance of 'Memory' in recapturing 'Thoughts of years gone by' (6) is already a recurring theme in the early volume, in which images of blighted nature also evoke English poets – 'In every rose of life, | Alas there lies a canker' (27–8). Looking back on 'Days of youth, now shaded | By twilight of long years' (9–10) is an unconvincing viewpoint for an adolescent poet; Tennyson therefore adopts the persona of age for venerable speakers with literary origins, such as 'Antony to Cleopatra', who prefigure the dramatic monologues, ballads and idyl/ls of later years. As the *Gentleman's Magazine* reviewer suggests, in 1827 Tennyson is a 'domestic' poet, but he is not yet an original English poet. In subsequent poems and volumes – and as reviewers increasingly recognize – Tennyson has the poetic maturity to 'steal . . . fire, | From the fountains of the past, | To glorify the present' ('Ode to Memory', 1830, 1–3) and, through original and exemplary representations of the classical, Elizabethan or medieval past, to interrogate and idealize nineteenth-century England.

Timbuctoo

The early volume's 'Advertisement', or Preface, was followed by an 'Introductory Poem' which begins: "Tis sweet to lead from stage to stage, | Like infancy to a maturer age'. The next 'stage' of Tennyson's poetic development took place at Cambridge. In November 1827 Tennyson followed his brothers Frederick and Charles to Cambridge University, which at that time exemplified the underpinning of Establishment Englishness by gender, class and religion; a masculine stronghold, with 'barriers of social rank' at every level of life including the three principal types of degree – Honours, Ordinary or Pass, and the Honorary Degree open only to 'noblemen and "fellow-commoners" who could prove their noble descent'.[31] Undergraduate studies were centred on classics and mathematics, daily chapel attendance was compulsory, and examinations largely involved repeating factual material. Tennyson entered Trinity, 'the most self-consciously grand' of Cambridge colleges,[32] and poems and letters reflect his initial unhappiness: 'what time my spirit was cold | And frozen at the fountain, my cheek white | As my own hope's quenched ashes' ('Playfellow Winds', 1828, 3–4).[33] However, in June 1829 Tennyson's prize poem *Timbuctoo* won the Chancellor's Medal for English Verse and the poem's success established him at Cambridge, leading to his election to the 'Apostles' (an informal essay and debating society, the Cambridge Conversazione Society, which 'existed to remedy a fault of our University education'[34]) and the intense friendship with Arthur Henry Hallam. Tennyson's name was printed with the poem in *Prolusiones Academicae* for 1829, the *Cambridge Chronicle and Journal and Huntingdonshire Gazette* published on 10 July 1829 and the *Classical Journal* for September 1829.[35] At Tennyson's request *Timbuctoo* was also included in collections of 'the Cambridge Prize Poems', even though he wrote dismissively to the publisher that 'Prize Poems . . . are not properly speak "Poems" at all and ought to be forgotten as soon as recited'.[36]

Tennyson's prize poem – recited by Charles Merivale, because of Tennyson's 'horror of publicity'[37] – was rapturously received by his Cambridge contemporaries. Hallam considered Tennyson 'as promising fair to be the greatest poet of our generation, perhaps of our century' and admired 'the splendid imaginative power' he could not emulate.[38] (Modern critics agree that Hallam's own prize poem is 'laboured and derivative'[39] and despite its Wordsworthian epigraph Hallam's *Timbuctoo* does not reflect 'a vision of our own'.[40]) Charles Wordsworth wrote to his brother Christopher, Master of Trinity College, 'if it had come out with Lord Byron's name, it would have been thought as fine as anything he ever wrote',[41] and Richard Monckton Milnes reported to his father than 'Tennyson's poem has made quite a sensation; it is certainly equal to most parts of Milton'.[42] Milnes is believed to be the author of an admiring notice in the *Athenaeum*, published in London on 22 July 1829.[43] The review, exemplifying the Apostles' high regard for Tennyson and wish to bring his work to a wider public, anticipates the critical debate on the future of poetry and the poetic succession which intensified when *Poems, Chiefly Lyrical* was published the following year.

Concern that the age was inimical to poetry had deepened during the 1820s. In 1819 Peacock satirized poetry's 'second childhood'; Macaulay concluded in 1825 that 'as civilization advances, poetry almost necessarily declines', and Carlyle in June 1829 declared that 'the Age of Machinery' had reduced poetry to 'a product of the smaller intestines'.[44] The decade also saw the deaths of Keats, Shelley and Byron; by 1830 Crabbe had only two more years to live and Wordsworth, as Bernard Richards remarks, was for many 'in a state . . . of living death'.[45] However, anticipating William Johnson Fox, who argued in 1831 that the age was not unpoetical, the *Athenaeum* reviewer regards as unfounded – held 'without any very good reason' – the belief that poetry is in decline, 'likely to perish among us for a considerable period after the great generation of poets which is now passing away'.[46] 'The age', he asserts, has unexpectedly refuted this belief, for 'it has put forth' a young man's prize poem, the imagery implying that Tennyson is the great poets' natural successor. Prize poems, the reviewer continues, 'have often been ingenious and elegant', but none has ever 'indicated really first-rate poetical genius' which 'would have done honour to any man that ever wrote'. The *Athenaeum* reviewer unhesitatingly affirms, with the examiners, that *Timbuctoo* is such a work and 'extract[s] a few lines' to justify his admiration. 'How many men have lived for a century', he asks rhetorically, 'who could equal this?'

Two years after *Poems by Two Brothers* had been welcomed as 'a graceful addition to our domestic poetry' Tennyson is hailed as its saviour, a potential heir to the passing generation of great poets, and equal to Byron and much of Milton. The *Athenaeum* reviewer regards and presents

Tennyson as an English poet and acknowledges his 'poetical genius'. Tennyson had entered the competition reluctantly and perhaps not seriously (the previous year he had failed to complete a prize poem on 'The Invasion of Russia by Napoleon Buonaparte'); he wrote in blank verse rather than the customary 'rhymed heroics'[47] and later spoke of 'turning' an 'old poem on "Armageddon" into "Timbuctoo" by a little alteration of the beginning and the end'.[48] However, *Timbuctoo* not only reflects a serious and recurring concern with 'The Poet's Mind' – exemplified by the Miltonic vision at the heart of both *Timbuctoo* and *Armageddon*, written when Tennyson was fifteen – but also heralds Laureate Tennyson's imperial views.

For *Armageddon* to become *Timbuctoo* required more than the 'little alteration' Tennyson suggested. He created a new beginning and ending, made significant changes to the central vision, removed all reference to religion and turned the speaker to face southwards, overlooking 'Wide Afric' (*Timbuctoo*, 57) rather than 'The valley of Megiddo' (*Armageddon*, 25). But as in Tennyson's contributions to *Poems by Two Brothers* the location is imprecise and Other, with 'Afric' distanced 'from green Europe' (*Timbuctoo*, 3) and the setting influenced by legend and the eighteenth- and early-nineteenth-century travel books by European writers which, Mary Louise Pratt argues, produced 'the rest of the world' for European readers.[49] 'Turning' the speaker transforms the prospect of a Biblical battle into a vision of Timbuctoo – and a Romantic view of poetry, as the 'fair City' (244) represents 'the Unattainable' (193) ultimately achievable through the transforming power of poetic imagination. This power is 'given' by 'the Spirit . . . of *Fable*' to the speaker who, 'raised nigher to the spheres of Heaven' – or set apart from 'the larger class of mankind' as the *Gentleman's Magazine* reviewer had suggested – is able to 'understand my presence, and to feel | My fullness' (209–15). Poetry is thus no longer a divine gift, as in *Armageddon*, but generated by the human capacity to recreate visionary experience. However, with the Spirit's warning that 'keen *Discovery*' may threaten the poet's vision, Tennyson first affirms then fears the loss of imaginative power. An age of scientific and geographic exploration may cause 'the brilliant towers' of *Timbuctoo* to 'shrink and shiver into huts' (240–2), leaving the speaker, abandoned by the Spirit, alone and 'darkling' (209), his desolation enhanced by the Shakespearean echo.

Timbuctoo's speaker, gazing on 'the Imperial height | Of Canopy o'ercanopied' (162–3), foreshadows the poet's – and England's – increasingly imperial vision when, as Laureate, Tennyson looks with 'imperial eyes' at countries other than his own. Mary Louise Pratt's

historical critique of eighteenth- and nineteenth-century travel writing links the aerial gaze with Victorian explorers of the African
interior, whose 'vivid imperial rhetoric' recorded for readers 'the
peak moments at which geographical "discoveries" were "won" for
England'.[50] Tennyson's speaker, standing 'upon the Mountain' (1, 77),
overlooking 'Wide Afric' (57) and the 'wilderness of spires' (159) of
legendary Timbuctoo, exemplifies 'the monarch-of-all-I-survey scene'
which recurs throughout their writings. The uninhabited landscape is
aestheticized – seen as in a painting – and adjectivally modified, the
broad panorama is centred on the observer, and the relationship is one
of mastery between the 'seer and the seen'.[51]

The Cambridge authorities' selection of Timbuctoo as the topical
subject for the 1829 prize poem links Establishment England with
nineteenth-century colonial expansion and commercial exploitation.
The African interior and Timbuctoo, the 'Unattainable' city at the
junction of its major trade routes, had been for centuries the subject
of rumour and legend; from 1778, when Sir Joseph Banks founded
the English African Association, they became the objects of extensive
and expensive exploration.[52] By 1830 failed expeditions to the African
interior had 'cost England . . . 720,000*l*'.[53] In 1824 Timbuctoo became a
prize city; the English and French raced to reach it and four years later
René Caillié returned to Paris to claim the reward. Caillié's *Journal*, published in France in 1829 and in English translation the following year
(when it was received with hostility and disbelief by English reviewers)
reports that 'Timbuctoo and its environs present the most monotonous
and barren scene I ever beheld'.[54] The grandeur and wealth of the fabled
city was an illusion and the dichotomy between imagination and reality
parallels the poetic dilemma at the heart of Tennyson's *Timbuctoo* – and
of much of his later poetry.

Tennyson's prize poem introduces themes which became recurring
poetic concerns and heralds his imperial themes, thus identifying
England and Englishness with imperial power. The *Athenaeum* review
predates the 'strenuous and self-conscious exercise in criticism' which
continued throughout 'the four decades between 1830 and 1870',[55]
and reveals that *Timbuctoo* captured the imagination of his Cambridge
contemporaries. Their encouragement led to Tennyson's first independent volume of poetry, published the following year while he was still
an undergraduate. By recognizing his 'first-rate poetical genius' and
asserting their belief that he was destined to succeed 'the great generation of poets which is now passing away', Hallam, the Apostles and the
Athenaeum critic define and shape Tennyson as an English poet.

Poems, Chiefly Lyrical

Tennyson's first independent volume of poetry was published by Effingham Wilson, an established London bookseller turned publisher, in June 1830, two months before the poet's twenty-first birthday. Apparently impatient for publication, Tennyson wrote to Wilson from Somersby on 18 June reporting 'complaints from various quarters that persons are not able to procure my book of the booksellers' and requesting him 'to disseminate it immediately, as everybody is leaving town'.[56] In fact, Wilson advertised the volume in the *Athenaeum* on 19 June and the *Literary Gazette* on 26 June,[57] and six hundred copies of the slim, duodecimo volume, containing fifty-six poems, were issued at a retail price of five shillings. As with *Poems by Two Brothers* it is not known why the publisher undertook the volume, or how many copies were sold, but in 1833 Tennyson appeared to owe the publisher eleven pounds. However, Hallam was 'confident the £11 will be found a mistake [and] you need not pay it',[58] which suggests that Hallam and perhaps others had guaranteed the publication costs. *Poems, Chiefly Lyrical* was intended to be a joint publication, following the example of *Lyrical Ballads* whose title it echoes, but with the poems in print and the Preface written, Hallam reluctantly withdrew his contributions at his father's request. Sending a copy of the volume to Tennyson's mother, Hallam wrote: 'To this joint publication, as a sort of seal of our friendship, I had long looked forward', adding that '[n]o labour on my part shall be wanting to bring his volume into general notice'.[59] Hallam (with Tennyson's approval) appointed himself Tennyson's business manager and, with other Apostles, circulated the published volume to poets and journal editors.[60]

June 1830 was an inauspicious time for an almost unknown author to publish a volume of poems. Newspapers had much to report, with intense political and social unrest at home and abroad. There was a deepening depression in the British book trade, lasting until 1833,[61] and George IV died on 26 June, widely unmourned,[62] which necessitated a parliamentary election. The following day, however, the first of three generally favourable early reviews of the volume appeared in the *Atlas* – a weekly 'General Newspaper and Journal of Literature on the Largest Sheet ever printed' – whose front page was edged in black to mark the King's passing. The anonymous reviewer (possibly the editor, Robert Bell) extracts as example three 'quaint and picturesque scraps', which 'forcibly' remind him of Herrick and Waller.[63] Tennyson successfully imitates 'the old English lyrical poets', although some poems are marred by 'affectation' – the archaic or artificial language which, critics believed, prevented the reader's sympathetic identification with the poem's subject. 'On the whole', however, the *Atlas* reviewer is 'greatly pleased with Tennyson', who returns readers 'to the pleasant times when there was a marvellous subtlety in verse'.

Two weeks later – on 21 August 1830 – the anonymous critic of the *Spectator*, a weekly periodical founded and edited by Robert Stephen Rintoul, welcomed 'a volume of very pleasant verses' which has achieved much and gives promise of more.[64] Although writing for 'an organ of educated radicalism' which supported the 1832 Reform Bill,[65] the *Spectator's* reviewer approves the seventeenth-century echoes he finds in 'little metaphysical pieces' reminiscent of Cowley. While regretting Tennyson's irregular rhyme schemes, 'fondness for old words' and archaic 'modes of pronunciation', the reviewer believes that Tennyson has the creative gift of a true poet, to give 'dignity to the simple and novelty to the common'. On 25 September 1830 a brief notice appeared in *Felix Farley's Bristol Journal*, written by an unidentified friend of Tennyson's.[66] Praising the poems' 'sterling merit', 'exquisite pathos, and undoubted genius', the reviewer concludes that the volume contains 'some of the most splendid gems of poetry we have met with for many, many years past'.

William Johnson Fox reviews *Poems, Chiefly Lyrical*

The early reviews of *Poems, Chiefly Lyrical* welcome Tennyson as a true poet, in whose work critics find strong echoes of the English literary past. However, the notices appeared in general or local newspapers rather than the literary journals for which Tennyson and Hallam had hoped. It was not until January 1831 that the first extended critique – by William Johnson Fox – was published in the *Westminster Review* which, with the *Edinburgh Review* and *Quarterly Review*, was regarded by contemporaries as the most influential critical periodical. As Fox's review inaugurated the critical debate on the future and role of poetry and the poet – foreshadowed in the *Athenaeum* review of *Timbuctoo* – which intensified following the publication of *Poems* (1832) and continued throughout the next four decades, his critique will be considered in some detail.

William Johnson Fox was a politician, author and nonconformist preacher and his review, which is remarkable for its optimism and praise of Tennyson's poetry, resounds with the rhetoric of public oratory.[67] Fox is concerned with poetry and the modern age, 'these supposed unpoetical days on which we are fallen' (212), a view he rejects. Poetry, which is dependent on 'physical organization' rather than 'supernatural gift' (211), is no exception to the law of human progression and the 'machinery of a poem is not less susceptible of improvement than the machinery of a cotton-mill' (210). Fox's image is appropriate to an industrial age and suggests the utilitarian spirit of both author and journal. He therefore sees no reason why poetry 'should retrograde from the days of Milton'. Victorian critics were preoccupied with poetry's effect, hence their overriding concern with its subjects and language. Fox believes that modern poets should explore modern themes. In a startling comparison for readers in an age of social unrest, he asks: 'Is not the French Revolution as good as the siege of Troy?' (212). Poets must also understand and apply psychology, the 'science of mind' that 'advances with the progress of society like all other sciences' and is 'the essence of poetic power' (213), a view revealing the unattributed influence of James Mill's *Analysis of the Phenomena of the Human Mind* (1829).[68] Successful recent poetry reflects this science, with much in Byron and Shelley, most of all in Coleridge and Wordsworth, and Fox concludes that Tennyson's 'little book' is as 'metaphysical and poetical in its spirit' as any of these poets, who 'are all going or gone' (213–14).

Fox thus presents *Poems, Chiefly Lyrical* to *Westminster Review* readers by comparing Tennyson with 'the great generation' of English poets which, as the *Athenaeum* critic of *Timbuctoo* had observed, 'is now passing away'. The sense of discovery Fox conveys links modern poets and poetry with the age of scientific and geographical exploration – and imperial expansion – exemplified by the Cambridge authorities' selection of the prize poem theme. A 'new world is discovered for [the poet] to conquer' as 'mental science' has pioneered 'the analysis of particular states of mind' (214–15). Therefore, Fox argues, the poet's delineations of action and character will be more truthful and effective and he will find an inexhaustible variety of subjects in the exploration of 'intellectual scenery', at which Tennyson excels. Tennyson enters 'a mind as he would . . . a landscape', and poems such as 'Supposed Confessions' – combining reflection, analysis, description and emotion – exemplify Fox's conviction that such topics are 'in accordance with the spirit and intellect of the age' (216). Fox anticipates by more than twenty years *Aurora Leigh*'s assertion that poets should 'represent the age, | Their age, not Charlemagne's' (1857, V, 202–3).[69]

Fox's critique also reveals the influence of Adam Smith (1723–90).[70] Tennyson, Fox declares, 'has the secret of the transmigration of the soul' (216). He can 'cast his own spirit into any living thing real or imaginary', assuming both their outward appearance and their inmost thoughts and emotions, leading to a moment of complete identification, an ability which exemplifies Adam Smith's concept of sympathy or dramatic projection – changing places with another in imagination – through which we gain understanding of ourselves and others. Fox illustrates his argument by analysing Tennyson's 'impersonations', concluding – like many later critics – that 'Mariana' is the volume's most perfect poem (219).

Fox greatly admires the volume's 'amatory' poems (220–1). The subject is 'of incalculable importance to society', a view which epitomizes contemporary concern with national character and moral conduct and the belief that women – with their influence on present and future generations – form the exemplary moral centre of the English home as a microcosm of society: 'Upon what love is, depends what woman is, and upon what woman is, depends what the world is'. More radically, however, Fox declares 'there is not a greater moral necessity in England than that of a reformation in female education', a subject Tennyson explored in *The Princess* (1847). Nonconformist Fox foreshadows the 'muscular Christianity' associated with Charles Kingsley by reassuring readers that the poems are 'the expression not of . . . sickly refinement but of manly love'. Tennyson's female portraits guide readers through 'the different gradations of emotion and passion', from flirtatious little 'Lilian' to the exemplary 'Isabel' – the 'stately flower of female fortitude and perfect wifehood' (222).

Fox anticipates reviewers' increasing demands for clarity and simplicity of poetic language and style. He admires the felicitous use of repetition to convey shades of meaning and create 'touching melodies' from very few words. Tennyson is 'a master of musical combinations' – among recent poets, surpassed only by Coleridge 'in the harmony of his versification' – and remarkable for 'the facility and grace with which [Tennyson] identifies himself with nature'. However, Fox echoes the *Atlas* reviewer's dislike of archaisms, which appear both indolent and affected, and Tennyson's tendency to use obscure words which modern 'young ladies . . . are not accustomed to read or sing in the parlour' (222–3).

Fox's ultimate concern – less lucidly expressed than his preceding arguments – is the future direction of Tennyson's poetic powers (223–4). Tennyson, he concludes, 'is a poet', and an English poet, compared throughout the critique with Wordsworth, Coleridge and the passing generation. Therefore he has a lasting national role, with 'deep responsibilities to his country and the world' and to 'present and future generations'. Victorian critics believed that poetry should have a moral purpose and a wide appeal. Although Fox fears that *Poems, Chiefly Lyrical* is too original to become popular, Tennyson should dedicate his art to

a nobler aim than mere amusement. By creating exemplary impersonations with which readers identify, Tennyson can 'command the sympathies' of countless minds and hearts and 'disseminate principles'.
Through their powerful but incalculable effect on 'national feelings
and character' poets can ultimately influence 'national happiness', and
by asserting that Tennyson's poetic powers can transform the English
nation, Fox uses his critical powers – and the pages of the influential
Westminster Review – to define and shape Tennyson as an English poet.

Encouraged by Fox's critique, Hallam continued to bring Tennyson's
volume 'into general notice'. He asked Leigh Hunt, editor of the *Tatler*,
to review *Poems, Chiefly Lyrical* and Charles Tennyson's *Sonnets*, published in March 1830, commending Alfred as 'a new prophet of those
true principles of Art' which Hunt himself had pioneered in England.[71]
Since the death of Keats, 'our English region of Parnassus' has been
ruled by unworthy kings; now, Hallam believes, 'the true heir is found'.
Hunt reviewed the volumes in late February 1831 (as Tennyson left
Cambridge for Somersby, where his father died in March), agreeing
that 'we have seen no such poetical writing since the last volume of
Mr Keats'.[72] He adds that the authors should be placed 'among the first
poets of the day' and Wordsworth and Coleridge should acknowledge
them as friends. In early March the *New Monthly Magazine*, edited during 1831 by Samuel Carter Hall, also recognized that *Poems, Chiefly
Lyrical* contained 'precisely the kind of poetry for which Mr. Keats was
assailed' and which the world is beginning to admire. The poems are
not equal to Keats's greatest, the critic concludes, but 'contain many
indications of a similar genius'.

The two remaining and extended reviews of *Poems, Chiefly Lyrical*
respond to the issues raised by Fox's critique. Hallam's own review was
published in the August 1831 issue of the *Englishman's Magazine*,[73] a
radical monthly literary journal edited by Edward Moxon which had
a brief existence from April to October 1831. The *Englishman's* guiding spirit was Daniel Defoe (1660–1731), admired in the Preface as a
'dauntless advocate of stubborn Truth . . . supported by the majesty of
conscious rectitude'[74] and reinterpreted to represent nineteenth-century
characteristics and concern with social reform and emancipation. From
'that intermediate class' which is the community's moral regulator,
Defoe turns 'in constancy and love towards the mild light of the domestic hearth' as – like a knight of the Victorian Medieval Revival[75] – he sets
forth with mailed glove and sword to 'do battle with error, intolerance
and oppression'. While the King deals 'with a party selfishly inimical to
the extension of popular rights', the *Englishman's* must emulate Defoe

and fight for 'Freedom of Trade' and 'of Conscience', for 'the Commons of England' and against 'iniquitous thraldom', especially the 'abominable system of Negro Slavery' as it is a truth 'inscribed upon the universal heart', although not yet universally acknowledged, that 'man can have no property in man'.

Arthur Henry Hallam reviews *Poems, Chiefly Lyrical*

Hallam's review – which he later dismissed as 'the hasty product of the evenings of one week'[76] – is persuasive, at times pedantic, and reveals his deep admiration for *Poems, Chiefly Lyrical*. Hallam's initial discussion of poetry and the age is centred on the distinction between reflective poets and poets of sensation. He rejects the view of Laureate Wordsworth's admirers that 'the highest species of poetry is the reflective', as the result 'is false in art' (85). By contrast, 'poets of sensation' such as Shelley and Keats – motivated solely by the desire for beauty – enrapture rather than reason, are picturesque not descriptive (86–7), and by advocating 'picturesque' poetry Hallam anticipates elements of the symbolist views which developed during the 1860s. Poets of sensation, he argues, live in 'immediate sympathy with the external universe' and recreate its multiple impressions. Thus able to attain 'the heights and depths of art' they not only cultivate their own poetic spirit but also fulfil the poet's transformative mission – to 'elevate inferior intellects into a higher and purer atmosphere' (88–90).

Hallam's conviction that poets of sensation cannot be popular (88) illustrates the intellectual and social class divisions in contemporary England. (Hallam's later Latin quotations (95, 100) exemplify the English gentleman's classical education.) As the *Gentleman's Magazine* reviewer argued in 1827, Hallam believes that a 'strong and immovable' barrier separates poets of sensation 'and all other persons' and for the great majority of readers it is '*morally* impossible to attain the author's point of vision' (89). Only occasional 'eminent spirits' such as Shakespeare and Milton have the power to reach the hearts and minds of all compatriots and to inform their Englishness (90). Their stirring – and apparently subliminal – influence became 'a part of our national existence; it was ours as Englishmen' and 'we retain unimpaired this privilege of intercourse with greatness' (91–2). Literature has degenerated since that golden age, but Hallam rejects Fox's view that the improvement of poetry and machinery is related and his plea for new subjects and language: 'The French Revolution may be a finer theme than the war of Troy; but it does not so evidently follow that Homer is to find his superior'. However, while modern poetry may have little influence on society, Hallam trusts 'Art herself . . . to raise up chosen spirits, who may . . . vindicate her title'.

Hallam then presents Tennyson to readers – as 'a poet in the truest and highest sense' and 'decidedly' a poet of sensation (92). Tennyson is thus placed in textual and poetic succession to Shakespeare and Milton, by implication chosen to restore literature's golden age. For Hallam, *Poems, Chiefly Lyrical* clearly reveals the 'features of original genius', reflecting 'the spirit of the age' but the influence of no other poet. Illustrating his argument by admiring analysis of selected poems, Hallam enumerates Tennyson's 'five distinctive excellencies' (93) although, as Carol T. Christ observes, without indicating whether the poet's emotion 'informs the objects of the external world' or results from the objects' own properties.[77] Reflecting on his critique, Hallam later commented: 'I thought more of myself and the Truth' than of 'whatever would do most good to Alfred', recognizing that it is difficult 'for a man to stop himself when he gets into full swing, and begins to write con amore'.[78] When he finally turns to the poems, Hallam also writes at length and *con amore*.

Appropriately for a critic who rejects modern themes, Hallam's chosen poems evoke the past. 'Recollections of the Arabian Nights' – a perfect picture gallery, often as majestic as Milton – returns readers to their happy childhood and old acquaintance Haroun Alraschid (94–5). Ballads were admired for their immediacy and simplicity of language,[79] and 'Oriana' is recommended to readers who delight in 'the heroic poems of Old England'. Hallam knows 'no more happy seizure of the antique spirit in the whole compass of our literature' (96). He shares Fox's admiration for 'the female characters', which for Hallam represent a new genre of poetry – 'a graft of the lyric on the dramatic' (99) – and foreshadow Victorian England's medievalist idealization of women. Defined by her beauty and mystery, 'Adeline' has taken Hallam's 'heart from out our breast'. As he remarks, however, the reviewer's 'trade is not that of mere enthusiasm': illustrating critics' wish for clarity and simplicity, Hallam points out the volume's few faults and Tennyson's occasionally ambiguous vocabulary (100).

Hallam's closing praise alludes to growing contemporary interest in the formation and derivation of the English language, which is suggested by reviews of *Poems* (1832) and discussed in Chapter 2. He notes approvingly that, with rare exceptions, the language of *Poems, Chiefly Lyrical* is 'thorough and sterling English' (100). This illustrates Tennyson's enthusiasm for the 'Saxon element', which gives 'our native tongue' its 'intrinsic freedom and nervousness', and the 'Latin and

Roman derivatives' from which Shakespearean speech drew its 'fertility of expression, and variety of harmony'. Concluding that English is, and can only continue to flourish as, a compound language, Hallam commends the volume to discerning readers.

In his critique, Hallam – even more than Fox, because he is writing as both friend and critic – defines and shapes Tennyson as an English poet. Tennyson is presented as 'a poet in the truest and highest sense', a man of superior sensibility, and a poet of sensation whose poetry, by implication, surpasses the reflective poetry of Laureate Wordsworth. He is also presented as successor to the past rather than the passing great generation of English poets – to Shakespeare, Milton and literature's golden age – a persuasive argument for a young poet with a 'passion for the past'. For Hallam as for Fox, the poet's role is of national importance, although stated more subtly and to be fulfilled less actively. Whereas Fox argues that poets should act with 'force', 'command sympathies' and 'blast' tyrants (224), Hallam's illuminating instant of dramatic projection is effected by beauty. The poet's role is to apply 'the transforming powers of high imagination' and the 'sterling' Englishness of language to restore both the spirit of modern poetry and the spirit of the nation (91).

Periodical press interest in *Poems, Chiefly Lyrical* continued in 1832. In February, John Wilson, professor of moral philosophy at Edinburgh University – writing as 'Christopher North' – praised Tennyson in his monthly column *Noctes Ambrosianae* in the widely read *Blackwood's Edinburgh Magazine* (known as 'the Maga').[80] Wilson shares Hallam's admiration for 'Oriana' and the 'Arabian Nights'. Commending Tennyson's 'fine ear for melody and harmony' and his 'rare and rich glimpses of imagination', Wilson concludes that, despite many affectations, Tennyson 'has – *genius*',[81] thus exemplifying the changing use of a 'slippery' word with 'no permanent definition'.[82] In England for much of the seventeenth and eighteenth centuries, *genius* was a God-given gift enabling talented people to excel in a particular field. With Goethe and other late-eighteenth- and early-nineteenth-century German Romantic writers, the word came to mean an exceptional man (despite feminine characteristics of intuition and imagination, geniuses were invariably male) set apart from society, whose 'flashes of inspiration' came from 'an internal creative urge' rather than from God.

John Wilson reviews *Poems, Chiefly Lyrical*

John Wilson's full-length review of *Poems, Chiefly Lyrical*, published in *Blackwood's* in May 1832,[83] introduces an initially dissonant voice into the chorus of critical approval and makes frequent use of the term *genius*, often sarcastically but finally with admiration. Again writing as 'Christopher North', Wilson assumes the persona of an irascible old man (725), inclined to administer his 'exorcising crutch' (727). Wilson shares earlier critics' concern with the poetic succession. He argues that 'England ought to be producing some young poets now, that there may be no dull interregnum, when the old shall have passed away' and, apparently echoing Fox, suggests that the 'moral and intellectual earthquake of the French Revolution' could produce 'the next age of poets' (723–4). Wilson's wish to prevent an interregnum also alludes to contemporary concern with the monarchical succession. His review appeared eight months after the coronation of William IV (born in 1765) and as the King's heir – thirteen-year-old Princess Victoria – began a series of 'annual, semi-royal tours during which she was formally presented to the nation'.[84]

Tennyson is presented to Wilson's readers as a little-known poet 'whom his friends call a Phoenix' but he designates 'merely a Swan' (724). Despite Hallam's disclaimer – that Tennyson had no connection 'with any political party, or peculiar system of opinions' (92–3) – Wilson, a Tory, wrongly assumes that Tennyson is 'the Pet of a Coterie . . . in Cockneydom',[85] inclined to radical views and affected verse. He had been reviewed by Leigh Hunt in the *Tatler*, in the utilitarian *Westminster Review* and the reformist *Englishman's Magazine*, receiving the extravagant praise Wilson regards as 'the besetting sin of all periodical criticism' (724). Wilson, by contrast, defines the poet's faults:

> At present he has small power over the common feelings and thoughts of men. His feebleness is distressing at all times when he makes an appeal to their ordinary sympathies. . . . What all the human race see and feel, he seems to think cannot be poetical; he is not aware of the transcendant [sic] and eternal grandeur of common-place and all-time truths, which are the staple of all poetry. (725)

Tennyson is therefore unlike Wordsworth, whose language 'records' rather than 'reveals, spiritualizing while it embodies' (725). Wilson attacks Hallam and Fox who, he believes, encourage Tennyson's affectation. Hallam's essay of 'superhuman . . . pomposity' sent the *Englishman's* to its untimely grave (724); Fox's admiration for 'The Merman' (728–9) represents a failure of sympathy which diverts the poet from his role – to defamiliarize, thus reaffirm, the shared, central and everyday experiences of humankind. However, Wilson retains his faith in 'genius', which can free itself 'even from the curse of Cockneyism' with the aid of his 'exorcising crutch' (726–7).

Wilson rejects as 'dismal drivel' (726) several poems Tennyson never reprinted, then demonstrates by 'judicious eulogy' that the poet is worthy of admiration (732). Selected poems evoke shared childhood memories of the rural scenes (738) that became increasingly iconic as the century progressed. Wilson extols the 'eminently beautiful' 'Ode to Memory' – by a young poet who sees that 'the bowers of paradise' are built on his native Lincolnshire landscape[86] – and commends the concise perfection of 'The Deserted House' and 'A Dirge', which intensify the landscape's pensive peace (732–3). He echoes Fox and Hallam's admiration for Tennyson's 'delicate perception of the purity of the female character' (734), while anticipating the symbolic floral imagery of John Ruskin's *Of Queens' Gardens* (1864).[87] Declaring a paternal devotion to all his 'ideal daughters' – 'seven lilies in one garland . . . Budding, blossoming, full-blown' – Wilson concludes that 'the rose is the queen of flowers', but should she die, 'the lily would wear the crown – and her name is "Isabel"'.

Wilson's ultimate examples, earlier admired in *Noctes Ambrosianae*, illustrate his wish for simplicity and shared experience. 'The Ballad of Oriana' is perhaps Tennyson's most beautiful poem (737). Although the immediate simplicity of ancient ballads – 'the music of the heart' – cannot be imitated in later centuries, 'rural dwellers' sometimes capture 'the spirit of the antique strain'. But Tennyson's greatest achievement is the visionary and romantic 'Recollections of the Arabian Nights' (738), which recaptures for Wilson as for Hallam childhood delight at discovering the tales. Tennyson, he believes, was long familiar 'with the Arabian Nights' Entertainments', otherwise 'he had not now so passionately and so imaginatively sung their wonders' (739).

Concluding his critique, Wilson is aware that its merit 'consists in the extracts', which are 'beautiful exceedingly' (740). He concedes that he may have exaggerated Tennyson's silliness, but is certain that he has not overstated Tennyson's strength and countless readers of 'the Maga' will confirm Wilson's judgement – 'Alfred Tennyson is a poet'. Wilson warns, however, that Tennyson has much to unlearn before 'his genius can achieve its destined triumphs': he must become less idiosyncratic and more selective (741). Wilson ends with an admonition. 'Nature is mighty' and 'poets should deal with her on a grand scale', in the manner of Wordsworth, who communed 'with the spirit "whose dwelling is the light of setting suns"'. In his critique Wilson refers to Scottish and English poets, but his principal and recurring comparisons are with

Wordsworth; he declares of 'Mariana', 'nor might Wordsworth's self . . . have disdained to indite such melancholy strain' (735). Through these comparisons, the exalted closing image and his concern to prevent 'a dull interregnum', Wilson attempts to shape Tennyson as a Wordsworthian English poet.

Inordinately sensitive to hostile criticism, Tennyson responded to Wilson's review with an epigram – 'a silly squib to Christopher North'[88] – in his next published volume. Although Tennyson later claimed that the critique was redeemed by the 'boisterous and picturesque humour such as I love', at the time he considered it 'too skittish and petulant'. Hallam's reaction was more realistic. He wrote to Tennyson that Wilson 'means well' and 'as he has extracted nearly your whole book, and has in his soberer mood spoken in terms as high as I could have used myself of some of your best poems, I think the Review will assist rather than hinder the march of your reputation.'[89] Subsequent press comment supports this view. On 1 May 1832 the *Sun*, a London evening daily, observed that '"Tennyson's Poems" is a review of some early poetical effusions of a young-man who bids fair, at no distant date, to become an ornament to the literature of his country'.[90] The *Edinburgh Observer* of 4 May 1832 described the critique as one in which 'well-merited castigation is inflicted upon egregious nonsense – but the poet receives ample compensation in the praise awarded to a few beauties, which were in considerable danger of not being observed at all'. The following day the *Athenaeum*, edited since 1830 by Charles Dilke, noted in its 'Weekly Gossip on Literature and Art' a 'bright article on Tennyson's poems', and the *Spectator* referred to the review as one of Wilson's 'extravaganzas', in which he first 'knocks down' and then extols 'The Poems of Alfred Tennyson (a young poet of genuine talent)'.[91]

Five years had elapsed between the *Gentleman's Magazine*'s welcome for the 'domestic poetry' of *Poems by Two Brothers* and the *Spectator*'s acceptance of the young poet's 'genuine talent'. During this period Tennyson's poems had been reviewed, briefly or at length, in a wide range of periodical publications, with his poetic 'genius' recognized as early as July 1829. Examination of the reviews confirms that the intense debate on the future and role of poetry and the poet, which followed the publication of *Poems, Chiefly Lyrical*, was anticipated by the *Athenaeum*. The reviews also reveal critics' increasing attempts to define and shape Tennyson as an English poet. He was first associated by comparison with past and passing English poets in the *Gentleman's Magazine*. With the *Athenaeum* review of *Timbuctoo* critics' comparisons became inseparable from their concern with the poetic succession.

For the three major critics of *Poems, Chiefly Lyrical* – Fox, Hallam and Wilson – writing in the political and social turmoil that preceded the 1832 Reform Act, poetry became inseparable from the condition of contemporary England. Fox argued that poetry, as susceptible to improvement as industry, should explore modern science and modern themes such as the French Revolution; Hallam rejected revolutionary themes, but reflected growing interest in the formation and derivation of the English language; Wilson suggested that the earthquake of the French Revolution could produce a new age of poets. All defined their differing views of the poet's national role.

The critics' views and their chosen poems illustrate contemporary themes and concerns which, as later chapters demonstrate, continued to preoccupy Tennyson and his reviewers. Extravagant praise for Tennyson's delicate female portraits not only exemplifies 'the woman question' but also foreshadows the prescribed gender roles of Victorian medievalism and the idealization of Queen Victoria. Wilson's nostalgia for childhood rural scenes anticipates the iconic images of England as a rural 'land of lost content' created to counter an age of industry and railways. Interest in Tennyson's sterling English language increased with the reviews of *Poems* (1832) – to be examined in Chapter 2 – and continued when, as Laureate, Tennyson achieved his national role and became the public voice of English poetry.

2
'Mr. Tennyson's Singular Genius': The Reception of *Poems* (1832)

Chapter 1 established that by May 1832 Tennyson had been recognized by a number of periodical critics as a young poet of genuine talent. Reviewers who praised the early poems perhaps awaited the volume which Tennyson published in December 1832, six months after the Reform Bill finally completed its troubled passage through Parliament and became law. In Chapter 2 I examine the critical reception of *Poems* (1832), Tennyson's second independent volume of poetry. I consider whether and how critics continued to define and shape Tennyson as an English poet and study the ways in which poems selected or rejected by reviewers reflect changing implications of English national identity in the wake of this significant moment of Englishness, which established inclusion and exclusion for the nation and formally defined the English political citizen as male.

Publication

Tennyson had been in no hurry to bring out another volume after the publication of *Poems, Chiefly Lyrical* in June 1830. However, Hallam's 'labour' to bring Tennyson's poems to wider notice continued. In August 1831 he asked Charles Merivale to enquire what Edward Moxon, publisher of the short-lived *Englishman's Magazine*, would give for the copyright if a new volume were 'ready to be published next season'.[1] By March 1832 Hallam thought he had persuaded Tennyson to publish a volume 'more free from blemishes and more masterly in power' than *Poems, Chiefly Lyrical*.[2] In June he was confident that 'Moxon would publish any volume Alfred might make up for him free of expense', believing that a second book would 'set Alfred high in public notice' and 'afford him the means of putting money in his pocket'.[3] Hallam's confidence had waned by September. He wrote to Tennyson of Moxon's impatience 'to begin the volume'[4] and, having received with 'a thrill of pleasure' some poems from Somersby, later admitted 'I had begun to despair of your volume getting on'.[5] Tennyson's first direct contact with Moxon was on 13 October, requesting duplicate proof sheets for correction. Aware that 'this proceeding would somewhat delay publication', he added, 'but I am in no hurry. My MSS . . . are far from being in proper order.'[6]

Last-minute changes during publication suggest Tennyson's poetic integrity. Despite Hallam's impassioned pleas – 'You must be pointblank mad. It will please vast numbers of people'[7] – and the prospect of public notice and remuneration, Tennyson withdrew *The Lover's Tale*, a blank verse poem of more than a thousand lines, intended to end the volume and already set up in print. 'After mature consideration', he wrote to Moxon, the poem 'is too full of faults and though I think it may conduce towards making me popular . . . to my eye it spoils the completeness of the book and is better away.'[8] The resulting slim volume of thirty poems was finally published at the beginning of December 1832. The title page, which stated simply 'Poems by Alfred Tennyson',[9] was dated 1833, perhaps because Moxon anticipated further delays. Tennyson was twenty-three and the publishing relationship lasted until Moxon's death in 1858. Four hundred and fifty copies of the volume were issued at six shillings each.[10] Almost one hundred copies were sold in the first two days and Hallam reported that 'the men of Cambridge have bought *seventy-five* copies; a fact infinitely to their credit'.[11] Reviewers appear to have anticipated the volume as the first critique appeared immediately and by mid-December 1832 *Poems* had been reviewed in four leading weekly journals. Although received less favourably than *Poems, Chiefly Lyrical*, the reception of *Poems* was not as severe as some twentieth-century critics and biographers have assumed.[12] Like 'Christopher North', reviewers 'mingle[d] blame and praise' (3).

Early reviewers and their concerns: the daily and weekly papers

Whether hostile or friendly, the reviews of *Poems* acknowledge Tennyson's poetic gift. They also reveal the reviewers' increasing preoccupation with the language of poetry, not only the affectations preventing a reader's sympathetic identification with a poem's subject but also the formation and derivation of the English language. The critics' concerns exemplify the remarkable development of language consciousness in the

eighteenth and nineteenth centuries, of which the movement towards –
and reaction against – the standardization of the English language was
an inseparable part. 'Standard Modern English' can be traced from
the Chancery English of the fifteenth-century Lancastrian court, with
spelling, punctuation and syntax gradually becoming standardized
during the sixteenth and seventeenth centuries and the preferred form
codified in eighteenth-century dictionaries and grammars.[13] Dr Johnson's
Dictionary (1755) 'fix[ed]' spelling and meaning; his successors Thomas
Sheridan (1780) and John Walker (1791) fulfilled Johnson's promise
'to fix the pronunciation' of the English language.[14] Although English
was never regulated by an Academy, it became increasingly associated
with Establishment authority. Walker's influential *Critical Pronouncing
Dictionary* introduced the term 'received' for the London accent of
court and gentry, long regarded as 'undoubtedly the best . . . not only
the best by courtesy, and because it happens to be the pronunciation
of the capital, but best by a better title; that of being more generally
received'.[15] Fashionable articulation was encouraged by orthoepists,
lectures and instruction manuals, both prescriptive and proscrip-
tive (George Jackson's *Popular Errors in English Grammar, Particularly
in Pronunciation* (1830) warned against using terms that were 'low' or
not 'gentlemanly') and fostered in public schools and Oxbridge – the
training ground for statesmen and Empire administrators – through
recitations, oral translations and, with the rise of English as an academic discipline, eventually the curriculum. By 1869, two years after
the Second Reform Act, the phonetician Alexander Ellis 'recognise[d] a
received pronunciation all over the country',[16] an apparently unifying
national language for an age of increasing democracy and an upwardly
mobile middle class. However, outside London and lower down the
social scale, regional variation persisted. Poets and linguists kept alive
local forms of speech. Between 1834 and 1867 William Barnes published
several volumes of poems in the Dorset dialect; in 'Northern Farmer, Old
Style' (1864) and later dialect poems, Tennyson explored his recurring
concerns in the local speech of his native Lincolnshire.

The first review of *Poems*, published in the *Athenaeum* on 1 December
1832, foreshadows critics' demands for a clear and simple style and
unaffected language. The anonymous reviewer declares that Tennyson
'is unquestionably a poet of fancy, feeling, and imagination', who is
'gifted with a deep sense of the beautiful', but unfortunately often
strays from the paths of true poetry in search of 'metaphysical subtilties,
and ingenious refinements'.[17] Remarking on Tennyson's evident love
of early English poets, the reviewer regrets that with their admirable

qualities – particularly the 'beautiful appreciation of the female character' – he has also captured their many 'affectations'. The critic concludes that the poetry is 'disfigured' by archaisms and words 'newly compounded after the German model', which 'hinder the due appreciation' of Tennyson's fine poetic spirit.

The *Athenaeum* reviewer's dislike of Germanic compounds illustrates the growing interest in etymology, which became increasingly inseparable from interest in national character. Reviewing *Poems, Chiefly Lyrical* in 1831, Hallam had commented favourably on Tennyson's 'thorough and sterling English' (100). In 'The Influence of Italian upon English Literature' – delivered as an address in 1831 and printed in 1832 – Hallam analysed the literatures' 'component parts', selecting a passage from Shakespeare containing equal numbers of 'Teutonic' and 'Roman' words as 'a beautiful specimen of pure English'.[18] The 'equipoise of Southern and Northern phraseology', he concludes, creates 'a natural harmony'. For Hallam, a nation's literature 'is the expression of its character' and literary analysis provides a lasting reminder 'of those divers influences by which the national character has been modified'.

Etymology and Englishness became closely linked to 'ever-broadening England' ('To the Queen', 1873, 30). Hallam and Tennyson's Cambridge friend Richard Chenevix Trench published *On the Study of Words* in 1851 and *English, Past and Present* four years later. Trench equates love of English with love of England and argues that patriotic Englishmen should develop 'a clear . . . harmonious . . . noble language' to reflect the speakers' 'corresponding merits'.[19] Trench and the authors he cites for support agree that English is 'compact in the main of [Saxon and Latin] elements'[20] whose 'intimate union', Jacob Grimm believes, creates its 'highly spiritual genius'. Grimm regards English as an incomparable modern language, which produced Shakespeare – 'the greatest . . . poet of modern times'; therefore, he argues, English 'may with all right be called a world-language', which 'like the English people appears destined hereafter to prevail with a sway more extensive even than its present over all the portions of the globe'.[21] Writing in praise of the English language and English poets in 1851, Grimm appears to foresee and justify the imperial expansion by which India had already been 'conquered and annexed and Englished!'[22] Gauri Viswanathan notes that 'English literature came into India . . . with the passing of the Charter Act of 1813' and English literature's introduction into India was formalized with the passing of the English Education Act in 1835.[23]

Richard Chenevix Trench shares Thomas de Quincey's view that 'situations which are homely, or at all connected with the domestic

affections' are heightened by the use of Saxon words'.[24] Hallam
Tennyson records that 'if [Tennyson] differentiated his style from that
of any other poet, he would remark on his use of English – in preference
to words derived from French and Latin'[25] and Tennyson's preferences
are apparent in the *Athenaeum* reviewer's chosen poems. 'The Miller's
Daughter' deals 'delightfully . . . with the moral and natural influences'[26] and the opening lines – with their profusion of monosyllables,
the alliterative 'while walking' (2) and the archaic English 'ivytod' for
'ivybush' (4) – establish immediately that Alice is the daughter of a
solidly Anglo-Saxon miller:

> I met in all the close green ways,
>   While walking with my line and rod,
> The wealthy miller's mealy face,
>   Like the moon in an ivytod.

> (1–4)

'Oenone' is the volume's 'poem of poems . . . chaste – and touching'.[27]
The origins of Oenone are mythological, familiar to the Apostles from
the English gentleman's classical education, yet when she appears
her characteristics are Anglo-Saxon: 'Hither came at noon | Mournful
Oenone, wandering forlorn' (14–15).

The reviews that followed in December 1832 and January 1833 confirm that reviewers were more concerned to shape Tennyson's poetry
than to define his role as a poet. Critics continued to focus on the poet's
language. On 8 December William Jerdan, editor of the *Literary Gazette*,
reproves Tennyson for imitating 'metaphysical' poets' worst faults.[28] In
the combative style of much contemporary journalism he mocks or mis-
construes sonnets and parodies 'The Lady of Shalott'. However, although
Jerdan considers the poetry misguided and the poet 'insane', he believes
that Tennyson's talents, properly directed, could bring the poet success.
He commends the volume's 'fine perception of rural objects and imagery'
and sentiments which are generally 'pure and natural' but sometimes
marred by 'affectation', an expression of critical disapproval which recurs
in reviews of *Poems*. In a brief notice in the *Spectator* on 15 December the
anonymous critic concedes that Tennyson excels in richness of language
and a 'minute taste for natural sounds and sights', but believes that these
qualities have been acquired from other poets rather than directly from
experience or observation.[29] The following day the *Atlas* contained an
extended review, possibly by the editor, Robert Bell, encapsulating the
early critics' views.[30] Reminding readers that the *Atlas* introduced *Poems*,

Chiefly Lyrical to the public, the reviewer declares that Tennyson's 'poetical nature is visible throughout every thing he does', but warns that he risks 'spoiling all its excellence by the varnish of affectation'. He reproaches Tennyson for picturesque 'coinages' which mar his meaning and for the over-refined 'metaphysics' of his unsurpassed portraits. However, the critic concludes that Tennyson makes 'ample amends' for his faults in the 'pure verse that will outlive the memory of his affectations'.

Reviewers' demands for a clear, simple style and distinct language were, as Isobel Armstrong observes, associated with demands for what is common and familiar.[31] Additionally, as the early reviews suggest, for what is rural and familiar and empirically observed, thus anticipating the critical reception of *Poems* (1842) and increasing concern with the changing English landscape. The critics' views – foreshadowed in May 1832 by John Wilson's wish for 'the simplest feelings' expressed in the 'simplest language' and belief that the 'transcendant and eternal grandeur of common-place and all-time truths . . . are the staple of all poetry' (725) – are encapsulated in the early reviewers' chosen poems. The *Athenaeum* and *Atlas* critics quote extensively and approvingly from 'The Death of the Old Year', 'New-Year's Eve' and 'The Miller's Daughter', and even William Jerdan commends Tennyson's 'rural imagery'. 'Rural' and 'pure' can be added to the list of words used approvingly by critics.[32]

Despite their dislike of 'affectation', the early critics admired Tennyson's pure verse. For John Forster, Tennyson had become a finer poet than Crabbe, regarded as one of the 'true poets among the moderns'.[33] Writing in the *True Sun* on 19 January 1833, Forster 'mingle[d] praise' and prediction.[34] Tennyson, he declares, has 'the true spirit of poetry' – feeling, imagination and, when he wishes, 'a most exquisite simplicity' – and is destined for the highest place in the ranks of poets if his youthful promise is fulfilled. No living poet has 'such a luxuriously intense feeling of beauty'. 'The Miller's Daughter' he finds 'exquisite throughout – full of the calm beauty of contented happiness . . . of heart-affection . . . simplicity and homely truth'. In June 1827, the *Gentleman's Magazine* critic had observed that *Poems by Two Brothers* lacked 'the perfect mastery of human passions which distinguishes Crabbe'.[35] Forster now concludes that 'The Miller's Daughter' contains 'the painting of Crabbe, but of deeper and finer colouring'.

Early reviewers and their concerns: the monthly journals

In January 1833 the monthly journals also responded promptly to the publication of *Poems*. Succinctly or at length, they echoed the daily and weekly papers' comments, concerns and selections. The *Metropolitan Magazine*, edited by Captain Frederick Marryat, welcomes the 'productions of one who has a deep feeling for poetical beauty'.[36] For *Tait's Edinburgh Magazine* the volume 'contains many good and a few beautiful poems', but 'scarcely comes up to the high-raised expectations of the author of *Poems, Chiefly Lyrical*'.[37] The *New Monthly Magazine* critic, believed to be the editor, Edward Bulwer-Lytton, focuses on faults exemplifying the affectation of recent poets. Tennyson imitates the Restoration poets' 'worst conceits', Elizabethans' 'most coxcombical euphuisms', and the style of Keats and Shelley.[38] Nevertheless, the reviewer sees more hope for Tennyson than for the poet's contemporaries, declaring that 'The May Queen' and its sequel 'New-Year's Eve' are 'very sweet and natural poems', with 'The Death of the Old Year' 'another poem of remarkable beauty'.

'New-Year's Eve' and 'The Miller's Daughter' receive the early reviewers' almost unanimous praise. The narrative poems – linked by close observation of the flora, fauna and customs of rural England, a central figure named Alice, and a 'box of mignonette' (48 and 83 respectively) – fulfil critical demands and show Tennyson as a human poet. The poems, and the reviewers' comments, also embody elements of nineteenth-century Englishness. Reviewing Tennyson's first published volume, the *Gentleman's Magazine* critic had welcomed 'a graceful addition to our domestic poetry'. Unlike his often Byronic contributions to *Poems by Two Brothers*, with their exotic locations and characters, 'The Miller's Daughter' and 'New-Year's Eve' are 'domestic' poems in two senses of the word; their setting is the English countryside and their concerns are the 'domestic affections' of the English home. William Jerdan, editor of the *Literary Gazette*, admired Tennyson's 'fine perception of rural objects and imagery', but the poems do not reflect the experience and observation required by the *Spectator* critic. Although not wholly idyllic, the often idealized pre-industrial landscape and way of life portrayed in 'The Miller's Daughter', evoked in 'New-Year's Eve' and welcomed by Jerdan are far removed from contemporary reality. Rural England in the early 1830s was disturbed by 'Swing' riots and rick-burning, increasingly crossed by railways, enduring rural depopulation and the abject poverty encountered during William Cobbett's *Rural Rides* (1830). 'The Miller's Daughter' in particular anticipates the ideology of rural Englishness, continuing beyond Housman into the Georgian era, in which England increasingly became a 'land of lost content', more imaginary than real.

The *Athenaeum* reviewer praised Tennyson's 'beautiful appreciation of the female character' and the poems' central characters prefigure

Victorians' increasingly dichotomous views of women. 'Little Alice' (7) – 'The May Queen' and the dying speaker of 'New-Year's Eve' – is a flirtatious rather than a fallen young woman who dies repenting her 'cruel-hearted' (19) behaviour; the suggestion of Christian contrition is enhanced in the 'Conclusion' which Tennyson added in 1842. Alice, 'The Miller's Daughter', is an idealized, shyly blushing (131–3) virgin who becomes a 'True wife' (215) embodying the exemplary domestic virtues of an 'Angel in the House'.[39] The miller's masculine identity is securely established by his labour, but Alice is both selfless and self-less, her identity as 'daughter' and 'wife' – with that of her real-life counterparts – defined by her relationship to masculine power, her story and 'sorrow' (224) narrated by her husband.

Recent critics observe that with the First Reform Act the political citizen was 'formally named as masculine'.[40] The Act, which finally became law on 7 June 1832, extended the franchise and redistributed seats among the constituencies, including northern industrial towns,[41] leading to greater awareness of other regions and classes and a developing interest in national character. In 1833, following his review of *Poems* in the *New Monthly Magazine*, Edward Bulwer-Lytton explored the 'national characteristics' of *England and the English* and attributed many of their foibles to 'the peculiar nature of our aristocratical [*sic*] influences'.[42] Matthew Reynolds argues that for Tennyson and many contemporaries the most important aspects of Englishness were national character and the liberty resulting from the parliamentary monarchy established in England in 1688,[43] although Bulwer-Lytton points out sharply that the 'Frenchman, indeed, has long enjoyed the . . . same consciousness of liberty' which is 'the boast of the Englishman'.[44]

Tennyson reflected on liberty, England and the English in a series of political and patriotic poems written during the social and political turmoil of the early 1830s. The poems describe, and prescribe, his political philosophy at the time – a belief that change is necessary, but should evolve slowly, guided by wise leaders who have due regard for precedent and a clear vision of the future – and define the leaders' moderating role.[45] Freedom and free speech are assumed to be English characteristics, implicitly shared by all thus uniting the nation. In 'Of old sat Freedom' (written *c*.1833), liberty has descended from the traditional heights to her English 'isle-altar' (14), acquiring as attributes 'the triple forks' and 'the crown' (15–16) and the qualities of gravity, majesty and the wisdom 'to scorn . . . | The falsehood of extremes!' (23–4). By associating freedom with religious and royal authority, Tennyson appears to counter Shelley's appeal to 'Men of England' (147) to rise

'In unvanquishable number, | . . . Ye are many – they are few' (151–5, 368–72).[46] 'The Mask of Anarchy', written in 1819 in angry response to Peterloo, had also been published in 1832 by Edward Moxon, the publisher of *Poems*.

The 1830s also saw the arrest and transportation of the Tolpuddle Martyrs (1834) and, from 1836, the origins of Chartism. Tennyson's early political poems reflect the fear of 'banded unions' ('You ask me, why', written *c*.1833, 17), political extremism and popular protest which recurs throughout his work. In Lucretius's later waking nightmare, 'crowds . . . in an hour | Of civic tumult jam the doors' ('Lucretius', 1865, 168–9). The speaker of 'I loving Freedom' (written 1832–34) considers the state's power to change its 'future form' and freedom (17–20) and sees two possible paths, the 'nobler' (25) which extends and the 'baser' (29) which restricts 'the lists of liberty'. In the early 1830s Tennyson's patriotic concern with liberty was not confined to England. *Poems* contained two sonnets written in angry response to the 'Muscovite Oppress[ion]' (10–11) of 'Poland' and the 'Polish Insurrection' which, as a 'noble' attempt to break their 'iron shackles' (9, 4) rather than popular protest, is to be encouraged not feared. The tyrannical Czar's 'iron sceptre' (196) reappears in 'Hail Briton!' (written 1831–33), the longest of three poems in the *In Memoriam* stanza form which portray the contrasting, 'nobler' path of English freedom. With their Miltonic echoes and formulaic appeals – 'O Just and Good' ('Poland', 11) – the Polish sonnets are impersonal; by contrast, the form and content of 'You ask me, why', 'Love thou thy land' (written 1833–34) and 'Hail Briton!' suggest that the poet's 'domestic affections' are deeply engaged. The self-contained stanza form – many contain a single idea, closed with a full stop or colon – is suited to Tennyson's vision of England as 'the land that freemen till' and a 'land of settled government' ('You ask me, why', 5, 9). His measured consideration of England and English character is enhanced by Anglo-Saxon words which resist elision and lines often unbroken by punctuation:

> True love turned round on fixèd poles,
> Love, that endures not sordid ends,
> For English natures, freemen, friends,
> Thy brothers and immortal souls.

> ('Love thou thy land', 5–8)

'Hail Briton!' reveals the poet's fear of the Celtic temperament. England is an 'agèd commonwealth' (35) with an exemplary national character – 'this great people . . . that hath finisht more | Than any other for mankind' (37–40) – but susceptible to the close and disruptive influence of 'that unstable Celtic blood | That never keeps an equal pulse' (19–20). Tennyson's true 'patriot' is therefore the patriarchal statesman who 'through the channels of the state | Convoys the people's wish' (144–7). Tennyson borrowed images from 'Hail Briton!' throughout his career, altered or intensified as his political views changed. The sea recurs, in controlled channels or sanctified by the 'Tory member's elder son' (50) for separating England from the 'revolts' and 'revolutions' (65) that rock France – 'God bless the narrow seas! | I wish they were a whole Atlantic broad' (*The Princess*, 1847, Conclusion, 70–1). Fear becomes terror of the Celt's 'blind hysterics' (*In Memoriam*, 1850, CIX, 16). The warships 'that blow | The battle from their oaken sides' (7–8) return to defend England in 'Britons, Guard Your Own' (1852, 38), written in response to Louis Napoleon's 1851 *coup d'état.* French revolts, and the revolution which William Johnson Fox and John Wilson believed could inspire modern poets, continued to influence Tennyson's patriotic defence of England and English freedom, which intensified at moments of crisis or change.

William Johnson Fox reviews *Poems* (1832)

William Johnson Fox's critique of 'Tennyson's Poems' – published in the *Monthly Repository* in January 1833 – immediately evokes the revolts and revolutions that rocked France in 1830 and brought Louis-Philippe to the throne.[47] Fox vividly recalls the time:

> When barricades were piled, and sabres clashed, and musketry and cannon roared, and Fury with her thousand weapons fought in the streets of Paris; when the rainbow tricolour again spanned the political heavens, and the shouts of French victory were echoed back by those of British gratulation. (30)

Stirred by the strife, 'the Spirit of Reform in this country' had rallied 'the friends of freedom' throughout England (30). As Fox remarks, he was not indifferent to 'the whirlwind, the earthquake, and the fire', but Tennyson's unheralded 'little book' – *Poems, Chiefly Lyrical* – allowed Fox to escape the tumultuous scene and recognize a young poet who:

> If true to himself and his vocation, might charm the sense and soul of humanity, and make the unhewn blocks in this our wilderness of society move into temples and palaces. (30)

He now welcomes the volume's 'brother book' *Poems*, 'so like and so lovely in its likeness' (31). Fox refers in his review to both volumes but quotes only, and extensively, from *Poems*.

Fox believes that English poetry has changed for the better since he reviewed *Poems, Chiefly Lyrical* in January 1831. Poetry has proved itself as 'susceptible of improvement' as 'the machinery of a cotton-mill' (1831, 210) and, he concludes, has 'advanced like any other art' (32). However, Fox's concern with the nature and role of poetry and the poet continues. The 'true poet' is both '*artiste*' and 'philosopher', creating poetry of outer beauty and inner meaning, and Tennyson's endowment of these qualities is exceeded only by Coleridge and Wordsworth (31). Much of Tennyson's poetry is unsurpassed and Fox is unconcerned by artifices and archaisms which enhance the music of his verse but risk the recurring charge of affectation (32–3). Fox believes that modern poetry has advanced because the human mind has progressed. By understanding and applying psychology, poetry has become 'philosophized' (33) and conquered the 'new and exhaustless worlds' he discerned in 1831 (1831, 214). Like all great poets Tennyson is a 'mental philosopher' and modern poetry's reflective nature is exemplified by 'The Palace of Art' – an allegory 'as profound in conception as it is gorgeous in execution' (34). Fox shares the early critics' admiration for 'The May Queen' and 'New-Year's Eve', with their rural English setting, and praises the portraits – both 'mental and material' – which abound in the volume (36–8). He finds humour in the exemplary miller – 'good, honest workyday man' – and Tennyson's finest powers in the medievalist 'Legend of the Lady of Shalott' (39–40).

However, unlike the early critics, Fox's ultimate aim is to define and shape Tennyson as an English poet. He is disappointed not to see a greater improvement in Tennyson's second volume (40). 'All great intellects are progressive' rather than self-absorbed and Tennyson must have a greater sense of purpose. Fox's belief that poetry must transform society's 'wilderness' is less forcefully expressed than in 1831, when poets could 'command' sympathies and 'blast the laurels of tyrants' (1831, 224). Poetry must have a civilizing influence; to influence 'national feelings and character, and consequently . . . national happiness' (1831, 224), poets must now 'charm' humanity's 'sense and soul' and enable society's 'unhewn blocks' to 'move into temples and palaces' (30). Tennyson's poetic power must therefore have a defined, specific and unifying purpose and Fox urges Tennyson to define and fulfil his mission and realize the aspirations of the volume's opening sonnet – 'Mine be the strength of spirit full and free' (40).

John Wilson Croker reviews *Poems* (1832)

Tennyson was mentioned briefly in the April 1833 issues of two monthly magazines. William Johnson Fox, discussing Browning's *Pauline* in the *Monthly Repository*, referred to Browning and Tennyson as 'fellow worshippers at the same shrine'.[48] John Wilson ('Christopher North'), reviewing William Motherwell's poems in *Blackwood's Edinburgh Magazine*, prophetically called Tennyson the new 'star of Little Britain', a City of London street once noted for its booksellers.[49] Tennyson responded, 'I do not rise or set there very cordially – I prefer vegetating in a very quiet garden' far from 'the great world of literature'. Tennyson refers only to its literary associations, but for Washington Irving 'Little Britain' – the 'heart's core' of London – epitomized Englishness. With its adherence to old customs it was 'the stronghold of John Bullism'.[50]

Fox and Wilson's comments were overshadowed by a savagely ironic article published on 6 April 1833 in the *Quarterly Review*.[51] The *Quarterly* – a Tory journal with a style reflected in the nickname 'hang, draw and quarterly' – was considered by many to be 'the next book to God's Bible'.[52] The author was John Wilson Croker, a prominent Tory politician and regular contributor to the *Quarterly*, which in 1818 had printed his notorious review of Keats's 'Endymion'. Tennyson's contemporaries, but not the poet himself, attributed the review to 'Christopher North', responding to Tennyson's epigram, or to the editor, John Lockhart, but authorship and intent are made clear in Croker's letter dated 7 January 1833 to John Murray the younger, son of the *Quarterly*'s publisher: 'Tell your father and Mr. Lockhart that I undertake Tennyson and hope to make another Keats of him'.[53]

Croker's review – published in the wake of Reform Bill turmoil and Continental revolts and revolutions – immediately links Tennyson with the 'Cockney School' of poetry and radicalism. He introduces to readers:

A new prodigy of genius – another and a brighter star of that galaxy or *milky way* of poetry of which the lamented Keats was the harbinger; and let us take this occasion to sing our palinode on the subject of 'Endymion'. (81–2)

Rather than writing a retraction, however, Croker directs his scathing sarcasm towards Tennyson, whose connections with Cambridge and radical publishers made him, in Croker's eyes, both a Cockney poet of humble origin and a radical in turbulent times. In 1828 Hallam had reported of Cambridge that '*Shelley* is the idol before which we are to be short by the knees'[54] and from 1828 to 1832 the Cambridge Union reflected reformist views.[55] Effingham Wilson, publisher of *Poems, Chiefly Lyrical*, was connected with radical publications and had protested against 'The Moral and Political Evils of the Taxes on Knowledge'.[56] Edward Moxon had owned the *Englishman's Magazine*, whose politics caused Hallam to regret that 'conservative principles cannot be *openly* maintained',[57] and in 1832 also published Shelley's polemical 'Mask of Anarchy'.

The publication of *Poems* strengthened Tennyson's association with radicalism. Many of the journals which reviewed *Poems* were liberal or radical in tone. The *Athenaeum*'s proprietor-editor, Charles Wentworth Dilke, 'considered himself a Radical'.[58] The *Spectator*, and the *New Monthly Magazine* edited by Edward Bulwer-Lytton, had been in favour of the Reform Bill. The *Metropolitan* had declared itself an 'unflinching' advocate of state and church reform, while the *Monthly Repository* – owned and edited by William Johnson Fox from 1831 – had been launched on a crusade for 'political and social reform'. *Tait's Edinburgh Magazine* was the Scottish equivalent of the *Westminster Review* and the *True Sun* was founded by Patrick Garland as a campaigning alternative to the Whig *Sun*. However, the first periodicals to review *Poems* in December 1832 were noted for their literary content and book reviews rather than politics, and critics 'mingle[d] blame and praise'. The critic of the liberal-radical *Athenaeum* declared that Tennyson's fine poetic spirit was marred by affectation. William Jerdan in the 'strongly conservative' *Literary Gazette* mocked many poems, but conceded that Tennyson's talents could lead to success. For the reformist *Spectator* and the radical *Tait's*, *Poems* was a disappointing successor to *Poems, Chiefly Lyrical*. Although the most fulsome praise of *Poems* appeared in the campaigning *True Sun*, Tennyson was not universally hailed as a radical poet by the radical press, nor wholly condemned by conservative reviewers with critical integrity.

John Wilson Croker wrote to Lockhart of his review, "'Tis too long, but really there is no convincing the world of such extravagant absurdity but by actual extracts'.[59] Selecting, for readers' delight, examples of 'Mr. Tennyson's singular genius' (82), Croker makes extensive use of quotations and misquotations – italicized for emphasis and interspersed with ironic comments – which are taken out of context and made to look ridiculous. He satirizes the opening sonnet and mocks the volume's weakest poems, 'To Christopher North' and 'O Darling Room', never reprinted by Tennyson. Croker rejects the poems which other critics praise, passing by much of the 'female gallery', of which he could make 'no intelligible extract' (86). The beauties of 'The Miller's Daughter' are comparable with Keats and represent the poetic 'truth to Nature' he particularly scorns (88). He objects at length to the language and rhythm of poems based on mythological subjects, complaining that Tennyson 'embroidered' (89) his classical sources which Croker, assuming the understanding of his gentleman readers, quotes but does not translate.

Tennyson's contemporaries and later biographers differ as to the effect of Croker's review. On 23 January 1833 Lockhart replied to Croker: 'you have most completely effected your purpose, and that as shortly as it could have been done'.[60] Later in the year Hallam reassured Tennyson that *Poems* 'continues to sell tolerably'[61] and James Spedding reported that the volume 'has paid its expenses and is making a clear profit'.[62] Moxon's belief that a review, 'even with a sprinkling of abuse in it', is 'worth a hundred advertisements' was apparently justified.[63] However, in 1923 Harold Nicolson declared that with the review 'Tennyson's reputation sank to zero'.[64] Charles Tennyson believed that the article had a disastrous effect, with sales of the volume irretrievably damaged.[65] Tennyson himself admitted in later life that the *Quarterly* review had almost crushed him, and his sensitivity to criticism increased. Learning that John Stuart Mill was to review *Poems*, Tennyson wrote to James Spedding: 'I do not wish to be dragged forward again in any shape before the reading public at present'.[66]

Although Harold Nicolson claimed that Mill alone raised his voice in protest against Croker, more than two years later, Tennyson's reputation was sufficiently established for a number of journals and literary figures to defy the *Quarterly*'s 'Biblical' authority by defending Tennyson in public and acknowledging his place in the poetic succession. On 9 April 1833 – three days after the *Quarterly* appeared – the *Sun* defended Tennyson against 'the stinging review of the productions of a young man' who, despite occasional lapses of taste, 'is unquestionably not devoid of the "vision and faculty divine"'.[67] Four days later the literary gossip columnist of the *Athenaeum*, finding the *Quarterly*'s review 'strangely provocative of comment', concluded that Tennyson 'has much fine poetry about him'.[68] Hallam wrote to Tennyson that Samuel Rogers 'defends you publicly as the most promising genius of the time'[69] and Allan Cunningham commented in the *Athenaeum* on 16 November that Tennyson 'is looked upon by sundry critics as the chief living hope of the Muse'.[70]

John Stuart Mill reviews *Poems, Chiefly Lyrical* and *Poems* (1832)

Tennyson need not have feared John Stuart Mill's measured and appreciative critique of *Poems, Chiefly Lyrical* and *Poems* (1832).[71] Published in the *London Review* in July 1835, Mill's review – the final response to the *Quarterly* – is of particular interest because, as Isobel Armstrong argues, he appears to balance the differing views of William Johnson Fox and Arthur Hallam with the ideas of earlier critics.[72] Although Mill believes that reviewers' interest in the volumes is confined to John Wilson's critique of *Poems, Chiefly Lyrical* in *Blackwood's* and Croker's review of *Poems* in the *Quarterly*, critical ideas were presumably widely discussed among contemporaries. Additionally, Mill writes with the intention of enhancing Tennyson's reputation and refuting Croker's criticism (86).

Mill's concern with the nature and role of poetry and the poet is more clearly structured and argued than earlier critics' ideas. He reminds readers that *Poems, Chiefly Lyrical* was the work of a young, unknown author with remarkable poetic powers (84). Tennyson's second volume reveals that his earlier faults, although still discernible, are diminishing, while 'the positive excellence' is 'not only greater and more uniformly sustained, but of a higher order'. The poet's imagination and intellect have both advanced. Aware that the poems have been gaining a considerable reputation, Mill wishes 'to accelerate this progress' and demonstrate the value of the *Quarterly*'s critical judgements (86). For Mill, Tennyson's greatest gift – particularly exemplified by 'Mariana' – is 'the power of *creating* scenery' which transcends mere description both to symbolize and evoke human emotion with a power surpassed only by reality. However, echoing Hallam's view of the barrier between poet and public, Mill doubts that 'Mariana' will be immediately appreciated by all poetry-lovers as only trite images and sentiments are instantly accepted. He believes that 'New-Year's Eve' will be the volumes' most popular poem (87–8), a choice which encapsulates Victorian critics' belief that:

> Simple, genuine pathos, arising out of the situations and feelings common to mankind . . . is of all kinds of poetic beauty that which can be most universally appreciated. (88)

Mill argues that the character of every true poet contains two essential elements – one inherent, the other cultivated (91). Deriving from nature a 'peculiar kind of nervous susceptibility', Mill's true poet resembles Hallam's poet of sensation, motivated solely by the desire for beauty. For Mill, however, every great poet – one who has influenced humankind – has also been a great thinker, echoing Fox's later view that poetry has become 'philosophized'. The poems prove incontestably that Tennyson is gifted with 'the poetic temperament' and his 'intellectual culture' is advancing steadily and rapidly. However, Mill warns, if Tennyson neglects the intellect necessary to discipline his imagination the resulting poems will give pleasure but not evoke sympathy. They will therefore fail to achieve poetry's noble aim – to influence human-kind's desires and characters through the emotions and 'raise them towards the perfection of their nature'. Mill successfully balances Fox and Hallam's differing views to reach a remarkably similar conclusion, that the true poet can transform the national character.

Mill concludes by discussing Tennyson's faults and, in footnotes, his failures (94–5) and by defining a critical view Hallam did not share:

> Let our philosophical system be what it may, human feelings exist: human nature, with all its enjoyments and sufferings, its strugglings, its victories and defeats, still remain to us; and these are the materials of all poetry. (96).

Poetry, he argues, requires 'the most finished perfection' to achieve lasting fame and the volumes are not without fault (96). Some short poems are meaningless, 'awkwardnesses and feeblenesses of expression' remain to be corrected (Mill appears to illustrate by example) and Tennyson's versification is not yet perfect. But these are minor imperfections, mentioned only to indicate where further effort is needed if Tennyson is to attain 'the high place in our poetic literature' for which he is already so well qualified (97).

Mill is disturbed by the volumes' most juvenile poems, the ballads 'English Warsong' and 'National Song' in *Poems, Chiefly Lyrical* and 'Buonaparte' in *Poems* (94). However, even Tennyson's weakest poems illustrate his recurring concerns with England and the English. Although 'Buonaparte' echoes the ballads' aggressive patriotism and preoccupation with English freedom, Tennyson's Francophobia is directed towards a military leader therefore 'dignified' by sonnet structure. For Mill, the inclusion of 'English Warsong' and 'National Song' is 'unaccountable', unless 'they are meant for the bitter ridicule of vulgar nationality, and of the poverty of intellect which usually accompanies it'.[73] 'National Song' dates from 1828–29 and Tennyson had recently completed a literary parody. However, 'I dare not write an Ode' (1827) is a mock ode revealing extensive knowledge of the classics, in which he explores with wry humour the difficulty of being an original English poet:

> I dare not write an Ode for fear Pimplaea
> Should fork me down the double-crested hill,

And sneering say that Fancy, like Astraea,
Has left the world to ignorance and ill – .

(1–4)

Awareness of Tennyson's later work and its recurring themes also rules out the suggestion of satire and Mill's query can be answered in the affirmative – the poems 'are to be taken as serious' (94). Discussing patriotism in 1833, Edward Bulwer-Lytton observed that the English and French 'are both eminently vain of country' with the Englishman rejoicing that 'so great a country belonged to himself'.[74] Tennyson's patriotism – like liberty in 'I loving Freedom' – followed two paths. The political poems of the early 1830s represent a measured, comparatively moderate consideration of English freedom, but in later years, whenever Tennyson perceived a threat to England's stability, he reverted to ballad form to encourage rather than ridicule 'vulgar nationality' (94) or popular patriotism. 'English Warsong' and 'National Song' are forerunners of Laureate Tennyson's ballads and drinking songs such as 'Hands All Round' (1852) and the bellicose and Francophobic poems of the 1850s.

Despite the childishness Mill deplores, 'English Warsong' and 'National Song' introduce themes which recur throughout Tennyson's career. In later works, the ballads' reiterated chauvinistic assertions – 'There are no men like Englishmen, | So tall and bold as they be' ('National Song', 7–8) – are transformed into chivalric ideals of political or military service to the nation. The 'Duke of Argyll' (1885) personifies Tennyson's 'Patriot Statesman' (1). Their unthinking celebration of English heroism and the military self-sacrifice Tennyson regards as inseparable from patriotism – 'Who fears to die? | Is there any here who fears to die?' ('English Warsong', 1–2) – anticipates the cavalry charges of the Light (1854) and Heavy (1882) Brigades and the insidious arguments of Tiresias praising those 'who dare | For that sweet mother land which gave them birth | Nobly to do, nobly to die' ('Tiresias', 1885, 117–19). The beauty and chastity of 'English maids' and 'wives' ('National Song', 25, 21) prefigure Laureate Tennyson's patriotic and increasingly idealized portraits of Victoria, to be revered as 'Mother, Wife, and Queen' ('To the Queen', 1851, 27–8). Ultimately, for Tennyson, 'there are no wives, like English' – royal – 'wives | So fair and chaste as they be' ('National Song', 21–2).

The reviews of *Poems* (1832) confirm that by July 1835 Tennyson was an acknowledged English poet. He was of sufficient stature to be 'undertake[n]' by the hostile Croker, regarded by friendly critics as equal to Coleridge, a finer artist than Crabbe and qualified for the 'high place' in English poetry he would attain in 1850. Tennyson was presented as the natural successor to the great and passing generation of English poets with whom he was compared; accordingly, critics sought to refine his language, direct his subjects and define his role. Fox and Mill's belief that poetry had a continuing, influential and ultimately unifying role in an age of industry echoed but intensified that of the *Athenaeum* reviewer, who in July 1829 rightly rejected the view that poetry was in decline, as throughout the nineteenth century Tennyson and his fellow poets continued to engage, directly or by allusion, with contemporary concerns.

The reviewers were writing in turbulent times. Their selections – and rejections – not only fulfil critical demands for clear and simple English, free from affectations which impede empathy, but also embody changing connotations of contemporary Englishness, including language and landscape, patriotism and perceptions of women, and Bulwer-Lytton's concern with 'our aristocratical influences'. Fox and Mill's preoccupation with transforming 'our wilderness of society' exemplifies the importance of national character to reviewers writing in an 'Age of Machinery' and 'reform of Government'.[75] Many of the English scenes and figures portrayed in *Poems* (1832) provide 'a precedent . . . | And an example' ('Hail Briton!', written 1831–33, 82–3). They evoke the imaginative identification Fox and Mill believe will raise society to its potential perfection. They also foreshadow the increasingly idealized and exemplary representations of England and the English to be considered in the following, predominantly theme-based chapters of this study.

3
'Mr. Tennyson's Truly English Spirit': Landscape and Nature in *Poems* (1842)

The two-volume edition of *Poems*, published by Edward Moxon in May 1842, laid the foundation-stone of Tennyson's fame. The volumes were favourably reviewed in a wide range of contemporary periodicals, many of whose critics comment approvingly on the poet's 'keen eye for the beauties of nature'.[1] In Chapters 1 and 2 I examined how reviewers of the early volumes attempted to define and shape Tennyson as an English poet in the context of contemporary concerns, and considered how poems selected or rejected by reviewers reflect changing aspects of nineteenth-century Englishness. In this chapter I argue that in *Poems* (1842) Tennyson constructs himself as a more English poet by changing from the sublime settings of earlier poems to a recognizably English landscape, and by using the English forms of popular ballad, and blank verse for the English Idyls, and suggest that he draws on a medieval past as a way of rejecting contemporary England's industrial landscapes. I also examine how poems contained in the two volumes embody new and emerging concepts of Englishness current in the mid-nineteenth century, and consider contemporary reviewers' responses to *Poems* (1842). Reviewers agreed that Tennyson had grown in poetic strength since his previous publication, but were less concerned with changing English society than reviewers of the early volumes.

'Taking the field'

During the 1830s progress towards the publication of *Poems* had been painfully slow. Despite the pleas of Moxon and the poet's brother Frederick, Tennyson had published no further volumes and had only reluctantly contributed poems to *The Keepsake* in 1836 and *The Tribute* the following year. Twentieth-century critics and biographers believe that the ten years' publishing silence was caused by fear of 'ridicule and misrepresentation'[2] following John Wilson Croker's savage attack on *Poems* (1832), although Arthur Hallam's death, and personal and family health and financial problems, must also have been contributory factors. As Tennyson himself remarked, '*I remember everything that has been said against me, and forget all the rest*'.[3] Towards the end of the 1830s Moxon intensified his efforts to persuade Tennyson to publish again. Friends echoed Moxon's pleas. In March 1838 Richard Chenevix Trench asked Richard Monckton Milnes to urge the poet 'to take the field', and George Stovin Venables warned Tennyson not to be 'so careless of fame and of influence'.[4] Edward FitzGerald complained in November 1839 that 'I want A.T. to publish another volume: as all his friends do . . . but he is too lazy and wayward to put his hand to the business'.[5] However, Tennyson's bitterly personal unfinished poem of 1839 confirms that disillusionment and insecurity rather than laziness lay behind his reluctance to republish:

> Wherefore, in these dark ages of the Press
> (As that old Teuton christened them) should I,
> Sane mind and body, wish to print my rhyme,
> Fame's millionth heir-apparent?[6]

An additional impetus to republish came from America where Tennyson's reputation had been growing steadily, with poems circulated in manuscript copies and by word of mouth.[7] Attempts to reprint the unrevised early volumes in Boston in 1838 came to nothing, but in December 1840 Charles Stearns Wheeler offered to edit the poems if Tennyson agreed to Little & Brown issuing an American edition. In February 1841, having 'corrected copies of most that was worth correcting' in *Poems, Chiefly Lyrical* and *Poems* (1832), Tennyson consented to 'republish these in England with several new poems and transmit copies to Little & Brown' and to Wheeler to 'do as you choose with them'.[8]

The publication of *Poems* owed much to Tennyson's friends. Tennyson and Edward FitzGerald had been contemporaries, but not acquainted, at Cambridge, where FitzGerald admired the poet's work,[9] and their 'first recorded meeting'[10] in April 1835 led to a lifelong friendship. Despite Tennyson's complaints – 'You bore me about my book'[11] – FitzGerald took over the practicalities of publication that Hallam had undertaken for the earlier volumes and experienced similar delays and difficulties. In September 1841 FitzGerald reported to Frederick Tennyson that 'Alfred is in London "busy preparing for the press"'.[12] Early the following year

Tennyson had still not sent his poems to the printer, so FitzGerald 'carried him off . . . with violence to Moxon's'[13] and, despite Tennyson's doubts and insecurities, pursued the volumes through to publication on 14 May 1842. Tennyson immediately sent copies to America, where they were published by W.D. Ticknor of Boston who had offered better terms than Little & Brown.[14] Ticknor's first edition consisted of between fifteen hundred and two thousand copies. Moxon was publishing in a continuing slump in the British book trade; he therefore issued a more cautious edition of eight hundred copies, bound in drab paper boards with a white spine label and priced at twelve shillings for the two volumes. In August 1842 FitzGerald confirmed to Frederick Tennyson that 'very many copies had been sold at Cambridge, which indeed will be the chief market for them'.[15] Four months after publication five hundred copies had been sold, and between 1843 and 1846 Moxon issued three successive and increasingly large editions.[16]

The first volume of *Poems* contained Tennyson's selection of poems previously published in 1830 and 1832, but with 'Mariana', 'The Lady of Shalott', 'Oenone' and other works extensively revised. In addition there were seven new poems, including the 'Conclusion' to 'The May Queen' and 'New-Year's Eve'. The second volume contained poems published for the first time – with the exception of 'The Sleeping Beauty' and 'St Agnes' Eve'[17] – many of which, as Tennyson's title page note points out, were written in 1833. Also included in the second volume were the blank verse poems later designated as 'English Idyls'. FitzGerald, a more demanding critic than Hallam, wished 'the new volume' could have been published separately, concerned that 'those everlasting Eleanores' and 'Isabels, – which always were, and are, and must be, a nuisance', would 'drag it down'.[18] However, as many twentieth-century critics conclude, the 1842 volumes 'established Tennyson as the foremost poet of his generation, that which succeeded Keats, Shelley and Byron'.[19] The first reviews appeared two weeks after publication, and although Tennyson feared 'the Press' the volumes were favourably received by critics in periodicals of differing political persuasions, intended for readers at all levels of society. Edgar F. Shannon lists eighteen reviews of the first edition alone, printed in daily, weekly and monthly newspapers and literary journals, in secular, religious and student publications, and in the three great quarterly reviews.[20] The reception of *Poems* fulfilled FitzGerald's prophecy, that 'with all his faults' Tennyson 'will publish such a volume as has not been published since the time of Keats' and 'will never be suffered to die',[21] and the hopes of earlier critics who had presented Tennyson as heir apparent to the passing generation of great English poets.

Early 'Nature-poems' and their context

The reviewers of *Poems* praised Tennyson's 'keen eye for the beauties of nature' and gift for 'English landscape-painting'.[22] As Tennyson wrote to Emily Sellwood in 1838, 'I have dim mystic sympathies with tree and hill reaching far back into childhood. A known landskip is to me an old friend.'[23] However, during the 1830s and 1840s, when *Poems* was prepared, published and reviewed, the English landscape and English rural society were changing; by 1851 more than half the population of England and Wales was living in urban areas. English agricultural society divided conventionally into three classes – landowners, farmers and labourers, 'who had nothing to sell but their labour power'.[24] This situation made inevitable the uprising of farm labourers which broke out in 1816 and 1822, as 'Swing' riots in late 1830 – predominantly in 'the low-wage South and East' – and recurred in 1834–35 and 1842–44, their object economic rather than revolutionary,[25] and which formed part of the varying movements of social protest which ebbed and flowed in the 1830s and Hungry Forties according to the cycle of booms and slumps.

England's physical landscape was also changing. An extensive network of canals had been constructed in the early decades of the nineteenth century; in the 1830s, as John Sterling observed in the *Quarterly Review*, 'seventy millions of pounds' created 'nearly fifteen hundred miles of railroads'[26] across the country. The enclosure of fields, commons and waste lands in the late eighteenth and early nineteenth century had introduced into the formerly open landscape walls, fences, trees and hedges, roads and drains, and the improved implements and chemical fertilizers of more intensive farming. Enclosure brought both drawbacks and advantages. For John Clare, 'Enclosure came and trampled on the grave, | Of Labours rights and left the poor a slave',[27] but the change had material benefits for Tennyson's 'Northern Farmer: Old Style', whose former bracken-covered 'waäste' had been transformed into valuable pasture land supporting a herd of eighty cows (1864, 37–40). Tennyson's childhood was rural rather than agricultural and he was touched only tangentially by the Swing riots which came close to Cambridge in November–December 1830.[28] However, always fearful of popular protest, he remembered until late in life the 'rick-fire days' of 'more than half a hundred years ago' ('To Mary Boyle', 1889, 27–8). Agrarian strife and the rural poor are largely absent from Tennyson's poems, in which the landscape is often idealized and which mirror the poet's closely observed delight in the flora and fauna that flourished in the trees and hedgerows of England's post-enclosure landscape.

The landscape settings of many poems Tennyson published in 1842 are notable for their Englishness, a resolution reflected in 'Ode to Memory'. Tennyson considered the 'Ode' to be 'one of the best of his early and peculiarly concentrated Nature-poems'[29] and James Spedding praised the poem as 'a sketch truly drawn from homeliest nature, which needs . . . no fancy dress to make it beautiful, but will remain for ever fresh'.[30] Its rhythms and theme – that childhood memories support us in later years – echo the 'Immortality Ode' and John Sterling commented drily that 'had it preceded . . . Mr. Wordsworth', Tennyson's 'Ode' 'would have been a memorable poem'.[31] However, the early 'Nature-poem' is memorable for the poetic manifesto at its heart – Tennyson's declaration that in future inspiration will be drawn from his memories of the English landscape. In Pauline Fletcher's apt phrase, Tennyson declares that he 'will dwell in the garden of his own mind rather than in the garden of literature',[32] although many 'Nature-poems' ultimately reveal the literary influence of his classical education. The poet of 'On Sublimity' (1827) had yearned for 'the wild cascade, the rugged scene, | The loud surge bursting o'er the purple sea' (3–4). In 'Ode to Memory' Tennyson consciously rejects the 'flaunting vines' and 'waterfall | which ever sounds and shines | . . . upon the wall | Of purple cliffs' (48–54) exemplifying the exotic settings of his early poems, many of which were inspired by the contents of Somersby's extensive library. The 'great artist Memory' (80) he invokes for inspiration in the 'Ode' is to 'Come from the woods that belt the gray hill-side' (55), the 'ridgèd wolds' (67) and 'waste enormous marsh' (101) of his native Lincolnshire, and from 'The seven elms, the poplars four | That stand beside my father's door' (55–7) as symbols of Somersby's idyllic garden.

An English 'garden bowered close | With plaited alleys of the trailing rose' evoked by 'Memory' ('Ode', 105–6) is the setting for 'The Gardener's Daughter'. One of the blank verse 'English Idyls' with contemporary themes whose debt to Theocritus is discussed later in the chapter, 'The Gardener's Daughter' embodies the Englishness of landscape, class and iconic Victorian womanhood prefigured by 'The Miller's Daughter', discussed in Chapter 2. The poem also exemplifies the nineteenth-century ideology of rural Englishness, in which poets and artists increasingly anticipate William Morris's injunction to 'Forget six counties overhung with smoke, | Forget the snorting steam and piston stroke, | Forget the spreading of the hideous town;' ('Introduction', *The Earthly Paradise*, 1868–70, 1–3)[33] to create a 'land of lost content', more imaginary than real. Tennyson was charmed by 'the distance . . . in the landscape, the picture and the past'[34] and the poem is set in the pre-industrial past and an idealized garden 'Not wholly in the busy world, nor quite | Beyond it' (33–4), a cultivated middle landscape safely distanced from industrializa-tion and agrarian strife. Christopher Ricks argues that 'it is the garden, not the girl, that fires the poem',[35] but both are essential to the vision at the heart of Tennyson's domestic idyl/l. The poet acknowledged that 'the descriptions of nature' are 'full and rich . . . to a fault', for 'the lover is an artist', but believed that 'the central picture must hold its place'.[36] The landscape surrounding the garden is languorous – the slow stream 'creeps' and lilies are 'lazy' (40–2). As the speaker nears 'that Eden where she dwelt' (187) the idyll intensifies: 'All the land . . . | Smelt of the coming summer' (75–7), and 'voices of the well-contented' and very English birds echo 'their joyful thoughts' (88–98). Nature and mood unite in harmony at the moment when the artist-speaker 'beheld her there' (121).

For John Sterling, 'The Gardener's Daughter' – subtitled 'The Pictures' – was an unsurpassable 'English landscape-painting'.[37] Leonée Ormond observes that the poem's painterly qualities and the artist-speaker's vision of Rose reflect the poet's admiration for Titian and 'the Titianic Flora' (167) in the Uffizi in Florence, noting that two deleted pas-sages 'suggest further connections with Titian'.[38] However, Tennyson's vision – unmoving and 'Gowned in pure while' (125) – is set in a recognizably English landscape and holds flowers that symbolize human love. His 'Rose | In roses' (141) also evokes an English Sleeping Beauty, an Anglicization of Charles Perrault's seventeenth-century nursery tale, *La Belle au Bois Dormant*, treated more traditionally in 'The Day Dream' where the princess and surrounding nature rest in suspended animation.

The vision of Rose is the 'prelude' (267) to a domestic idyll that crosses class barriers and foreshadows Victorian England's preoccupa-tion with home and family. In 1864 John Ruskin idealized the home as 'a sacred place, a vestal temple, a temple of the hearth'[39] and, as Laureate, Tennyson revered Victoria as 'Mother, Wife, and Queen' ('To the Queen', 1851, 27–8). Like Alice, 'The Miller's Daughter', Rose is a white-clad virgin 'suffused by blushes' (151) who becomes a true wife. She is similarly given identity by her father's profession, and a voice by the male speaker, and is subject to the male gaze, the artist-speaker's 'pencil' lingering over the physical beauty and potential fertility of her 'bounteous' breast (138). As Michael Timko remarks – citing 'The Sisters', whose narrator avenges her sister's betrayal by murdering the Earl – not all Tennyson's 'idyllic ladies' are mere 'lilies or roses', afraid to take action.[40] Rose both moves and acts, although less dramatically than the avenging sister, thus appearing to be a stronger character than Alice. While the speaker gazes, Rose – although silent – retains sufficient self-possession to 'braid' her hair and 'grant' a symbolic rose, an action that leaves him transfixed and 'statue-like' (155–8). Eustace's later wedding vow is '[b]reathed, like the covenant of a God, to hold | From thence through all the worlds' (203–5) and the poem's central vision also encapsulates Tennyson's view of marriage as a 'two-celled heart' and of the woman's role in the relationship – 'Nor equal, nor unequal' (*The Princess*, 1847, VII, 285–9). The flower granted by Rose symbolizes her 'greatest gift, | A woman's heart' (224–5) and willingness, despite her conventionally 'faltering' voice (230), to 'enter on' what the poet later termed 'the larger woman-world | Of wives and mothers' ('The Ring', 1889, 443–4). Tennyson does not 'tell . . . | Of that which came between' (246–7) the meeting and the unveiled portrait; he is concerned only with 'love at first sight, first-born' (185) and the transcendent moment of recognition and acceptance.

'The Gardener's Daughter' is set in an idealized landscape, in which mood and nature are fused. In 'Mariana', by contrast, Tennyson portrays a psychological landscape, a landscape of the mind which mirrors Mariana's desolation and symbolizes her unfulfilled sexuality. The poem received contemporary critics' particular praise. For the *Sun* reviewer, 'every line is instinct with the truest feeling'.[41] Leigh Hunt admired the 'images all painted from nature, and true to the feeling of the subject'.[42] Charles Kingsley marvelled at the way 'in which the scenery is drawn, simply and faithfully, from those counties which the world considers the quintessence of the prosaic – the English fens'.[43] More recent critics have demonstrated that nineteenth-century views of women became increasingly dichotomous, and Mariana is a fallen woman, the mirror image of Rose, the virginal 'Gardener's Daughter', and 'Isabel', a model of marital chastity and the poem with which 'Mariana' was juxtaposed in all editions supervised by Tennyson. As the critic of *Tait's Edinburgh Magazine* recognized, one of the poet's 'most peculiar gifts' is the 'power of making the picturesque delineation of external nature illustrate the mood of mind portrayed'.[44] The house, garden and surrounding landscape are seen through Mariana's eyes and the natural images reflect her state of mind, a use of landscape which anticipates the symbolist poets. The *'moated grange . . .* rose to the music of Shakespeare's words',[45] but Tennyson invented the stanza form with its ballad-like refrains and for Leigh Hunt the recurring sighs of 'aweary, aweary' 'help us to sympathise with the fatigue of the inhabitant'.[46] However, although the subject of the poem is Mariana's sensibility the narrative voice is male, and

the poem's imagery emphasizes Mariana's repeatedly 'dreary' and desolate life. She has been deserted, is punished for her sexuality and serves
as a warning not an example. Landscape and nature in 'The Gardener's
Daughter' are fertile, bountiful and basking in summer warmth; the
contrasting natural images in 'Mariana' suggest sterility, darkness and
decay, emblematic of her exclusion from the Tennysonian world of
wives and mothers – 'blackest moss' (1), 'thickest dark' (18). A flat and
almost treeless 'dark fen' (28) surrounds the 'lonely moated grange' (8,
32), resembling the 'waste enormous' Lincolnshire 'marsh' evoked by
the poet's 'Memory' ('Ode to Memory', 101), and in the desolate house
time passes slowly. Whereas Rose's silent movement to grant the symbolic flower is positive and life-affirming, the altered tense and decisive
tone of Mariana's final refrain signal the death of hope – 'Then, said she,
"I am very dreary, | He will not come," she said;' (81–2).

The 'English Idyls' and critical interpretations of
the idyll form

Tennyson created a uniquely English form of the classical idyll. In Robert
Pattison's view, part of the fascination of 'Mariana' is 'its playful distinction of form':[47] neither wholly a ballad nor truly a lyric, 'Mariana', he
concludes, 'is an idyll', although unlike 'The Gardener's Daughter' not
included among the poems later designated as 'English Idyls'. Tennyson
used to spell 'English Idyls' and 'the shorter Idyls' (which he pro-
nounced 'eye-dls') with one 'l', to distinguish them from the epic *Idylls
of the King*.[48] However, he did not define the purpose of the two terms
which, like the poems themselves, are open to differing interpretations,
with critics focusing variously on form, content and context. Pattison,
for example, notes that in Tennyson's work 'idyll . . . designates poems
that might more strictly be classified as dramatic monologue, dialogue,
epyllion, elegy, satire or lyric', which were created by Theocritus and
other Alexandrian poets and later came to be called idylls. Idyll, from
the Greek *eidyllion*, can mean 'little picture' or, from its root *eidos*, reflect
interest in poetic structure and visual imagery. There is no general agree-
ment on the term in English and as it is rarely used in titles of English
poems before Tennyson there is no clear English tradition on which the
poet could draw.[49]

The Englishness of 'Mariana' thus consists not only in its landscape
and Shakespearean source but also in the poem's form. Observing that
the idyll's originality lies in its adaptation of existing forms, Robert
Pattison analyses its characteristics and the contradictions he describes

are reflected in 'Mariana' and the 'English Idyls', in which Tennyson reworked his classical sources to create a uniquely English idyl/l. The idyll is self-conscious in its erudition and distance – Pattison cites the Theocritean framing device and the development of allegory[50] – and eclectic in its re-use of tradition. Grander than the lyric, the idyll often uses the lyric first person, and characters sometimes sing. Idylls focus on events isolated from a larger context; contain a limited number of characters, with action affecting only the protagonist/s. An idyll may create a dramatic situation, but may also be a monologue. It is a realistic form, but not didactic, and the idyll's ironic detachment belies a complete seriousness of purpose.

The influence of Theocritus on the 'English Idyls' is examined by Angela O'Donnell, who argues that by emulating Theocritus Tennyson learned to use language and imagery more precisely and with greater restraint.[51] The poet's study of Theocritus developed with the nineteenth century's increasing scholarly interest in Hellenism. As a child Tennyson was taught Latin and Greek by his father and during his Cambridge years Trinity College became England's most important institution for the study of Greek. In 1842 Walter Savage Landor published a critical commentary on *The Idyls of Theocritus*, emphasizing their variety of subjects and genres. Tennyson and Browning both understood the form's flexibility, the latter defining 'an idyl' as 'a succinct little story complete in itself; not necessarily concerning pastoral matters . . . although from the prevalence of such topics in the idyls of Theocritus, such is the general notion'.

As Angela O'Donnell observes, modern and contemporary critics differ as to which poems can be designated 'English Idyls'.[52] She also notes that many modern critics, influenced by Hallam Tennyson's *Memoir* and Aubrey de Vere's discussion of the early poems, assume that the 'English Idyls' are 'pictures of English home and country life'.[53] However, this misinterpretation began with the volumes' early reviewers – classically educated English gentlemen familiar with the pastoral tradition. John Sterling, for example, praises Tennyson's 'Idylls' as 'compositions drawn from the heart of our actual English life'.[54] Tracing the poems' publication history, O'Donnell echoes Robert Pattison in concluding that the 'Idyls' are 'English' in form rather than content, with the Greek dactylic hexameters of Theocritus becoming English blank verse.[55]

William E. Fredeman is concerned with content rather than form. For Fredeman, Tennyson is 'the domestic poet *par excellence* in English',[56] with the 'English Idyls' and other 'domestic idyls' unified by an underlying vision that first evolved in 'The Miller's Daughter' and recurs throughout

Tennyson's work. The idyls' domestic themes – friendship, love, marriage and family relationships, viewed in contemporary settings – go beyond Victorian domestic ideology to present Tennyson's vision of an ideally ordered but rarely realizable world that Fredeman defines as a hierarchical ladder, ascending from 'personal security, through familial stability, to a higher order in the state and in the cosmos'. Fredeman's view of this ideal is exemplified by King Arthur's 'model for the mighty world' (*Guinevere*, 1859, 462) and encapsulated in Hallam Tennyson's observation that 'Upon the sacredness of home life [Tennyson] would maintain that the stability and greatness of a nation largely depend'.[57]

Michael Timko agrees that domesticity is equated with civilization and culture in Tennyson's idyllic vision.[58] In Timko's view, the idyls reflect Tennyson's recurring concern with problems prevailing in England's rapidly changing society; thus the exemplary values and virtues portrayed in the poems are to preserve 'that which is best, most "civilized".' For Herbert F. Tucker, the 'English idylls' also aim to articulate 'an acceptable world'.[59] However, the poems reflect the tensions created by Tennyson's need to endorse such values, shared with middle-class readers, without aligning himself to any particular interest and while fulfilling the idylls' requirement for resolution. His polemical purpose is therefore concealed in detailed description of the physical world, which ultimately unites individuals in a familiar landscape.

Elizabeth K. Helsinger similarly regards the 'English Idyls' as both descriptive and prescriptive, but argues that Tennyson's rural scenes make 'imperfect icons'.[60] Helsinger believes that in writing the 'English Idyls' Tennyson was responding to 'the pressure exerted on him to write as a national poet' (clearly by critics of the earlier volumes) – by turning to English subjects and framing stories of an English past with a contemporary English audience – and exploring the possibility of poems becoming 'public symbols creating collective bonds of national feeling'. Although the 'English Idyls' were welcomed on publication as expressions of a uniquely English appreciation of rural life and landscape, Helsinger argues that the poems reflect Tennyson's ambiguous relationship with landed power (his family were not wholly dependent on land) and his complex view of the poet's role. The poems' narration of past events is often framed by a contemporary audience of young male friends, mirroring the Cambridge Apostles who encouraged the publication of Tennyson's early volumes. This ideal relationship between poet and audience-as-community ended when Tennyson's father and grandfather died in the 1830s, forcing him to consider a commercial relationship with an increasingly democratized reading public.

Roger Ebbatson also suggests that any reading of the 'English Idylls' should consider the poems' preparation and publication in the 1830s and their 'political unconscious'.[61] For Ebbatson as for Herbert F. Tucker, the 'Idylls' serve 'a middle-class drive for power'. They are 'English' because their 'narrativisation of nationhood' unites in responsive recognition the English middle-class readers who welcomed the poems' publication, thus marginalizing disruptive social forces. Despite the Idylls' 'domesticating trajectory', however, gaps and changes in the narrative structure betray Tennyson's difficulty in representing his imagined community. Ebbatson finds the recurring Theocritean themes of 'erotic frustration and verbal competition' reflected in the poems and echoes Robert Pattison in noting that Tennyson follows Theocritus's example by creatively reworking his 'founding classical model'.

The 'English Idyls': 'Dora'

The rural settings, flora and fauna inseparable from the 'English Idyls' and other poems in the 1842 volumes form a unifying English 'language' which Elizabeth K. Helsinger, quoting George Eliot, terms the 'mother tongue of our imagination'.[62] She argues that 'rural things (flowers, bird notes, fields and hedgerows)' create a shared national language, which is subtly and inextricably associated with our childhood. However, Helsinger's 'rural things' should also include customs and occasions central to the rural year, including the 'harvest time' (53) that forms the setting of 'Dora', accepted as an 'English Idyl' by all the modern critics discussed above. Although critics justly focus on the influence of Theocritus when discussing the 'English Idyls', A. Dwight Culler regards Robert Southey's nine *English Eclogues* (1799) as the Idyls' formal precedent.[63] Tennyson was also indebted to Mary Russell Mitford's prose idyl *Our Village: Sketches of Rural Character and Scenery*, published in five volumes between 1824 and 1832; 'Dora', written by 1835, was partly suggested by Mitford's story *Dora Cresswell*.

'Dora' is both descriptive and prescriptive. Tennyson's 'tale of a nobly simple country girl, had to be told in the simplest possible poetical language, and therefore . . . gave most trouble'.[64] The resulting experiment in decorum, in which the poet reworked his English, classical and Biblical models, was praised by contemporary reviewers and later critics, although only more recent critics have discerned the underlying social and political concerns. In 'Dora' the blank verse is pared down to the austerity appropriate to a narrative of self-denial and humility that Edward FitzGerald believed 'comes near the Book of Ruth'[65] and

Tennyson employs a nobly simple language resonant with the authority of the King James Bible not only to portray but also to advocate a rural English patriarchy:

> With farmer Allan at the farm abode
> William and Dora. William was his son,
> And she his niece.

> (1–3)

Reviewing the volume in the *Examiner* in May 1842, John Forster commented that 'Dora' has 'the homely beauty, without the trivial detail, of one of Wordsworth's ballads',[66] but Elizabeth K. Helsinger regards the poem as both homage and critique of the Poet Laureate, because in 'Dora' – as in 'The Gardener's Daughter' – rural English virtues are embodied in idealized women.[67]

Contemporary critics also link 'Dora' with the exemplary figure of Rose. John Sterling argued that the two poems are equal to 'the eclogues of Theocritus and Virgil' as 'anecdotes drawn from rustic life and rounded into song', but reveal 'all the gain that Christianity and civilization have brought to the relation of the sexes, and to the characters of women'.[68] For Charles Kingsley, Tennyson was 'not merely the only English rival of Theocritus and Bion', but 'much their superior'.[69] In 'Dora', as in other 'English Idyls', the relation of the sexes is attended with sadness and loss, perhaps mirroring Tennyson's own experience of family conflict and mourning. 'Dora' can be seen as a third and final 'daughter' poem, in which an adopted daughter is a moral exemplar. Rose and Dora are idealized young Englishwomen who exemplify or effect Tennyson's hierarchical domestic vision, with Rose representing a future 'Angel in the House'. Dora herself creates the poem's central vision of a female figure in an English landscape. For an unmarried young Victorian Englishwoman, her father or guardian's 'will is law' (43) and Dora defies patriarchal authority to reconstruct the family – again a microcosm of society. Once her reconciliatory role is fulfilled, Dora must live 'unmarried till her death' (167).

Tennyson altered his English literary source to foreground the central vision in 'Dora'. Class divisions are widened. The farming family's wealth and respectability are symbolized by 'the golden seal, that hung | From Allan's watch' (132–3) but William, an undutiful son, disobeys his father and rejects Dora to marry a 'labourer's daughter' (38), not the daughter of the village schoolmistress as in Mary Russell Mitford. Thus William's unfilial behaviour, rather than social-economic conditions, is the implied cause of the unspecified 'distresses' – and death – that 'came upon him' (47). The lives of Farmer Allan and his family are inseparable from the English landscape and the poem's events are centred on the culmination of the farming year. William dies 'in harvest time' (53) and the transforming vision of Dora with the fatherless child – in a field among the poppies that epitomize the unifying language of Englishness – recurs, in 'Dora' but not in Mitford, when 'there has not been for these five years | So full a harvest' (63–4):

> And Dora took the child, and went her way
> Across the wheat, and sat upon a mound
> That was unsown, where many poppies grew.
>
> (69–71)

However, the natural abundance suggested by the repeatedly 'full harvest' (67) is delusory. England in the 1830s and Hungry Forties endured a cycle of booms and slumps, and the good harvests and trade boom ended in 1836. The poem's full harvests are idealized rather than actual, appropriate to Tennyson's parable of restored relations within the family.

Medieval landscapes

Echoes of the 'mother tongue' of Englishness, inextricably associated with Tennyson's Lincolnshire childhood, recur throughout the volumes. As the *Cambridge University Magazine* critic commented in October 1842, 'an affectionate observation of nature' is among the 'elements of the true poet . . . abundantly manifested in Tennyson'.[70] Fleeting images or detailed descriptions of the natural world, often reflecting Tennyson's myopically close vision, are used to establish settings, enhance description, heighten comparison or provide consolation. The initial vision of 'a boundless universe' (26), offered to the suicidal speaker of 'The Two Voices' to 'solace woe' (433), is the image of an emerging and iridescent 'dragon-fly' (8–15); by the poem's close, 'Nature's living motion lent | The pulse of hope to discontent' (449–50). With her 'pensive thought and aspect pale', melancholy 'Margaret' is 'sweet and frail' as the meadow 'cuckooflower' (6–8). Margaret's 'twin-sister, Adeline' (48) evokes a subtle Shakespearean allusion to 'the language wherewith Spring | Letters cowslips on the hill' (61–2),[71] anticipating Tennyson's overtly erotic use of natural imagery in poems such as 'Now sleeps the crimson petal, now the white', one of the six intercalated songs from *The Princess* (1847).

Several poems depict the emerging medievalism that epitomizes Tennyson's rejection of nineteenth-century England's industrial landscapes and culminates in the epic *Idylls of the King*. The opening lines of 'The Lady of Shalott' immediately place Camelot in a Lincolnshire landscape:

> On either side the river lie
> Long fields of barley and of rye,
> That clothe the wold and meet the sky;
> And through the field the road runs by
> To many-towered Camelot;

> (1–5)

The landscape is naturalistic – neither idealized nor symbolic – and described simply, in the 'short and Saxon words' Charles Kingsley admired in 'Mariana'.[72] In his laudatory critique of *In Memoriam*, *The Princess* and *Poems* (1842), Kingsley analyses Tennyson's observation of nature, concluding that 'he has become the greatest naturalistic poet which England has seen for several centuries'. For Kingsley, it is Tennyson's 'subjective and transcendental mysticism' which enables him to describe nature with such simplicity: 'it is the mystic . . . , who will describe Nature most simply, because he sees most in her'. Tennyson's description of Camelot's landscape, and the changing seasons – from summer sunshine (91) to autumn storms (118–20) – which prefigure the seasonal cycle central to *Idylls of the King*, perfectly reflects the medieval spirit; it captures the objectivity and mysticism of 'the old ballad writers' and their delight in nature for its own sake. Defining Tennyson's Englishness in a judgement that mirrors his own Anglocentric and Anglican viewpoint, and homogenizes the English landscape, Kingsley comments that unlike poets 'from Keats and Byron down to Browning', who have rushed abroad to revive their creative imagination, 'Mr. Tennyson's truly English spirit' finds the perfect setting for an ideal myth in the scenery to be found in 'every parish in England'.

'Sir Launcelot and Queen Guinevere: A Fragment' is an early Arthurian poem depicting the chivalrous relationship between a man and a married woman, which was closely related to courtly love and inseparable from Victorian England's medieval revival. As John Mitchell Kemble noted in 1833, the poem is a 'companion to *The Lady of Shalott*'.[73] The connection is suggested by Tennyson's use of the same stanza form, but with lines five and nine as rhyming lines rather than refrains, thus removing popular ballad elements inappropriate to the titled couple. In 'the Spring, Queen Guinevere and Sir Lancelot ride through the forest green, fayre and amorous'; their love is suggested by the burgeoning and very English natural world – 'linnet' (10) and 'throstle' (11), the 'violet' (30) and the 'chestnut buds' which 'spread into a perfect fan, | Above the teeming ground' (16–18) – and apparently approved by the laughing 'Blue isles of heaven' (6) and 'happy winds' (38). (In 1856 John Ruskin coined the term *pathetic fallacy* for similar attributions of human emotions and sympathies to nature.) Both ride through the forest, singing, but only Guinevere is described. She is seen through Lancelot's eyes, in harmony with spring and nature in her 'gown of grass-green silk' (24), and the vocabulary evokes joy and femininity – 'blissful' (22), 'ringlet' (39), 'dainty' (41). She is 'Queen' Guinevere, her marriage symbolized by the 'golden ring' which holds the 'plumes she bore' (26–7), but there is no allusion to the 'shameful sin' which, for Arthur, destroyed the 'fair Order of my Table Round' (*Guinevere*, 1859, 484 and 460). The closing kiss is anonymous and conditional:

> A man had given all other bliss,
> And all his worldly worth for this,
> To waste his whole heart in one kiss
> Upon her perfect lips.
>
> (42–5)

However, the verb 'to waste' and the wheeling 'sparhawk' (12) suggest that their woodland idyll is threatened.

'Morte d'Arthur' was Tennyson's first major poem on what many regarded as 'the good old English subject of King Arthur'.[74] The poem was later shaped into *The Passing of Arthur* (1869), which ends the *Idylls of the King*. 'Morte d'Arthur' was published five years into a new reign, and with the Ecclesiastical Commission established in 1835, and the contemporary concerns which Tennyson explored in the *Idylls* – monarchy, religious faith, human conduct and morality – are foreshadowed in the poem and its frame, 'The Epic'. Written during the winter that followed Arthur Hallam's death, 'Morte d'Arthur' is very different from the early Arthurian poems: restrained, elegiac and in the iambic blank verse whose rhythms evoke Shakespeare. Tennyson altered his literary source in Malory; Arthur dies in the winter, which is appropriate to his defeat and death and was eventually to complete the *Idylls*' seasonal cycle. The bleakness of subject and season is established immediately – 'the winter sea' (2) – and symbolized by the landscape.

Sir Bedivere, who challenges, then accepts Arthur's monarchical 'Authority' (121), twice carries the wounded king. He is taken first to the abandoned 'chapel' (8) which stands for 'the general decay of faith | Right through the world' ('The Epic', 18–19) and contrasts with Arthur's belief that the world 'is every way | Bound by gold chains about the feet of God' (254–5). The chapel stands on 'a dark strait of barren land' (10) emblematic of the morally and spiritually sterile 'waste land' (202) – far distant from Camelot, the epitome of human civilization – from which Arthur had reclaimed 'this isle' (*The Coming of Arthur*, 6, 10–12) and to which, he fears, it will return after his death. The harsh and desolate landscape comes into sharper focus as Bedivere carries Arthur from 'the place of tombs' (46) to the funereal barge, swiftly striding across the ridges of 'the frozen hills' (183), his armour echoing in their 'icy caves | And barren chasms' (186–7). By contrast, Arthur's final vision of 'the island-valley of Avilion', where 'I will heal me of my grievous wound' (259–64), portrays an idealized landscape which encapsulates Tennyson's rejection of nineteenth-century industrial England: it is an 'English Idyl' in miniature. Blessed with a temperate climate – 'falls not hail, or rain, or any snow' – Avilion lies 'Deep-meadowed, happy, fair with orchard-lawns | And bowery hollows crowned with summer sea'. For many in the industrial England of the 1840s and 1860s, the vision of Avilion, which was incorporated unchanged into *The Passing of Arthur* in 1869 (427–32), represented a rural landscape that was more imaginary than real.

Satirical 'bird notes'

Tennyson uses the 'bird notes' inseparable from the unifying language of rural Englishness to humorously critical effect in *Poems*: in 'The Goose' and 'The Blackbird' he alludes satirically to contemporary legislation and the condition of England. But as Edward FitzGerald remarked, 'Alfred, whatever he may think, cannot trifle'; 'His smile is rather a grim one'[75] and the bird notes are both discordant and melodic. The *Cambridge University Magazine* critic and John Forster, *Poems*' first and otherwise favourable reviewer, regret the publication of 'The Goose', which they regard respectively as a pebble among the volumes' 'pearls' and 'ammunition' for Tennyson's foes.[76] John Sterling, by contrast, considers 'The Blackbird' to be 'sufficiently good for publication, but not for detailed criticism'.[77] However, the poems' position in the volumes and the stanza form indicate that 'The Goose' and 'The Blackbird', with other new poems written by 1834, deal directly or indirectly with contemporary concerns. The three early political poems referred to in Chapter 2 – 'You ask me, why', 'Of old sat Freedom' and 'Love thou thy land' – are measured reflections on English liberty, revealing the 'peculiarly radical conservatism' which fears change, yet sees its necessity.[78] (As with Wordsworth, the radical element of Tennyson's conservatism passed with the years.) 'The Goose' and 'The Blackbird' are familiar domestic birds, associated with the nursery rhymes and folk tales of English popular culture. Accordingly Tennyson used the rapid narrative, regular rhymes and incantatory rhythms of popular ballad form to allude satirically to the turbulent condition of England at the time of the 1832 Reform Act and the Poor Law Amendment Act of 1834, which Thomas Carlyle interpreted in *Chartism* (1839) as 'an announcement, sufficiently distinct, that whosoever will not work ought not to live'.[79]

'The Goose' was placed immediately after the three early political poems to close Volume 1 of *Poems*, strongly suggesting that its simplicity is deceptive. Paul Turner notes the probable influence of Sir Thomas More's prose *Dialogue of Comfort against Tribulation*, based on Aesop.[80] Tennyson Anglicizes and transforms the Aesop fable of the goose that laid the golden egg into a popular ballad-like poem satirizing both the equal distribution of wealth and radical agitation symbolized by the 'windy weather' (4, 40). 'The Goose' is given by an apparently kindly stranger to the 'old wife . . . | Her rags scarce held together' (1–2), who embodies the labouring poor generally absent from Tennyson's poems, to provide warmth in 'a stormy season' (8). The radical stranger's 'rhyme and reason' (6) are delusory, however. Morally corrupted by sudden wealth, the woman becomes idle and proud and moves out of her former social sphere:

> And feeding high, and living soft,
>   Grew plump and able-bodied;
> Until the grave churchwarden doffed,
>   The parson smirked and nodded.

> (17–20)

The 'old wife', annoyed by its cackling, threatens to strangle the goose. Taking back his gift, the stranger departs as he arrives, in turbulent weather and with the characteristic suddenness of the popular ballad.

'The Goose' and 'The Blackbird' exemplify nineteenth-century England's ballad revival. Analysing the ballad form and its history, W.W. Robson notes that the revival began with the publication of the three-volume *Reliques of Ancient English Poetry* (1765), collected and sometimes

fabricated by Thomas Percy.[81] Romanticism gave new life to two traditions of medieval story-telling. The first merged ballad with romance,
softening the ballad's original form which nineteenth-century readers
found harshly unattractive, to create poetry that is inward-looking
and privileges the poet's reactions, although some poems tell a story.
The second, more outward-looking and publicly orientated balladry is
concerned with a communal rather than an individual response. Robson
believes that much of Tennyson's popular or demotic balladry should be
re-evaluated, as many ballads reflect poetry's origins in song, riddle and
proverb, and he divides the popular poems into three groups – 'dramatic
monologues of common life', 'celebratory', and 'homiletic'. Tennyson's
homilies are often overtly moralistic, hence perhaps the *Christian Teacher*
critic's praise for the poet's exceptional ability to 'write a real simple
and natural *ballad*'.[82] For example, the speaker reprovingly reminds the
flirtatious 'Lady Clara Vere de Vere', who 'thought to break a country
heart | For pastime ere you went to town' (3–4), that 'Kind hearts are
more than coronets, | And simple faith than Norman blood' (55–6),
illuminating contemporary gender roles for rich and poor when he rec-
ommends that she 'teach the orphan-boy to read, | Or teach the orphan-
girl to sew' (69–70). Lady Clara is reproved at length, but as Robson
remarks, Tennyson's advice is generally more succinct when delivered in
a regional accent. This could also be said of Tennyson's political views;
his extended and fearful explorations of working-class agitation are
concisely expressed in the later comment of the 'Northern Farmer: New
Style' that 'the poor in a loomp is bad' (1869, 48).

'The Goose' and 'The Blackbird' are more subtly homiletic than 'Lady
Clara', their serious subtext suggested by grouping, metre and a force
of nature. As mentioned above, 'The Goose' is placed after the three
political poems at the end of Volume 1. 'The wild wind', which in 'The
Goose' accompanies the radical stranger and 'rang from park and plain'
(45), appears more powerfully in the preceding poem, 'Love thou thy
land', when 'the soul | Of Discord' threatens 'to race the rising wind'
(67–8). 'The Blackbird' was sent to James Spedding with 'Love thou thy
land' in early October 1834 – soon after the passing of the Poor Law
Amendment Act on 14 August – and Tennyson pointed out that the
poem is 'in another strain but the same metre'.[83] 'The Blackbird' is linked
with 'Love thou thy land', 'You ask me, why' and the contemporary but
unpublished 'Hail Briton!' by the measured *In Memoriam* stanza form
and metre in which Tennyson explored English political freedom. 'The
Blackbird', like the old wife, is reproached for ingratitude. Left free to
feed on abundant fruit in the speaker's ordered and very English garden,

the bird also eats the poet's early summer apples, but ceases to sing. 'Plenty' again leads to idleness and 'corrupts the melody | That made thee famous once when young' (15–16). The speaker's closing warning to the bird foreshadows Carlyle's 1839 comment on the Act – if the labouring classes do not work, they should not live:

> Take warning! he that will not sing,
>   While yon sun prospers in the blue,
>   Shall sing for want, ere leaves are new,
> Caught in the frozen palms of Spring.

> (21–4)

An experimental tree and final 'bird notes'

This chapter will conclude with discussion of two poems, often over-looked by modern critics, in which Tennyson experiments with nature and nature has the last word, and with a brief survey of contemporary reviewers' responses to the 1842 volumes. 'The Talking Oak' (written 1837–38) was Tennyson's 'experiment' to 'test the degree in which it was in [his] power as a poet to humanise external nature'.[84] John Forster appeared to think the experiment successful – '"The Talking Oak" is "filled with quaint fancy and voluptuous beauty"' – whereas for Richard Monckton Milnes, although written with 'grace and care', the poem 'certainly appears somewhat too long'.[85] Several more recent critics, including Robert Pattison and William E. Fredeman, include 'The Talking Oak' among the 'English Idyls'. Paul Turner describes it as a light-hearted companion to 'St Simeon Stylites', on the rather tenuous grounds that the poem surveys five hundred years of English history from 'a height approximately equal to that of the saint's pillar'.[86] Tennyson's source was literary, the oracular talking oaks of Aeschylus' *Prometheus Vinctus* (832),[87] familiar to the poet from his classical education, with echoes of *As You Like It* in 'the name | I carved with many vows' (153–4). 'The Talking Oak' has the rhyme scheme and rhythm of a popular ballad, but Tennyson alters the narrative form – from third person to dialogue – to give the oak a voice, causing John Sterling to complain that an ancient oak would 'hardly . . . be so prolix and minute in its responses'.[88]

Tennyson's experimental oak is a very English, and Tennysonian, tree. Oaks are conventional symbols of England elsewhere in the volume – 'Eleänore' was born 'far from our oaken glades' (10) – and are inseparable from English popular culture and naval history: the patriotic sea song 'Heart of Oak', with words by Garrick and music by Boyce, was written in 1759 to celebrate 'the year of victories'.[89] Looking back over 'good old Summers, year by year' (39), the talking tree shares the poet's passion for the past, but an actual oak would not have survived to 'circle in the grain | Five hundred rings of years' (83–4). By the end of the Napoleonic wars, England and Wales were among the least-wooded countries in the world: shipbuilding 'had denuded maritime counties of free-standing oaks'[90] and turned them into Tennyson's nautical symbols of Englishness – the 'ships of war that blow | The battle from their oaken sides' ('Hail Briton!', 7–8) to defend England. 'The Talking Oak', which has 'shadowed' and lovingly describes 'many a group | Of beauties' (61–2), also shares the poet's idealized view of marriageable young English womanhood, embodied in the central vision of Rose, 'The Gardener's Daughter', whose social standing is defined by her father's profession. With her 'novel' and 'new piano' (117–19), Olivia has the leisure interests of a young Victorian woman from a different social class. Walter, the oak's interlocutor, accepts without question the distant but constant presence of Olivia's home, 'Sumner-place', discernible from the oak's 'topmost branches' (31–2, 95–6, 151–2, 247–8) and symbolizing the hierarchical class structure of mid-nineteenth-century England. Walter and the oak are monarchists and echo Tennyson's mistrust of radicalism. The Tory oak rejects 'the gloomy brewer', Cromwell, whose soul departs on the 'wild wind' which now represents republicanism (54–6); Walter will praise the oak more than 'England honours' its 'famous brother-oak', which sheltered Charles I from the Roundheads and their 'surly' hymns (295–300).

The volumes end appropriately with English nature in a valedictory mood. Although a short poem of just sixteen lines, 'The Poet's Song' echoes the themes of other poems discussed in this chapter and exemplifies the poetic manifesto at the heart of 'Ode to Memory': Tennyson's classically influenced poet figure is placed in a rural English landscape. 'The Poet' leaves the town for the country, in characteristically changeable English weather – 'rain had fallen', 'sun' and 'shadow' alternate and the wind, no longer a political symbol, blows gently (1–4). He is an Orpheus figure, familiar to Tennyson and classically educated readers, but the Poet's 'melody loud and sweet' (6) entrances an unlikely and very English avian audience: songbirds and a raptor, diurnal and nocturnal birds gather round the Poet. As in the central vision of 'The Gardener's Daughter' and 'Dora', an idealized nature is held in suspended animation to heighten the moment:

> And he sat him down in a lonely place,
>   And chanted a melody loud and sweet,

> That made the wild-swan pause in her cloud,
> And the lark drop down at his feet.

(5–8)

Despite its brevity, the volumes' final poem also betrays the doubts and uncertainties that delayed its publication for so long. The nightingale finally acknowledges the Poet's supremacy in song and his prophetic role: 'For he sings of what the world will be | When the years have died away' (15–16). However, although not overtly feral, nature carries an underlying threat – the hawk stares 'with his foot on the prey' (12) and Tennyson's English Eden conceals a 'snake' which slips 'under a spray' (10). Although necessary for poetic creativity, the country is 'a lonely place' (5); the Poet is both isolated and vulnerable, evoking the fear of becoming 'prey' (12) to critics and the public – 'my name | Shot like a racketball from mouth to mouth | And bandied in the barren lips of fools' – evident in Tennyson's bitterly personal unfinished early poem.[91] 'The Poet's Song' proves to be a rather bitter-sweet melody.

The 1842 volumes reflect Tennyson's decision – articulated in 'Ode to Memory' and epitomized in 'The Poet's Song' – to construct himself as a more English poet. He moves from a sublime to a domestic landscape: inseparable from the poems discussed in this chapter are the elements of English nature and landscape which create a unifying language of Englishness. Close readings also reveal a more subtle and underlying Englishness – often enhanced by the use of blank verse, with its Shakespearean echoes, or the contrasting popular ballad form – and the literary influences of Tennyson's classical, and class-based, gentleman's education. Anticipating the *Idylls of the King*'s 'parabolic drift',[92] Tennyson uses English nature and landscape to explore – however tangentially, and in a variety of ways – both private and public contemporary concerns. 'The Poet's Song' suggests Tennyson's ambivalent view of the poet's role; 'The Goose' and 'The Blackbird' allude satirically to the dangers of rapid social reform.

Critics of the early volumes had attempted to define and shape Tennyson as a national poet to succeed 'the great generation of poets which is now passing away'.[93] For reviewers of the 1842 volumes, the poetic succession appeared secure. Tennyson was accepted as a great, or potentially great, English poet and critics shared John Forster's 'conviction that Mr Tennyson has not only redeemed the promise of his early writings; but given forth a new pledge, to be hereafter yet more worthily redeemed'.[94] The first edition of *Poems* was favourably reviewed in a wide range of contemporary periodicals, intended for readers of all classes, and within a few months the *Morning Post* critic declared that Tennyson was entitled 'to take his stand at once amongst the most famous of our living poets'.[95] Almost without exception, reviewers approved the revisions to early poems reprinted in 1842; for John Sterling, Tennyson 'has sifted . . . his earlier harvests, and kept the better grain'.[96] Where fault was found, there was little hostility. Critics passed over the weaker poems to focus on Tennyson's finer work, printed extended extracts and entire poems, or referred readers to the volumes. Reviewers no longer regarded Tennyson as a radical poet. Although the Whig *Sun* initially linked Tennyson with Shelley and found him at times obscure, complaint turned to praise, particularly of 'Locksley Hall', unhesitatingly given 'preference over the majority' of poems published 'within the last ten years'.[97] The *Spectator* critic regarded the poet's most obvious defect as his occasional 'Cockney' diction, but conceded that Tennyson's powers, 'properly cultivated', would 'place him among the first rank of living poets'.[98]

Reviewers commented approvingly on Tennyson's poetic progress and the exemplary Englishness of his language and thought. John Forster found in the volumes 'matured taste and greatly strengthened power'; he believed that Tennyson was acquiring the valuable art of 'selection and compression' and that his 'sense of the beautiful' had become 'more chastened, more intellectual'.[99] For the anonymous critic of the *Atlas* – as for many reviewers – Tennyson's intellectual development was particularly apparent in the second volume, and he welcomed the poems' increased sincerity and 'solid thoughtfulness'.[100] Whereas critics of the early poems had regretted Tennyson's 'affectations', reviewers of the 1842 volumes praised his 'perfect mastery over the English language'. Francis Garden, co-editor of the High Church *Christian Remembrancer*, similarly commended the poet for writing 'such genuine and vigorous English' and confirmed that Tennyson was 'generally acknowledged to hold the foremost place' among poets of 'the rising generation'.[101] The *Morning Post* – a Tory and High Church journal which 'catered to the fashionable world', poetry's largest market – also extolled the second volume poems for the strength, brilliance and 'perfect mastery of language',[102] while the *Weekly Dispatch* – a radical newspaper 'dedicated to the denunciation of abuses' – brought Tennyson to the attention of its vast and contrasting readership of 'artisans and operatives' by printing extended extracts from 'The Vision of Sin' and the 'really beautiful' 'Day Dream'.[103]

Critics appeared anxious to associate the Englishness of Tennyson's thought, and his increased poetic power, with masculinity. Their anxiety was more than appreciation of Tennyson's poetic decorum. It suggests not only contemporary concern with gender roles – exemplified by Tennyson's domestic ideology, idealized women and the chivalrous gentlemen to be discussed in Chapter 5 – but also the ambiguous cultural space occupied by male poets: as Thaïs E. Morgan observes, male poets were expected to articulate the deep feelings and 'private states of consciousness' identified 'as the preserve of femininity'.[104] For Henry Chorley in the *Athenaeum*, 'the new volume is so thickly studded with evidences of manly force and exquisite tenderness . . . as to substantiate Mr. Tennyson's claim to a high place among modern poets'.[105] John Forster praised 'Locksley Hall' as 'a piece of strong, full-blooded, man's writing',[106] while Leigh Hunt, writing in the *Church of England Quarterly Review*, anticipated 'muscular Christianity' – a term first used in 1857 and associated with Charles Kingsley – by describing 'The Two Voices' as 'genuine, Christian, manly, and poetical philosophy'.[107]

The volumes were reviewed seriously and at length in the three powerful and partisan quarterly reviews. John Sterling's extended critique in the *Quarterly Review*, published in September 1842, was followed by Richard Monckton Milnes's essay in the *Westminster Review* a month later; James Spedding's article in the April 1843 *Edinburgh Review* was the final review to appear before the publication of a second edition of *Poems*. Sterling's critique has been defined as the most significant contribution to the contemporary debate on 'poetry and the age', because he attempts to define why the question is relevant and what form of poetry is appropriate to the age.[108] The critique's publication is additionally significant because it was seen by the literary world of the time as repudiating John Wilson Croker's virulent attack on *Poems* (1832). As Croker's letter to the *Quarterly Review* editor, John Lockhart, makes clear, 'the Tennyson article' was 'understood by others as a broad hint that my influence in the *Quarterly* was gone, and by myself, as an intimation that our connection was drawing to a close'.[109]

John Sterling and Tennyson, with Richard Monckton Milnes and James Spedding, had been friends since Cambridge, but the *Quarterly* critique is not wholly laudatory. Sterling's belief that poets should respond creatively to the age influences his view of some of the volumes' finest poems – 'we know not why . . . a modern English poet should write of Ulysses rather than of the great voyagers of the modern world', whose 'feelings and aims' are closer to 'our comprehension'.[110] Sterling was also constrained by the *Quarterly* editor's refusal to allow praise of any poem ridiculed by Croker, although he argues eloquently on Tennyson's behalf. Initially conceding that the age could be considered 'essentially unpoetic' (386), Sterling surveys the political, commercial and religious life of contemporary England to conclude that poets should 'find in this huge, harassed, and luxurious national existence the nourishment, not the poison, of creative art' (385).

Anticipating *Aurora Leigh* (1857), Sterling argues that poetry 'must wear a new form'. The poet should 'give us back our age' in all its aspects 'transmuted into crystalline clearness and lustre' (395), and he believes that Tennyson has accomplished this more than most modern poets. The second volume 'is on the whole, far advanced in merit beyond the first', with the blank verse poems 'among the riches of our recent literature' (396). Seeking evidence of the age, Sterling reviews the collection in four distinct groups – 'Idylls', 'purely Lyrical' poems, 'Fancies' and 'Moralities' – of which the Idylls are 'the most valuable part of Mr. Tennyson's writings, a real addition to our literature' (406). In the Idylls Sterling finds 'a clear and faithful eye for visible nature . . . and a mould of verse which for smoothness and play of melody has seldom been equalled in the language' (406). With their tenderness, grace and power, the Idylls – 'compositions, drawn from the heart of our actual English life' – surpass Tennyson's 'mythological romances', at first sight 'the most striking portion of his works'. For Sterling, 'to bewitch us with our own daily realities, and not with their unreal opposites', is a 'still higher task' which 'could not be more thoroughly performed' (401).

John Sterling requires the poet to transform the age, as in poetry 'we seek, and find, a refuge from the hardness and narrowness of the actual world' (394). However, he is less concerned with changing society than earlier critics who, with John Stuart Mill in 1835, directed Tennyson towards the transformation of the national character. Comparing Tennyson's Idylls with Wordsworth's poems 'on similar themes, of present human existence in the country', Sterling argues that the older poet's profoundly reflective 'English Idylls' (415) would have been freer, creating greater delight, 'had the moral been less *obtruded* as its constant aim' (416). Tennyson, he believes, 'is a very different stamp of soul'; his better and later poems, underpinned but not dominated by a morality which few other contemporary critics appear to discern, are a fusion of 'affection, imagination, intellect' with 'the fairest images of the real world as it lies before us all to-day'. Among Tennyson's Idylls 'two are pre-eminent' – 'The Gardener's Daughter' and 'Dora' (406) – and the poems epitomize Sterling's apposite concluding description of Tennyson as 'the most genial poet of English rural life that we know' (416).

In 'The Gardener's Daughter' and other poems discussed in this chapter Tennyson fabricates a myth of rural Englishness. He does not portray the reality of agrarian strife or poverty, but presents only the fairest images of a contemporary England in which the poor, like Rose's father, are absent or, as in 'The Goose' and 'Dora', serve only as satirical or moral symbols. Tennyson's exemplary figures set in an idealized, pre-industrial landscape, created at the height of the Hungry Forties, represent an England that is more imaginary than real. However, the imagery of other rural representations, and the volumes' delayed publication, suggest ideological and perhaps emotional faultlines symbolized by remarkably similar images. The 'English Idyls' are not wholly idyllic. A fear of underlying rural unrest is encapsulated in Sir Edward Head's nightmare of 'the raw mechanic's bloody thumbs | Sweat[ing] on his blazoned chairs', an image which recurs in the bitterly unfinished poem written in 1839 when Tennyson was being urged to publish again: 'Why desire . . . the public thumb | Of our good pamphlet-pampered age to fret | And sweat upon mine honest thoughts in type, | The children of the silence?'[111] Perhaps in the late 1830s Tennyson was neither wholly committed to republishing nor to a rural ideology, his ambivalent position akin to the idealized garden of Rose, 'The Gardener's Daughter' – 'Not wholly in the busy world, nor quite | Beyond it, blooms the garden that I love' (33–4).

4
'Fair Victoria's Golden Age': Tennyson and Monarchy

Tennyson was twenty-eight when Victoria acceded to the throne in 1837 at the age of eighteen; when he died in 1892 the Queen had eight more years to live and reign. During these decades, particularly as Poet Laureate, Tennyson wrote many 'royal poems', addressed or dedicated to Victoria and Albert, and 'royal occasion poems' to mark or mourn royal events. Critics' and historians' perceptions of Victoria's reign have changed in recent decades. John Lucas argues that during the second half of the nineteenth century – Tennyson's Laureate years – the Queen became 'identified as an embodiment of England' and England became a royalist nation.[1] Whereas Victoria's immediate predecessors had been regarded as 'private nuisances and public dangers', Lucas believes that Victoria's reign transformed popular views of monarchy, uniting classes and regions and virtually eliminating republican elements. In this chapter I examine Tennyson's poetic portrayals of the monarchy, discussing the context in which they were written, to consider the poet's role in this perceived transformation and the new or contested ideas of Englishness they represent. I also consider Tennyson's 'royal poems' in the light of Elizabeth Langland's view that, as the century progressed, Englishness took on an increasingly masculine construction.[2] Finally, I read Tennyson's poetry of monarchy in relation to the conclusions of Richard Williams and other recent historians, who challenge Lucas's view of the linear progression of royal popularity.[3] However, to provide a framework for the poems I first outline the critics' differing views, before moving on to consider the critical views in relation to Tennyson's poetry of monarchy.

Royal popularity: a linear progression?

John Lucas asserts that by the late nineteenth century patriotism 'meant almost exclusively love of England as embodied in and by Victoria'.[4] He explains the processes by which, through successive imagery, the Queen became an emblem of England and English values. These involve not only 'the creation of Victoria as England' but also 'of England as Victorian, that is, as a royalist nation', a transformation achieved against considerable odds and exemplified by the term *Victorian*, first used in 1875. Before Victoria's accession many assumed that England would follow a European pattern and become a republic. The aristocracy disdained Victoria's Hanoverian antecedents and were to consider Albert un-English; there was fear of working-class anti-monarchism, particularly where radicalism was associated with regionalism, and later of provincial republican groups which resurfaced briefly in the early 1870s. In Lucas's view, 'the construction of patriotism on royalist terms' was largely 'the work of the middle class'. This process was driven by desire for a unified nation and belief that, by evoking loyalty to Victoria as Queen rather than to abstract ideas of nation, conflicting class or regional interests could more easily be suppressed. Accordingly, almost from her accession Victoria was presented in terms appropriate to middle-class values, with imagery emphasizing ideals of family life. Later images of Victoria as medieval queen or Liberty invited 'chivalric defence', while Victoria as Britannia commanded 'deferential awe'. By the 1870s Victoria had come to be considered above politics and party interest, therefore 'capable of being an embodiment of England as a whole'; the figure of Victoria/ Liberty/Britannia was loved and venerated and, Lucas concludes, when Victoria died the possibility of England becoming a republic had virtually disappeared.

Elizabeth Langland challenges John Lucas's argument. Arguing that 'to be an emblem of England and to embody the essence of Englishness . . . are not the same thing', Langland attempts to untangle Victoria's relationship to the increasingly diverging but interwoven narratives of nineteenth-century Englishness and Victorianism.[5] Although English identity was at issue on Victoria's accession and marriage, anxiety abated after the Great Exhibition (1851) whose success brought distinction to England and national gratitude to Albert. Perhaps as a result, in royal representations in English art of the 1850s and 1860s 'Victoria is consort, Albert the king'. These depictions – for Lucas 'chivalric', for Langland 'Anglo-Saxon' – mirror earlier idealized images of Victoria as middle-class mother and conflict with portraits of her as queen regnant. Langland locates similarly gendered imagery in the Victorian novel. Thomas Hughes's *Tom Brown's Schooldays* (1857) in particular establishes a 'gendered ethos of Englishness': public school-educated Englishmen reflect the active virtues that build the Empire; Englishwomen as mothers, wives and widows have the passive virtues of love and self-sacrifice. For Langland, the 'domestication of the monarch'[6] perpetuated an ideology which became increasingly defined as Victorianism rather than Englishness once the term *Victorian* came into use in 1851 (some years earlier than John Lucas suggests). As wife, mother and widow, the Queen embodied Victorianism, while developing ideas of Englishness became associated with masculine and imperial representations. Defining Englishness by quoting Lytton Strachey's biography of Victoria (1921), Langland contrasts Albert with the Foreign Secretary Lord Palmerston, whose Englishness is characterized by 'happy valiance', or conduct simultaneously 'bold and prudent in the pursuit of international affairs'. The Prince Consort, tied to European monarchical interests, was Victorian but not English; the Queen – although 'Victorian to the core' and the 'image of England' – could not possess the 'masculine insouciance' that epitomized nineteenth-century Englishness.

Richard Williams and later historians examine at length issues touched on by John Lucas and Elizabeth Langland. Williams analyses attitudes to the monarchy throughout Victoria's reign, using public writings to demonstrate the frequency and variety of discussion. His particular concern is republicanism – 'a school of thought in the late 1840s and 1850s and an organised movement in the 1870s'[7] – which used newspapers and pamphlets to reach an increasingly literate society. Williams's belief that two strands of discussion of the monarchy – one reverential, the other critical – co-existed throughout Victoria's reign challenges the 'linear progression of royal popularity' postulated by John Lucas and earlier by Kingsley Martin.[8] This holds that in the first half of Victoria's reign the Crown was regarded as expensive, outdated, un-English and as interfering in politics; by 1901 the monarch had been elevated above socio-political conflict and was venerated as the emblem of England and empire. Williams's investigations considerably modify this linear, chronological view. He examines Chartism and middle-class radicalism between 1837 and 1861, the emergence of republicanism in the late 1840s and its development and decline from 1861 to 1887, with the criticism of the monarchy that persisted until Victoria's death. He traces the veneration of Victoria as monarch and woman through its successive stages. Williams demonstrates that a critical, questioning attitude to the monarchy persisted throughout Victoria's reign, co-existing with a reverence for the monarchy similar to that associated with the reign's final years which promoted Victoria as 'the universally popular emblem of national consensus'. 'That in reality she could never be', Williams concludes, although by 1901 'the balance in the perception of the monarchy had moved decisively in this direction'.

Essays edited by David Nash and Antony Taylor – published to explain 'the breadth, depth and little-known complexity of republicanism'[9] – amplify aspects of Richard Williams's investigations. Introductory and concluding sections outline the context, heritage and legacy of Victorian republicanism. The central section examines contemporary interpretations of republicanism and to whom the different formulations appealed, contrasting the intellectual, classically influenced 'patrician republicanism' of Sir Charles Dilke with an apparently antithetical and broader 'plebeian radicalism' with which, however, it shares traditions and concerns. The collection engages with contemporary writings on monarchy, noting that Walter Bagehot's *The English Constitution* (1867) provided inspiration to the royals but was largely ignored outside governing circles. The editors conclude that for most republicans – and for the radicals whose hostility to corruption continued beyond the 1870s – a 'modern monarchy' was a contradiction in terms and their ultimate concern was to correct 'the excesses of the monarchical state'.

Frank Prochaska's study of the historic relationship between republicans and the monarchy also aims to illuminate the differing strands of republican opinion.[10] Referring to republicanism's 'protean' nature, Prochaska defines its three most prominent, often overlapping forms. 'Classical' or 'civic virtue' republicans generally accepted a limited and public-spirited monarchy, 'theoretical' republicans contemplated but did not pursue the end of the monarchy, whereas the minority of 'pure' or anti-monarchical republicans called explicitly – and sometimes violently – for the monarchy's abolition. Criticism of court corruption, allowances to the royal family and Crown finance created an additional strand of 'Civil List' republicanism. The monarchy survived troubled times; in Victoria's reign 1848 and 1870–72 were particularly turbulent years. This was not simply due to the power of tradition, or the gradual transfer of power from the monarch to elected ministers. Prochaska concludes that the monarchy was often active in its own defence and at 'critical historic moments' insured against potential trouble through 'highly visible, public-spirited social service'.

Frank Prochaska's analysis of nineteenth-century republicanism, together with Richard Williams' investigations and the essays edited by David Nash and Antony Taylor, have been discussed at some length as they counter the linear, chronological view of the progression of royal popularity held by John Lucas and earlier historians and illuminate the 'critical historic moments' in Victoria's reign which are often commemorated in Tennyson's poems of monarchy.

'The Queen of the Isles'

Tennyson's first 'royal poem' was written for Victoria's accession on 20 June 1837. 'The Queen of the Isles' was scribbled in haste, 'within this last half hour', sent to James Spedding and intended for anonymous publication in 'the Times or some paper with a circulation'.[11] Conceding that '[i]t is little more than newspaper verse', Tennyson thought 'it might have an effect if good music went along with it', and the poem has the rhymes, rhythm and refrain – 'a health to the Queen of the Isles' – through which oral poetry and drinking songs are remembered and transmitted.

'The Queen of the Isles' exemplifies nineteenth-century England's ballad revival, discussed in Chapter 3. The accession poem's hopeful anticipation is mirrored in the many poems, prints and street ballads which appeared at the time, all idealizing Victoria and confirming by their existence Richard Williams's view that reverence for the monarchy existed from the outset of her reign. Victoria was believed to share the Whig views of her widowed mother, the Duchess of Kent, and she was welcomed for the supposedly reforming sympathies expressed, for example, in the street ballad 'Queen Victoria':

> She doth declare it her intent
> To extend reform in parliament,
> On doing good she's firmly bent,
> While she is Queen of England.
>
> (17–20)[12]

Despite its apparent light-heartedness, 'The Queen of the Isles' not only captures the popular mood but also alludes to serious contemporary concerns. Ballads were often used to attack people and institutions and, as the second stanza indicates, Victoria's predecessors were not held in high regard:

> The reigns of her fathers were long or were short,
> They plagued us in anger or vext us in sport.
>
> (5–6)

Tennyson's acerbic comments foreshadow the views of historians such as Sir Sidney Lee, Victoria's first biographer, who declared that the English throne had been successively occupied by 'an imbecile, a profligate and a buffoon',[13] and echo the newspaper obituaries on Victoria's Hanoverian uncles, the brothers of George III, Shelley's 'old, mad, blind, despised, and dying king' ('Sonnet – England in 1919', 1). Of George IV (1820–30) *The Times* declared: 'There never was an individual less regretted by his fellow-creatures than the deceased King. What eye has wept for him? What heart has heaved one throb of unmercenary sorrow?'[14] For the *Spectator*, William IV (1830–37) 'though at times a jovial and, for a king, an honest man' was 'a weak, ignorant, commonplace sort of person', his apparent and paradoxical 'popularity . . . acquired at the price of something like public contempt'. However, in June 1837 many contemporaries agreed, with Tennyson, to 'Let them sleep in their good or their evil report' (7) and pledge Victoria's health, for 'the blessing of promise is on her like dew' (35). As *The Times* declared, 'the accession of a youthful sovereign to the throne is wont to fill the hearts of nations with eager faith and sanguine assurance of prosperity'.[15]

Although John Plunkett argues that the accession created 'a rage for royal representations' that characterized the first two decades of Victoria's reign,[16] the contrast between Victoria's elderly, reactionary uncles and the new queen was heralded in earlier iconography. Even before her entry into public life, the young Princess Victoria was portrayed as 'the rose of England'; the Dulwich Picture Gallery's delightful portrait of 'Queen Victoria, aged Four' shows a rose placed by her feet. The flower, which is particularly associated with the Virgin Mary – 'the rose without thorns',[17] that is, sinless – represents a simple but powerfully ideological image to eclipse the Georgian era and, Lynne Vallone believes, a significant aspect of the 'visualization campaign – waged by the Duchess of Kent . . . as much as by the press'.[18] The refrain to the street ballad 'Queen Victoria' confirms that the image was well-established by 1837:

> Of all the flowers in full bloom,
>   Adorn'd with beauty and perfume,
> The fairest is the rose in June,
>   Victoria, Queen of England.

Tennyson reflects the contemporary ideology of separate spheres by assuming that Victoria will reign but not rule:

> May those in her council that have the chief voice
> Be true hearts of oak that the land may rejoice

And her people may love her the more for her choice –
So a health to the Queen of the Isles.

(9–12)

His concern with the moderating role of statesmen, explored in greater
detail in the early political poems (discussed in Chapter 2), is a preoccupation that recurs throughout Tennyson's career. In the accession
ballad, Victoria's 'council' will 'have the chief voice' (9), their masculine Englishness exemplified by the 'true hearts of oak' (10) of English
naval tradition – and the 'happy valiance', bold but prudent conduct in
both international and domestic affairs – with which they 'balance the
nations in Peace' (23) and maintain 'a satisfied people' (17) at home.
Even in 1885, Tennyson continued to urge the 'Patriot statesman' to be
'wise to know | The limits of resistance, and the bounds | Determining
concession' ('To the Duke of Argyll', 1–3).

In 1837, Tennyson's contemporaries were also concerned with leadership and maintaining a stable society. The turmoil surrounding the troubled passage of the Reform Bill through Parliament was a recent memory,
the Poor Law Amendment Act of 1834 was in force, a bank crisis in 1837
slowed the railway boom, and in 1837 and 1838 harvests were poor and
winters harsh.[19] The years from 1839 to 1842 were to be of particular
political turbulence as calls for social reform were given impetus by severe
social and economic conditions. The 1830s and 1840s were the decades
of utilitarianism and Chartism, with the movement towards the six-
point Chartist petition – drawn up in 1837 and presented in 1839, 1842
and 1848 – beginning in June 1836 when the London Working Men's
Association was founded to promote political education. Richard Williams
explores in turn middle- and working-class radical movements during
these decades and summarizes their differing positions. In middle-class
radicalism, both parliamentary and journalistic, intellectual criticisms of
the monarchy were based on utilitarian principles – that 'government
should be rational and economical'.[20] MPs such as Joseph Hume and
periodicals such as *Punch* also attacked the additional financial burden
of 'royal annuities'. Williams points out that, while Chartists professed
loyalty to Victoria, they wished the Crown to identify with the people,
rather than 'the narrow, oppressive governing class'. For many people, the
Chartist movement revived fears of the French Revolution and they echoed Thomas Carlyle's call for strong national leadership to be a 'bulwark
against social disintegration'.[21] In a series of six lectures, delivered in 1840
and published in 1841, Carlyle argues that the loyalty created by 'hero-
worship' of such leaders would unite rather than fragment society.

Tennyson's concluding wish in the accession ballad is for a long reign and heirs to the throne:

> God bless her! and long may she hold the command
> Till the hair of the boy shall be gray in the land
> And the ball and the sceptre shall pass from her hand
>   To the race of the Queen of the Isles.

(37–40)

George IV and William IV had ruled for only ten years and seven years respectively and Tennyson's concern with 'the race of the Queen of the Isles' (40) touches on contemporary anxiety for the future of the monarchy. Alexandrina Victoria was the only child of Victoria, Princess of Saxe-Coburg-Gotha, and Edward, Duke of Kent – the fourth son of George III – destined to the throne from infancy as death, childlessness or illegitimacy debarred the closer kindred of George III and led to fears that his large family was becoming extinct. The succession was secured by Victoria's marriage in 1840 to Prince Albert – a Saxe-Coburg-Gotha cousin, welcomed at birth as 'the pendant to the little cousin [Victoria]'[22] – and the births of nine children between 1840 and 1857, all of whom survived to adulthood and to marry, and to influence in their turn both veneration for and criticism of the monarchy.

'To the Queen' (1851)

As Laureate, Tennyson published two poems entitled 'To the Queen' – the first in 1851 dedicating the seventh edition of *Poems* (1842) issued in April, the second in 1873 as the epilogue to *Idylls of the King*. 'To the Queen' was Tennyson's first publication as Poet Laureate and reveals a complete change in attitude towards the monarch whose accession he had greeted with a popular ballad. Between 1837 and 1851 Tennyson's career had advanced. He prepared and published the two-volume *Poems* (1842) and *The Princess*, issued on Christmas Day 1847 and, Christopher Ricks suggests, 'obliquely commemorative' in its concern with the Prince's role in a forthcoming royal marriage.[23] Tennyson also completed *In Memoriam*, which was published anonymously at the end of May 1850. In September 1845 he was granted an annual Civil List pension, and in June 1850 he and Emily Sellwood were finally married. However, during the 1840s Tennyson also experienced financial difficulties[24] and the physical and psychological problems (fear of inheriting his father's instability) for which he sought frequent water cures.[25] In March 1847, after 'some abortive attempts', he declined to provide an ode for Prince Albert's installation as Chancellor of Cambridge University, because 'the work does not seem to prosper in my hands'.[26] Tennyson concluded that despite 'Household affections' and 'filial regard toward' Trinity and Cambridge, and 'loyal touches towards Queens and Princes', Cambridge contained many 'far more capable than myself of doing justice to so grave a theme as the Installation of a Prince-Consort'. Although 'strongly sensible of the compliment involved', he declined 'from sheer dread of breaking down'. Tennyson wrote in April 1847 that he was 'lying sick of more than one ailment',[27] and his strongly worded refusal appears to confirm Robert Bernard Martin's view that 'it was general nervousness for which he needed treatment'.[28]

Tennyson's doubts about taking on a public role continued when he was offered the Laureateship in 1850. He prepared two replies, one accepting and the other rejecting the appointment, but in September 1850 he succeeded William Wordsworth as Poet Laureate. He was appointed, Hallam Tennyson believed, 'owing chiefly to Prince Albert's admiration for "In Memoriam"':[29] Victoria took no part in the decision and a relationship of trust and mutual respect between poet and monarch developed only after Albert's death in 1861. On succeeding to the Laureateship, Tennyson became the public voice of English poetry and part of a literary tradition reaching back beyond John Dryden, the first official Poet Laureate, to Ben Jonson, who was granted a court pension by James I in 1616. 'To the Queen', dated 'March 1851', was Tennyson's first Laureate poem. An early draft, first published in 1895 and known as the 'Drexel text',[30] reflects on the role of 'kingly poets' (19), mirroring his initial uncertainty by opening with an assertion and closing with a doubt, and is therefore worth discussing alongside the published poem.

The Drexel text and 'To the Queen' (1851) represent the earliest stages of a unique literary relationship. Tennyson's 'friendship and respect for Queen Victoria'[31] can be traced in Hallam Tennyson's *Memoir* and Charles Tennyson's biography, with additional insights to be gained from the poet's later letters to close friends or family. Charles Tennyson writes that 'Alfred had felt a deep and romantic respect for the Queen ever since . . . her accession' and their first meeting after Albert's death began a 'romantic and chivalrous relation between the Queen and her Poet Laureate', which he regards as 'a unique and touching episode in the story of English literature'.[32] Although the Drexel text reproduces sentiments contained in 'The Queen of the Isles' and earlier patriotic ballads – its opening assertion, 'The noblest men are born and bred | Among the Saxo-Norman race' (1–2), echoes the boast that 'there are no men like Englishmen' ('National

Song', 1828–29, 7) – the tone and pace are remarkably different. The Drexel text's courtly language, and the measured *In Memoriam* stanza form used in major patriotic poems such as 'Hail Briton!', exemplify Tennyson's enhanced regard for Victoria and subtly underline his loyalty: 'And in this world the noblest place | Madam, is yours, our Queen and Head' (3–4).

The Drexel text also suggests a high regard for the poets' role. Although poets often appear 'wretched' (10), Tennyson compares them with the monarchy:

> The poets, they that often seem
> So wretched, touching mournful strings,
> They likewise are a kind of kings,
> Nor is their empire all a dream.
>
> (9–12)

Like Victoria's 'flag' (6), flying over the expanding 'empire' (12) to be discussed in Chapter 6, the poets' words fly over land and sea, to delight the distant and enhance for posterity 'a glorious reign' (16):

> Their words fly over land and main,
> Their warblings make the distance glad,
> Their voices heard hereafter add
> A glory to a glorious reign.
>
> (13–16)

In the Drexel text Tennyson considers the Laureate's role in classical terms. The Laureateship is not for flatterers, nor for 'taskwork' odes (21), and 'kingly' poets (19) should believe monarchs worthy of their royal role. Although addressed 'To the Queen', the Drexel text often refers to 'the king':

> A work not done by flattering state,
> Nor such a lay should kings receive,
> And kingly poets should believe
> The king's heart true as he is great.
>
> The taskwork ode has ever failed:
> Not less the king in time to come
> Will seem the greater under whom
> The sacred poets have prevailed.
>
> (17–24)

As in other poems, Tennyson turns to the past to consider the present. He alludes to classical literature's recurring nostalgia for an idealized Arcadian past by wishing to be 'as those of old' (29), able to reawaken succeeding generations to 'fair Victoria's golden age':

> I would I were as those of old,
>   A mellow mouth of song to fill
>   Your reign with music which might still
> Be music when my lips were cold.
>
> That after-men might turn the page
>   And light on fancies true and sweet,
>   And kindle with a loyal heat
> To fair Victoria's golden age.
>
>   (29–36)

Ultimately, however, the poet of the Drexel text doubts his ability to succeed Wordsworth, believing himself a poor player on the reed pipes of Pan (37–40), Arcadia's god of nature and – from classical times – the patron of pastoral poets:

> But he your Laureate who succeeds
>   A master such as all men quote
>   Must feel as one of slender note
> And piping low among the reeds.
>
>   (37–40)

In the poem published in 1851 the 'romantic and chivalrous' relationship develops and the doubts diminish. Classical allusions recede and the poem becomes a chivalrously deferential address 'To the Queen', now 'Revered Victoria' (1). Two years later Tennyson again altered the opening stanza, further enhancing the Queen's status and establishing his role as an English courtier-poet in the tradition of Sir Philip Sidney and Sir Thomas Wyatt. In 1853 the Queen is 'Revered, beloved' and her name follows the stanza break:

> Revered, beloved – O you that hold
>   A nobler office upon earth
>   Than arms, or power of brain, or birth
> Could give the warrior kings of old,

> Victoria, – since your Royal grace
> To one of less desert allows
> This laurel greener from the brows
> Of him that uttered nothing base;
>
> (1–8)

Tennyson thus creates a suitably reverential pause – 'the syntactical and rhythmical equivalent of a courtly bow'[33] in Christopher Ricks's apt phrase – between the opening address to the Queen, her Royal status enhanced by capitalization, and the following reference to her Laureate, still 'of less desert' than Wordsworth, who 'uttered nothing base' (6–8). The Laureate does not presume on the sovereign's 'greatness': 'should' there be time from 'the care | That yokes with [the] empire' (9–10) he no longer seems to question, Tennyson 'could' trust Victoria's kindness to discern 'aught of ancient worth' (12) in the dedicatory volumes. The humility of the poet's offering 'To the Queen' evokes the chivalrous relationship related to courtly love which became an inseparable element of Victorian medievalism (to be discussed in Chapter 5), increasingly focused on the figure of Victoria and exemplified by royal events such as the *Bal Costumé* of 1842. The 'kingly poet' has become the Queen's faithful servant:

> Take, Madam, this poor book of song;
> For though the faults were thick as dust
> In vacant chambers, I could trust
> Your kindness.
>
> (17–20)

Chivalric touches are added as 'To the Queen' echoes the accession ballad's wish for a long reign and 'noble' heirs (22) and in its concern with the monarch's reputation for 'lasting good' (24). Victoria should be remembered for her peaceful 'life' and 'land' and the 'pure' court (25–6) which prefigures the Arthurian Camelot of *Idylls of the King*. (The purity which Tennyson and muscular Christianity 'grafted' onto Victorian chivalry was not celibacy, but required faithfulness within marriage.[34]) Above all, Tennyson suggests, Victoria – by 1851 the mother of seven children – should be revered 'as Mother, Wife, and Queen' (28), roles which not only require chivalric devotion but also reflect the mid-nineteenth-century idealization of woman- and motherhood epitomized in Tennyson's earlier poem *The Princess* (1847): 'No Angel, but a dearer being, all dipt | In Angel instincts, breathing Paradise' (VII, 301–2). The word order also reflects Victoria's preferred public image. In portraits she often chose to be shown with her children, personifying 'our happy domestic life – which gives such a good example':[35]

> Her court was pure; her life serene;
> God gave her peace; her land reposed;
> A thousand claims to reverence closed
> In her as Mother, Wife, and Queen;
>
> (25–8)

Gendered images of the Queen as wife and mother – of her family and later of the nation – proliferated throughout the reign. Such representations were prefigured in two poems written by Elizabeth Barrett Browning for Victoria's coronation on 28 June 1837, which was seen as symbolically inaugurating the new era. 'The Young Queen' represents Victoria as mother of a nation, whose 'grateful isles | Shall give thee back their smiles, | And as thy mother joys in thee, in them shalt *thou* rejoice;' (49–51).[36] 'Victoria's Tears' foresees a 'well beloved' (32) Queen – who repeatedly 'wept, to wear a crown' (10, 20, 30, 40) – influencing her nation by 'pure tears' rather than 'tyrant's sceptre' (33–4), a sentimental image belied by contemporary reports and representations of the self-possessed young Victoria.[37]

John Plunkett's comprehensive study of Victoria as the 'first media monarch' demonstrates that the royal family 'enjoyed an exceptional degree of publicity' throughout her reign.[38] The 'royal image' became a constant – and constructed – presence on a wide variety of media. Focusing on the period from 1837 to 1870 (which spans the years between Tennyson's accession ballad and 'To the Queen', published as the epilogue to *Idylls of the King* in 1873) Plunkett traces the growth of the newspaper and periodical press, including the development of an illustrated press in the early 1840s, which was aided by technological advances, and the reduction and removal of Newspaper Stamp Duty in 1836 and 1855 respectively. In August 1860 'the royal image became photographic'[39] and Plunkett notes that the resulting profusion of newspapers, prints and photographs offered Victoria's subjects 'an intimate and personal interaction with the monarchy'.[40] However, the relationship was shaped by Victoria, who personally approved the publication of her photographs, which were habitually and extensively retouched.

John Plunkett argues that Victoria's manipulation of the media helps to explain why 'she was simultaneously revered, reviled, fetishized, ignored, and gossiped about'. This view both encapsulates Richard Williams's belief that differing forms of veneration and criticism co-existed throughout Victoria's reign, and counters John Lucas's linear, progressive view of royal popularity. Williams comments that Victoria and Albert's wedding on 10 February 1840, minutely covered in the London and provincial middle-class press, 'launched the Victorian monarchy on its domestic career'.[41] Plunkett agrees that the marriage was part of a movement towards royal populism but focuses on critics of the wedding, who were suspicious of Victoria's 'high-profile role', feared the involvement of 'a foreign confederacy', or satirized *The German Bridegroom*.[42] Williams examines newspapers and periodicals throughout the 1840s and 1850s to conclude that Victorian domes-tic ideology was at its most intense in relation to the Royal Family. Tennyson's idealized 'Mother, Wife, and Queen' (28) thus embodies two aspects of nineteenth-century Englishness, as the English were remarkable not only 'for their appreciation of home comforts'[43] but also their intense and 'innate . . . veneration' for the monarchy.[44] However, Williams also discusses the critical writings and events which belie the vision presented in 'To the Queen' (1851) of Victoria's peaceful 'land' (26) and 'unshaken' throne (34). Working-class counter-ceremonial was organized for coronation day and for the wedding day which coincided with the sentencing of the Newport rising's Chartist leaders[45] and the Queen survived an assassination attempt on 10 June 1840. Chartist reaction to royal events during the Hungry Forties reflected anger at the monarchy's 'obscene luxury', particularly when contrasting the luxury surrounding royal births with working-class infant mortality.[46]

Frank Prochaska examines the policy of popularizing the monarchy. Initiated by Albert (to be idealized by Tennyson in the 'Dedication' to *Idylls of the King* (1862)), this policy was pursued throughout the 1840s, continued during the rise of republican ideas in the early 1850s among radicals disillusioned by the failure of Chartism, and as republican-ism failed to flourish in a relatively prosperous era.[47] Whereas Richard Williams believes that Albert's political legacy was ambivalent and should be reappraised,[48] Prochaska argues that to ensure social equilib-rium and prevent criticism of the Royal Family – including accusations that he received a lavish allowance for doing nothing – Albert 'steered the monarchy towards [political] neutrality' and social service and brought the Crown into greater contact with the people, initially 'with respect-able society' and after 1848 seeking to reach 'the common people'.[49] Prochaska believes that by broadening its social appeal through public service, which complemented Victoria's admired domestic and family values, Albert was directing the monarchy towards 'civic republicanism', in the classical sense of seeking 'social stability through public spirit, a balance of powers and respect for the rule of law'.[50]

'Dedication: To the Prince Consort'

Albert wrote to 'My dear Mr Tennyson' on 17 May 1860 asking the poet to inscribe his copy of 'your "Idylls of the King"'.[51] When Albert died, on 14 December 1861 aged forty-two, Tennyson dedicated a new edition of the *Idylls* 'to His Memory – since he held them dear' (1). 'Dedication: To the Prince Consort' was written 'by about Christmas 1861 and sent on 7 January 1862'.[52] By 23 January Tennyson was 'altogether . . . out of love with my Dedication', but 'as the Queen has approved of it' the loyal Laureate, glad to 'have soothed her sorrow', supposed 'it must stand as it is'.[53]

Tennyson's dedicatory poem pays tribute to Albert in content and form. By using Shakespearean blank verse, the poet links with English literary tradition a Prince Consort many had considered 'un-English'.[54] The poem – in four sections of unequal length – opens with a short dedication whose hesitant lines are broken as if in grief:

> These to His Memory – since he held them dear,
> Perchance as finding there unconsciously
> Some image of himself – I dedicate,
> I dedicate, I consecrate with tears –
> These Idylls.
>
> (1–5)

The archaic but hopeful 'Perchance' (2) foreshadows both the Arthurian *Idylls*, to which 'Dedication' is the prologue, and the extended section extolling Albert's virtues that follows after a break suggesting the poet has paused to gather strength.

Tennyson shared Princess Alice's 'strong desire that I should in some way "idealize" our lamented Prince', but doubted his ability to 'idealize a life which was in itself an ideal' and again reported ill-health.[55] However, the poet's romantic and chivalrous relationship with Victoria is echoed in the resulting eulogy of Albert – who 'seems to me | Scarce other than my king's ideal knight' (5–6) – a comparison Tennyson heightens by paraphrasing the oath sworn to Arthur by his 'glorious' and exemplary 'company', formed 'To serve as model for the mighty world' (*Guinevere*, 1859, 461–2).[56] A model of chivalric purity, the Prince Consort 'clave' only to the Queen, over 'whose realms to their last isle', the poet assumes, is cast 'The shadow of His loss', together with 'the gloom of imminent war' (10–13). Richard Williams counters Frank Prochaska's view of Albert's neutrality, pointing out that his 'political activities continued to be viewed with suspicion in the final years of his life'[57] – despite the Great Exhibition's success – and one of Albert's last acts was to intervene in 'the Trent affair'.[58] For Tennyson, Albert is an exemplary patriot-statesman, with the qualities of the English gentlemen to be discussed in Chapter 5:

> How modest, kindly, all-accomplished, wise,
> With what sublime repression of himself,
> And in what limits, and how tenderly;
> Not swaying to this faction or to that;
> Not making his high place the lawless perch
> Of winged ambitions, nor a vantage-ground
> For pleasure;
>
> (17–23)

Both 'modest' and 'wise', he is self-contained and impartial, neither self-seeking nor self-indulgent. Amidst the Court's intrigues and jealousies, and under intense public scrutiny, he continues to wear the symbolic 'white flower of a blameless life', throughout the 'tract of years' (23–4) that implies an often desolate crusade. 'England's hope, the poet believes, is for '*his* sons' (30) to inherit his qualities.

Albert's title encapsulates his ambiguous position and reflects contemporary concerns with patriarchal authority and gender roles. In June 1857 Victoria created Albert Prince Consort – by letters patent, as ministers did not accede to the Queen's request for the appropriate parliamentary bill to be introduced.[59] Although Victoria became Queen at nineteen, the first female monarch since Queen Anne (1702–14) proved to be a strong and determined ruler. Albert became Victoria's unofficial secretary and confidential adviser and by 1857 'the firm which had started as "I and Albert", behind the scenes had become "Albert and I"'.[60] Officially, however, he was the Queen's husband, his most important role as 'noble Father of [England's] Kings to be' (33). 1857 also saw the introduction of the Matrimonial Causes Act which, when followed in 1870 by the Married Women's Property Act, gave married women a limited degree of autonomy. Legislation began to challenge the ideology

of separate spheres, represented at its most extreme by the old King in
The Princess (1847), who sees:

> Man for the field and woman for the hearth:
> Man for the sword and for the needle she:
> Man with the head and woman with the heart:
> Man to command and woman to obey;
> All else confusion.

(V.437–41)

Personal experience of the 'black blood' of the Tennyson family[61] –
his disinherited and embittered father's drunken violence and mental
instability – led the poet to mistrust the patriarchal relationship.
Tennyson subverts masculine authority in *The Princess* through the
character of the young Prince, prone to life-threatening 'weird seizures'
which are an 'old and strange affection of the house' (I.13–14), until
released through his love for Princess Ida. In 'Dedication', royal authority is qualified by analogies between the framing poem's Prince Consort
and the *Idylls*' King Arthur, husband to the adulterous Guinevere
whose 'foul ensample' (*Guinevere*, 1859, 487) led to the dissolution of
'the whole Round Table' (*The Passing of Arthur*, 1869, 402). The Prince
Consort is a patriarchal figure whose power is qualified; ultimately, for
Albert – as for the Poet Laureate – it is the Queen 'to command'.

'To the Queen' (1873)

As Tennyson wrote, 'Dedication' 'conclude[s] with an address to our
beloved Queen';[62] Victoria 'commands' both the poem's close and
the later epilogue to *Idylls of the King*. Although 'the Crown' is now
represented as 'a lonely splendour' ('Dedication', 48), the poet urges
sovereignty to triumph over the assumed frailty of her 'woman's-heart'
(43) and, echoing the Anglican liturgy of whose church 'the Crown' is
head, he prays that the love of her family and people will comfort the
Queen until divine love reunites her with Albert. The publication of
'Dedication', which 'had soothed her aching, bleeding heart',[63] led to
Tennyson's first meeting with Victoria on 14 April 1862 and began an
understanding, firmly grounded in mutual respect and enhanced by
their experience of deep and extended mourning, between two difficult
and egocentric people. Tennyson wrote in May 1863 that the Queen
was 'in every way worthy of England's love and honour'.[64] His second
poem entitled 'To the Queen' – written at Emily Tennyson's suggestion

in December 1872 and published in 1873 as the epilogue to *Idylls of the King* – is in the iambic blank verse which carries resonant echoes of Shakespeare and exemplifies the Laureate's increasingly intense personal allegiance to Victoria, now addressed directly as 'thou, my Queen' (33).

For Tennyson, the closing prayer of 'Dedication' has been triumphantly fulfilled. The nineteenth-century revival of chivalry made loyalty a much-admired virtue and, since Albert's death, the Queen has remained: 'O loyal to the royal in thyself, | And loyal to thy land, as this to thee' (1–2). The poet cites as 'witness, that rememberable day' (3), the National Thanksgiving held at St Paul's Cathedral on 27 February 1872 following the illness (typhoid) which had taken the 'flickering life' of the Prince of Wales 'halfway down the shadow of the grave' (5–6). As Richard Williams notes, the upsurge of sympathy which followed the Prince's recovery – derided by radicals as 'typhoid loyalty' – was 'viewed in many quarters as the death-blow to republicanism'.[65] Albert had died of typhoid in 1861 and the Royal Family was seen not to be immune from diseases still prevalent in late nineteenth-century England.[66]

London's cheering crowds are represented as one 'roll[ing] tide of joy through all | Her trebled millions' (8–9). They embody both 'thy people and their love' (7), an implied unity which echoes John Lucas's view of late-Victorian England as 'a royalist nation'. However, Tennyson's view of the 1860s and early 1870s as a linear progression of royal duty supported by loyal subjects is partial in two senses of the word: he reflects the veneration without the co-existing criticism. Victoria took to extremes the protracted mourning often inseparable from Victorian domestic ideology and withdrew almost completely from public life, although – as Margaret Homans points out – she 'did make exceptions for one kind of public ceremonial: unveiling or dedicating statues and other memorials of Albert'.[67] During the 1860s Victoria was increasingly criticized for living in retired seclusion at Civil List expense, her attachment to her Balmoral servant John Brown gave rise to salacious rumours, the Prince of Wales's involvement in successive scandals gave cause for concern, and in 1870 Gladstone wrote of the 'royalty question' that 'the Queen is invisible and the Prince of Wales is not respected'.[68] The cost of the monarchy – and the resulting economic criticisms – continued to increase as the royal children, whose births had in turn been celebrated and criticized, received annuities on their maturity and marriage.

The dowry and marriage on 21 February 1871 of Princess Louise – Victoria's sixth child – was a particular catalyst. It led both to intense royal 'fever' and the organization into a republican movement of the more prominent branch of the 'two distinct republicanisms' which, Richard Williams argues, developed from different sources in the 1860s and 1870s.[69] This 'mainstream republicanism' – an alliance of middle-class radicals and artisans – was radicalized by the Queen's seclusion and her heir's unpopularity. The alternative, 'proletarian and socialist' republicanism originated in the small socialist groups of the late 1860s and developed from domestic social concerns: unrest accompanied the Second Reform Bill and Act in 1865 and 1867, with a financial crisis in 1866 and an agricultural, trade and industrial depression in 1869 and 1870. Both republicanisms were additionally influenced by events in France, the fall of Napoleon III (1870) and the Paris Commune (1871). Tracing the divergence and subsequent contraction of the two republicanisms between late 1872 and 1874, Williams concludes that republicanism had little chance of achieving its ultimate aim in the early 1870s as it failed to become a large-scale popular movement and, predominantly, because most liberals and radicals believed that the desired reforms could be achieved under a British constitutional monarchy.[70]

'To the Queen' demonstrates an increasingly intense allegiance to the Empire. The Laureate ignores contemporary republicanism and domestic social conditions to challenge the Empire's economic critics, thus forming part of the vocal defence of the empire which developed during the 1860s and 1870s. As 'witness' to the mutual loyalty of Queen and people, Tennyson also cites: 'the silent cry, | The prayer of many a race and creed, and clime . . . From sunset and sunrise of all thy realm, | And that true North' (10–14). The countries of the Empire – including Canada, 'that true North' (14) – are assumed to share England's emotions. Three letters to *The Times* in January 1870 from 'A Colonist', later identified as Sir John Rose, had advocated that on grounds of cost Canada should sever her connection with Britain, a view Tennyson rejected as 'Villa[i]nous!'[71] In a series of staccato statements and rhetorical questions, 'To the Queen' similarly rebukes the separatists, or 'Little Englanders':

> A strain to shame us 'keep you to yourselves;
> So loyal is too costly! friends – your love
> Is but a burthen: loose the bond, and go.'
> Is this the tone of empire? here the faith
> That made us rulers? This, indeed, her voice
> And meaning, whom the roar of Hougoumont [Waterloo]
> Left mightiest of all peoples under heaven?
>
> (15–21)

He reassures Victoria that the true 'voice of Britain' – and of the Poet Laureate[72] – is that of England's capital, 'the full city', celebrating 'Thee and thy Prince' (24–7).

For the poet of 'To the Queen' (1873), loyalty to crown and country is inseparable from loyalty to the Empire and its administrators and settlers:

> The loyal to their crown
> Are loyal to their own far sons, who love
> Our ocean-empire with her boundless homes
> For ever-broadening England, and her throne
> In our vast Orient, and one isle, one isle,
> That knows not her own greatness: if she knows
> And dreads it we are fallen.
>
> (27–33)

'To the Queen' not only exemplifies the Orientalism to be discussed in Chapter 6 but also represents a change of definition and attitude. In early Victorian England the phrase 'British Empire' referred only to the British Isles and the term *imperialism* was first used in 1851 to criticize Louis Napoleon.[73] 'Dedication' and earlier royal poems merely allude to the Empire – Victoria's 'realms to their last isle' ('Dedication', 1862, 11). However, by 1872 the 'peculiarly radical' element of Tennyson's 'conservatism', which fears change yet sees its necessity,[74] is no longer apparent and 'To the Queen' defends an imperialist policy against its critics and the perceived threat of dissolution. The aggressive patriotism with which the poet rejects dissent as disloyalty to the Crown is enhanced by the allusion to past military victory and through subliminal echoes of Shakespearean blank verse. Tennyson fabricates a myth of England and the Empire – an idealized representation which ignores the realities of domestic depression to assert that the 'mightiest of all peoples under heaven' are 'wealthier – wealthier – hour by hour!' (21–3), while the image of 'ever-broadening England' (30) implies a process of organic growth rather than territorial expansion through annexation or wars.

Tennyson then reverts to the chivalric poetic humility of 'To the Queen' (1851). He asks Victoria – 'thou, my Queen' (33) – to accept the *Idylls* for love of Albert:

> Not for itself, but through thy living love
> For one to whom I made it o'er his grave

Sacred, accept this old imperfect tale,
New-old, and shadowing Sense at war with Soul,
Ideal manhood closed in real man

(34–8)

Tennyson heightens Arthur's – and by analogy, Albert's – chivalric purity
by excising the relationship between the King and Mordred, Arthur's son
by his half-sister Morgause. Victoria should also accept her Laureate's
'blessing' and 'his trust that Heaven', apparently favouring the Empire,
will avert the distant storm of debate that threatens 'thine and ours'
(46–8). He notes with scorn that 'some are scared' (48) by signs of doubt
or dissent, are overcautious, self-interested or susceptible to malign
influences which – as so often in Tennyson – come 'from France' (56).
The poem's conditional ending echoes the themes and language of the
early political poems and encapsulates Tennyson's ideal of England as a
hierarchically structured and stable society, ruled by moderate patriot-
statesmen and crowned by an ideal – and idealized – monarch, the vision
heightened by the measured pace, repetition and visual links between
the words. The purpose of 'this great world' (59) cannot be seen, 'yet – if'
our 'slowly-grown | And crowned Republic's crowning common-sense'
(60–1) does not fail, such fears are merely 'morning shadows' (63), dis-
proportionately larger than the shapes that cast them, not the threaten-
ing shadows which prefigure the death of Arthur and his empire.

Royal occasion poems

Tennyson, unlike earlier Poets Laureate, was not required to commemorate the sovereign's birthday or great public events. He also 'hate[d] a
subject given me . . . still more if that subject be a public one',[75] but
during his Laureateship Tennyson wrote many poems to celebrate royal
occasions, including the contentious marriages of Victoria's children.
Critics generally dismiss these poems,[76] often written at the Queen's
request and betraying the tension between loyalty and dislike of 'given'
subjects. However, they exemplify both Tennyson's increasing allegiance
to Victoria and the linear progression of his creation of a myth of monarchy and Empire and – in one instance – evoke his deepest emotions.

Through politically judicious marriages, which Tennyson invariably
idealizes as love-matches, the Queen's daughters and sons became allied
to many of the crowned heads of Europe. 'A Welcome to Alexandra:
March 7, 1863' – greeting the 'Blissful bride of a blissful heir' (27) – was
published in *The Times* on 10 March 1863 to mark the marriage of

Princess Alexandra of Denmark and the Prince of Wales who, as Edward VII, failed to fulfil Tennyson's hope that Victoria's successors would prove 'as noble till the latest day' ('To the Queen' 1851, 22). Tennyson described the poem, which received the Queen's 'warmest thanks', as 'a little lyrical flash, an impromptu'.[77] The imperative verbs and relentless rhythm of 'A Welcome', which retains the popular ballad's rapid pace and regular rhymes, attempt to recreate the thunderous sound of royal salute, bells, brass and fireworks – 'Welcome her, thunder of fort and of fleet!' (6). Tennyson was notably hostile to the Celtic temperament[78] and the poem's awkward conclusion, with its emphasis on the differing origins of 'the people', appears to question the anticipated national unity:

> O joy to the people and joy to the throne,
> Come to us, love us and make us your own:
> For Saxon or Dane or Norman we,
> Teuton or Celt, or whatever we be
> We are each all Dane in our welcome of thee,
>
> > Alexandra! (29–34)

Many of Tennyson's poems were written in pairs, or 'pendants', which complement or oppose each other. The welcome to Alexandra required 'A Welcome' to her sister-in-law 'Her Royal Highness Marie Alexandrovna, Duchess of Edinburgh: March 7, 1874' published in *The Times* exactly eleven years later. Grand Duchess Marie Alexandrovna – 'Russian flower' (6) – who married Victoria's second son Alfred in Russia in January 1874, was the granddaughter of Tsar Nicholas I, descendant of the 'Czar' who ruled with an 'iron sceptre' ('Hail Briton!', 196). The marriage united two empires; accordingly the later, more measured 'Welcome' is in the double *In Memoriam* stanza form. Tennyson assumes that the marriage is known and welcomed 'along the steppes' (11) and throughout the British Empire – by 'India . . . | On capes of Afric as on cliffs of Kent' (14–17), by the 'pines of Canada', still believed 'loyal', and by 'the Maoris' (18–19), which ignores the reality of three Maori Wars (1843–47, 1863–64 and 1869–70). The marriage of monarchy and empire is symbolized by the final union of names, 'Alfred – Alexandrovna!' (50). However, celebration is subverted by the third stanza's pessimistic tone which, as Robin L. Inboden observes, appears to foreshadow the decline of the empires embodied by the bride and groom:[79]

> Fair empires branching, both, in lusty life! –
> Yet Harold's England fell to Norman swords;

> Yet thine own land has bowed to Tartar hordes
> Since English Harold gave its throne a wife,
>   Alexandrovna!
> For thrones and peoples are as waifs that swing,
>   And float or fall, in endless ebb and flow;
>   But who love best have best the grace to know
> That Love by right divine is deathless king,
>   Marie Alexandrovna!
>
>   (21–30)

Royal occasion poems written in the 1880s carry echoes of 'Vastness' (1885), in which Tennyson questions – 'All new-old revolutions of Empire . . . what is all of it worth?' (30) – finally to affirm the importance of love and the hope of life after death: 'Peace, let it be! for I loved him, and love him for ever: the dead are not dead but alive' (36). 'Love' in 'Marie Alexandrovna' is an absolute monarch – 'by right divine is deathless king' (29); in Tennyson's final royal marriage poem 'Love' is equated with 'the Sun', also an attribute of royalty. 'To H.R.H. Princess Beatrice' was written at the Queen's request to celebrate her youngest daughter's marriage to Prince Henry of Battenberg. Tennyson responded with a measured poem in blank verse, published in *The Times* on 23 July 1885, in which the poet appears more concerned with death than life. 'Two Suns of Love' (1), maternal and spousal, lighten human life, 'Which else with all its pains, and griefs, and deaths, | Were utter darkness' (1–3). Even the wedding ceremony is 'that white funeral of the single life' at which 'The Mother weeps' (8–9). Victoria insisted that after the wedding 'dear Beatrice will live with me as heretofore, without which I *never* could have *allowed* the marriage',[80] a sacrifice which Tennyson idealizes as 'all-faithful, filial' loyalty, with the 'True daughter' (13) moving between:

> The two that love thee . . .
> Swayed by each Love, and swaying to each Love,
> Like some conjectured planet in mid heaven
> Between two Suns, and drawing down from both
> The light and genial warmth of double day.
>
>   (18–22)

On three occasions Tennyson commemorated the premature deaths of 'the race of the Queen of the Isles' (40). 'Prince Leopold', Victoria's youngest and haemophiliac son, who died in March 1884 aged thirty-one, received as 'An Epitaph' eight lines of unexceptional rhyming couplets which suggest that he is reunited with the father he resembles:

> Wherefore should your eyes be dim?
> I am here again with him.

> (5–6)

Tennyson's final royal occasion poem mourns 'The Death of the Duke of Clarence and Avondale', the Prince of Wales's heir, who died at the age of twenty-eight. The blank verse poem, written to comfort Alexandra, Princess of Wales (welcomed to England in 1863) was published in the *Nineteenth Century* in February 1892, eight months before the poet's own death. Although a grief to his family the Duke's death was a relief to the Establishment, continually concerned by his 'combination of a below-average intellect with an above-average sexual appetite',[81] but in a chivalric tribute Tennyson praises him as 'princely, tender, truthful, reverent, pure' (4) and laments 'his brief range of blameless days' (9). That 'a world-wide Empire mourns' with the Royal Family (5) has also become a poetic convention. Tennyson is increasingly aware that the 'face of Death' is now turned 'toward the Sun of Life' (12). Visiting the poet in January 1892 the composer Hubert Parry found him 'much exercised about eternal punishment'[82] and the poem's conclusion is ambiguous – the family should 'Mourn in hope' rather than certainty of reunion in 'the great Hereafter' (17). Despite his age, however, Tennyson was still sufficiently interested in the work of younger poets to 'congratulate Kipling on his "English Flag"'.

The flag as symbol of England inspired one of Tennyson's most considered royal occasion poems, which proves that when his deepest feelings are touched the 'taskwork ode' does not 'ever fail' (Drexel text, 21). 'Dedicatory Poem to the Princess Alice' was written in March 1879, three months after the Princess had 'died of kissing her child, who was ill with diphtheria'.[83] By marriage Alice, Victoria's second daughter, was Grand Duchess of Hesse-Darmstadt, but her deathbed request, reported to Tennyson from the Queen, was for an English flag to be put on her coffin. The poem was published in the April 1879 edition of *Nineteenth Century* dedicating 'The Defence of Lucknow', which commemorates the uprising known to contemporaries as the 'Indian Mutiny', and whose refrain rejoices that 'And ever upon the topmost roof our banner of England blew'. By the late 1870s, monarchy and empire were inextricably linked.

The blank verse 'Dedicatory Poem' forms an extended and almost unbroken question. Qualifying words and phrases recur – 'if' (1, 2, 4), 'perhaps' (6), 'may' (14, 19), 'who can tell' (14) – as Tennyson meditates on the inter-relationship of the living and the dead. Alice is both 'Dead Princess' and 'living Power' if she 'live[s] on' (1–2) and is not separated from 'earthly love and life' (4–6), when perhaps the praise of her native and adopted lands may rise towards her. March 1879 also saw the marriage of Alice's brother Prince Arthur, Victoria's third son. In a startling image, which both symbolizes the recent royal marriage and funeral and evokes the poet's own, much earlier loss, Tennyson visualizes 'Thy Soldier-brother's bridal orange-bloom | Break through the yews and cypress of thy grave' (11–12) echoing the 'Old Yew' whose 'roots are wrapt about the bones' of Arthur Hallam (*In Memoriam*, 1850, II, 1–4). Tennyson hopes the light of 'this March morn' (10), which saw 'thine Imperial mother smile again', may ascend to Alice (13–14). (Amidst considerable controversy, touched on below, Victoria had been proclaimed Empress of India on 1 May 1876 and she joined Europe's Emperors – the Tsar, the Emperor of Austria and, from 1870, the Emperor of Germany, father-in-law of her eldest daughter Victoria.) As Tennyson contemplates the royal death, the lines become broken as if by emotion. Alice is 'England's England-loving daughter', her Englishness exemplified by England's 'flag | Borne on thy coffin' (15–17):

> Thou – England's England-loving daughter – thou
> Dying so English thou wouldst have her flag
> Borne on thy coffin – where is he can swear
> But that some broken gleam from our poor earth
> May touch thee, while remembering thee, I lay
> At thy pale feet this ballad of the deeds
> Of England, and her banner in the East?
>
> (15–21)

Returning to the hope of *In Memoriam*, the poet again anxiously questions whether 'some broken gleam from our poor earth | May touch thee' (18–19), even though 'dear words of human speech | . . . communicate no more' (*In Memoriam*, LXXXV, 83–4). By 1879 sentiments expressed in the early patriotic ballads have become personified by the Laureate's idealizations of Victoria and her daughter – 'there are no wives, like English' royal 'wives | So fair and chaste as they be' ('National Song', written 1828–29, 21–2). In poetic homage which mirrors the chivalric tributes 'To the Queen', Tennyson lays at Alice's feet his 'ballad of the deeds | Of England, and her banner in the East' (20–1).

'On the Jubilee of Queen Victoria'

By 1887 the accession ballad's wish for a long reign had been fulfilled. Tennyson's extended and formal 'Ode' to celebrate the fiftieth anniversary of Victoria's coronation was published in April 1887, eight years after 'Dedicatory Poem to the Princess Alice'. In the intervening years, from the mid-1870s to the late 1880s, the criticism and veneration of the monarchy which had been apparent since the accession continued to co-exist. Although republicanism as an organized movement had largely disappeared by 1874 criticism persisted in the radical press and parliament, often strengthened by the protesting voices of Irish MPs, still heard on the eve of the Golden Jubilee. The royal 'fever' which surrounded Princess Louise's wedding in 1871 was perpetuated during the 1870s and 1880s by the mainstream and loyalist press, dominating but not silencing the dissent. Therefore, as Richard Williams argues, *The Times'* description of the monarchy as a 'universally popular institution' – and John Lucas's view of England as a unitedly royalist nation – 'could not hold true'.[84]

The dynastic royal marriages which Tennyson idealized as love-matches generated both criticism and enthusiasm. The loyal press praised the entry into London in March 1874 of Prince Alfred and his Russian bride, Marie Alexandrovna, for its imposing ceremonial and strong military element – 'an inspiring body of troops . . . of whom any nation might be proud'[85] – but the marriage grant made to Alfred in 1873 led to a republican protest rally in Hyde Park, and *Reynold's Newspaper* contrasted the lavish royal wedding with contemporary destitution in Clerkenwell.[86] Protests against the annuity to Prince Arthur – Princess Alice's 'Soldier-brother' (11) – on his majority in 1871 intensified with his 1878 marriage allowance and he was attacked as a 'sinecurist' and 'counterfeit soldier'. In 1882 the marriage of the chronically ill Prince Leopold was seen as 'a device to pension his [German] bride' and when Princess Beatrice married in 1885 thirty-eight MPs voted against the grant, including several Irish MPs for whom the Royal Family epitomized England's attitude towards Ireland.

However, attacks on the cost of the Crown and Royal Family were not channelled into a consistent critique of the institution of monarchy. The Prince of Wales, denounced as debauched and debt-ridden by the radical press, was increasingly seen by the mainstream loyalist press as 'the industrious inheritor of his father's mantle': his 1875–76 tour of India was a 'special personal triumph'[87] and he was more popular at the 1887 Jubilee than the 1872 Thanksgiving. Additionally, Victoria had overcome the controversy surrounding the Royal Titles Act of 1876.[88] Introducing the measure, Disraeli did not immediately announce the Queen's new title – Empress of India – nor include in the Bill and Proclamation a clause confining its usage to India. Parliament and the press attacked the title as un-English and 'imperialistic', in the contemporary sense of authoritarian rule, and Disraeli was accused of undermining Parliament and exalting the Crown.

Richard Williams's exhaustive survey of press coverage up to and including the Golden Jubilee concludes that it was 'the sovereign herself who was lauded extravagantly'.[89] The lavish praise of Victoria contained in the middle-class press is given authoritative utterance by Tennyson's ode 'On the Jubilee of Queen Victoria', written between December 1886 and February 1887 and published in the April 1887 edition of *Macmillan's Magazine* as *Carmen Saeculare: An Ode in Honour of the Jubilee*.[90] A public ode for a ceremonial occasion was intended to be sung and, at Tennyson's request, Sir Charles Stanford provided a musical setting.

Tennyson had greeted Victoria's accession with a hastily-written popular ballad. In 1883 the poet accepted a peerage, taking his seat in the House of Lords in 1884 as Baron Tennyson of Aldworth and Freshwater. The Laureate celebrated the Jubilee with a ceremonial ode epitomizing his perception of Victoria's dignity as woman and monarch, and his final tribute to the Queen is consciously classical in both form and content: 'I wrote a great part of my "Jubilee Ode"' in the 'beautiful metre' of Catullus' *Collis O Heliconii*' and Horace's *Carmen Saeculare* 'is a similar celebratory prayer'.[91] The public ode was developed by Pindar and the patterned stanza structure of the 'Jubilee Ode' – alternating three-line stanzas addressed to the Queen with five stanzas of eight, ten or eleven lines exhorting her subjects – suggests the formalized movement of Greek choric song. The diction is formal, often Latinate, with the measured pace appropriate to the dignity of an ageing monarch. Many lines end with a three-syllable word reflecting the rhythm of 'Jubilee' and its sense of celebration, and each long stanza ends with a resounding reminder of the occasion – 'year of her Jubilee':

> She beloved for a kindliness
> Rare in Fable or History,
> Queen, and Empress of India,
> Crowned so long with a diadem
> Never worn by a worthier,

> Now with prosperous auguries
> Comes at last to the bounteous
> Crowning year of her Jubilee.
>
> (4–11)

Fifty years have passed 'Since our Queen assumed the globe, the sceptre' (3) and Tennyson commands nationwide celebration. Illuminations
and fireworks which echo Alexandra's 'Welcome' (1863) are to 'Shoot
your stars to the firmament' (17) and each town's 'multitude' – assumed
'Loyal' – should raise 'One full voice of allegiance' (21–2). The Laureate
reminds her people of Victoria's virtues: the 'Queen, as true to womanhood as Queenhood', shares their 'glories' and the 'sorrows' (25–7)
suggested by ordering the affluent to be 'bountiful' to 'the lowly, the
destitute' and 'to the Hospital' (28–33). With justification, Tennyson
sees the reign as fifty years of commercial and scientific development
and of 'ever-widening Empire' (52–4). He exhorts all classes and nations
to unite in celebratory song, from the lords of land and industry to the
'Patient children of Albion' (59), by implication obedient to their parent and their wished-for patience an English attribute. Although the
Empire's different nationalities are finally acknowledged, their separate
identities are to be subsumed in the English-language 'Jubilee Ode':

> You, the Mighty, the Fortunate,
> You, the Lord-territorial,
> You, the Lord-manufacturer,
> You, the hardy, laborious,
> Patient children of Albion,
> You, Canadian, Indian,
> Australasian, African,
> All your hearts be in harmony,
> All your voices in unison,
> Singing 'Hail to the glorious
> Golden year of her Jubilee!'
>
> (55–65)

In the final stanza – extended 'with the Queen's express approval'[92] –
the poet commands her people's 'Trust' (68). Should distant 'thunders'
and spectral 'darkness' threaten:

> Trust the Hand of Light will lead her people,
> Till the thunders pass, the spectres vanish,

And the Light is Victor, and the darkness
Dawns into the Jubilee of the Ages.

(68–71)

'To the Queen' (1873) had trusted 'Heaven' to avert the distant 'tempest' of doubt and dissent (46–7). In the 'Jubilee Ode' Tennyson pays a final tribute to the name the Queen chose on accession, enhancing the suggestion of divinity which makes her additionally worthy of veneration – 'Light' is not only a metaphor for royalty, but related to 'the Light of the World'. The 'Hand of Light' which leads 'her people' is specifically feminine, but linked by capitalization to 'the Light' as 'Victor'. The 'Victor' is therefore Victoria, an implied androgyny with a Christian subtext. When discussing 'The Holy Grail's concluding reference to 'that One | Who rose again' (1869, 914–15), Tennyson had commented: 'They will not easily beat the character of Christ, that union of man and woman, strength and sweetness'.[93]

The 'Jubilee Ode's concluding, androgynous image finally interweaves Elizabeth Langland's differing concepts of Victorianism (Victoria as ruler and mother) and masculine Englishness.[94] Paradoxically, the image also partially confirms John Lucas's initial argument, which Langland had challenged. As Richard Williams demonstrates, by 1887 England was not wholly 'a royalist nation'[95] – the co-existing strands of veneration and criticism continued after the Golden Jubilee[96] – but for Tennyson, Victoria had become both an emblem of England and the essence of Englishness. Written during more than five decades of Victoria's long reign, the poems of monarchy are an important part of Tennyson's oeuvre. The form and content of the rapidly written accession ballad and contrasting, consciously classical Jubilee ode exemplify the linear progression of Tennyson's allegiance to the institution of monarchy and to Victoria herself, as she progressed from young royal motherhood to imperial matriarchy. For the Laureate, as for the Prince Consort, it was the Queen 'to command' and Tennyson's loyalty is represented by the idealized portraits of Victoria and Albert, the moving memorial to their daughter Alice, and the often unsuccessful attempts to attribute their perceived chivalric virtues to other descendants. At times, the poems of monarchy betray the poet's concerns, but despite his early fears Tennyson fulfils the role of 'kingly poet' defined in the Drexel text of 1851 and – although the gender is changed – he has come to 'believe | The king's heart true as he is great' (19–20).

The poems of monarchy both mirror and perpetuate the veneration of the monarchy, which increased during Victoria's reign. The co-existing, often intense criticism of the monarchy does not make its appearance in Tennyson's poetry and the unified England he portrays is thus a fabrication – an invented and exemplary realm – to be encouraged at times of depression, division or debate. The 'Jubilee Ode's 'one full voice of allegiance' (22) conceals regional, class and religious differences, and the unequal distribution of wealth revealed by reference to 'the destitute' (31). The ennobled poet's early ambivalent view of the 'ermined pall | Of Empire' ('Hail Briton!', 1831–33, 10–11) has long vanished, but Tennyson's imperial vision is also a myth, which rejects the signs of protest. In the 'Jubilee Ode' the Laureate finally gives the Empire's subjects a presence and voice, but the voice is his own and the language English.

5
'To Serve as Model for the Mighty World': Tennyson and Medievalism

Critics and historians agree that in nineteenth-century England the Medieval Revival was not only a powerful imaginative force in art and literature, politics and culture – most immediately apparent in the architecture of the age – but also 'a territory of the mind',[1] inseparably interwoven with the fabric of nineteenth-century thought and touching all classes of Victorian society. There is also critical consensus that the nineteenth-century Medieval Revival was difficult to define and delimit (the term *Middle Ages* spans and apparently unifies many centuries) and had 'no single significance or use',[2] and in generalist essays and volumes and specialist studies critics analyse the differing aspects of Medievalism's variety of forms, particularly the Arthurianism which preoccupied Tennyson for more than fifty years.

In this chapter I consider how Tennyson uses aspects of the medieval past to explore new models of Englishness, to celebrate contemporary and historical figures, and to create a 'model for the mighty world' (*Guinevere*, 1859, 462). 'Mythic Uther's deeply-wounded son' (105) first appears in 'The Palace of Art', written by April 1832, published in *Poems* (1832) and much revised for the 1842 volumes. 'Clouds and darkness' finally 'Closed upon Camelot' (75–6) in 'Merlin and the Gleam', written and published in 1889, three years before the poet's death. To trace Tennyson's developing use of medievalism the poems are examined in generally chronological order, with reference to the poet's letters and to the views of critics and historians, who outline the medievalist context in which the poems were written and whose views are touched on below.

A nineteenth-century dream of order?

As Hilary Fraser points out, 'historicism itself was subject to the movement of history'.[3] Critics such as Robin Gilmour and David Newsome trace the movement of the Medieval Revival through the nineteenth century,[4] from the early literary influence of Sir Walter Scott, in turn influenced by Romanticism's revolt against the rational and ordered tone of eighteenth-century thought and culture.[5] Gilmour regards the medievalism of the 1830s and 1840s – the decades of Tennyson's growing fame – as a 'consciously reactionary movement, High Church and often Catholic in religion, Tory-radical in politics'.[6] Suggesting a dualism discussed at greater length in critics' specialist studies, Gilmour argues that Thomas Carlyle's *Past and Present* (1843) – which juxtaposed the moral order of life in a feudal monastery with the social anarchy of 1840s England – established an 'authoritarian social criticism' which was developed in the medievalism of John Ruskin and William Morris. Within this tradition, Gilmour suggests, 'the Middle Ages pass from being the property of Tory radicalism to being the property of socialism'. In literature and painting after 1850 – Tennyson's Laureate years – medievalism became domesticated and the Arthurian legends were rediscovered, and from the late 1860s the Middle Ages, used unhistorically for much of the nineteenth century, became the subject of scholarly study by historians such as Edward Freeman and J.R. Green. Newsome adds that the age of late Victorian medieval scholarship barely survived the century, but throughout Victoria's reign medievalism 'never lacked a powerful spokesman'.[7] As Newsome's comment implies, masculine discourse dominated Victorian medievalism. However, in her more recent study Clare Broome Saunders analyses a coexisting female medievalism and considers how women writers, poets and artists used the medieval motifs, forms and settings which enabled them to comment on contemporary issues without incurring career-destroying censure.[8]

Specialist studies examine more closely the origins and diverse aspects of the Victorian Medieval Revival. Clare A. Simmons is one of several critics to observe that *medievalism* – with *medieval* a nineteenth-century term and defined as 'the later reception of the Middle Ages' – was not confined to England.[9] However, Simmons believes that as a nation 'filled with the relics of deliberate disjunction from the Medieval', England's relationship with its medieval past is particularly complex. In England, she suggests, medievalism 'seems to encode desire or mourning for loss', for 'the Saxon kingdom, the ordered society of the Middle Ages', or an age of chivalry and romance. For Alice Chandler, much of medievalism's complexity and creativity similarly lies in 'the tension between its use of the imagined past as a metaphor and the persistence of the real past as a fact'.[10] Chandler traces two important strands of the medieval myth. The first – also argued by Simmons – is 'the quest for order'[11] exemplified by nineteenth-century idealization of feudalism's hierarchically ordered and land-based society. The second is medievalism's 'darker aspect', the elements of disorder and violence which intensified its 'literary and psychological impact'[12] and appeared to echo the turbulence of England's industrializing and increasingly fragmented society.

Charles Dellheim examines medievalism in the context of nineteenth-century England's complex class and political divisions. Defining medievalism as 'the appeal to, and the appeal of, the styles, symbols, and survivals of the Middle Ages', Dellheim concludes that Victorians adopted the Middle Ages to criticize and to affirm their own age.[13] Conservative medievalists – exemplified by the aristocratic and neo-feudalist 'Young England' movement of the early 1840s[14] – sought to reassert 'feudal ideals of social hierarchy and communal responsibility'; middle-class social critics, including William Morris, admired medieval aesthetic achievements and rejected the 'Age of Makeshift'; working-class representatives mourned their lost 'rights', 'liberties' and 'cooperative society'.[15] However, although Victorian society turned to the medieval world to protest against the social and cultural impact of industrialization, Dellheim argues that Victorians also invoked the Middle Ages to celebrate modernity, framing the railway age in the Gothic architecture of stations such as St Pancras.[16]

The working-class lament for lost liberties, to which Charles Dellheim refers, evokes an essential element of nineteenth-century medievalism – 'the English national myth of origin known as Anglo-Saxonism, Teutonism or Gothicism'.[17] For Hugh A. MacDougall, Anglo-Saxonism is 'the second great national myth'[18] of English history, superseding traditional accounts represented by Geoffrey of Monmouth's twelfth-century *History* and widely accepted throughout the late Middle Ages, which elaborated the Arthurian legends and located the origins of England's early inhabitants in Troy. Reginald Horsman defines Anglo-Saxonism as the concept of a separate, superior Anglo-Saxon race, 'with innate endowments enabling it to achieve a perfection of governmental institutions and world dominance'.[19] Although an inseparable part of nineteenth-century thought, its origins were in the sixteenth-century English Reformation, and Horsman traces the complex process by which the early stress on Anglo-Saxon liberties was transformed into the belief in Anglo-Saxon racial superiority which was also inseparable from nineteenth-century English thought.[20]

Rosemary Jann examines the democratic myths of nineteenth-century medievalism. She concludes that the three strands of Victorian medievalism – conservative, Whig and Socialist/radical – yearned to create 'a sense of organic unity with the past in order to sanction and control change in the present', but their reconstructions of the past were ultimately shaped by differing class ideals.[21] Class is also inseparable from the Arthurianism discussed by many critics. Although Arthurian stories were not associated with aristocratic educational tradition, the mourning for the lost age of romance and chivalry referred to by Clare A. Simmons was confined to the upper levels of nineteenth-century English society. Peter Mandler – one of the few critics to discuss medievalism in the mass culture market – follows popular culture's move away from medievalism in the 1830s, arguing that as chivalry became closely identified with the hyper-aristocracy, the expanding 'penny press' began to celebrate 'Tudor England' as 'Merry England'.[22] Stephanie L. Barczewski examines nineteenth-century interpretations of King Arthur and the popular but conflicting legend of Robin Hood – the 'medieval outlaw who seemed to represent everything that Arthur opposed' – which, she believes, paralleled the conflict between inclusion and exclusion in nineteenth-century England.[23]

As Norris J. Lacy concludes, 'Arthurian scholarship has virtually exploded in recent decades'.[24] Arthurian scholarship has also changed since the 1980s. Earlier criticism focused on the work of pre-Raphaelite artists and poets and *Idylls of the King*, the title later given to Tennyson's sequence of Arthurian poems published between 1859 and 1885. The view that *Idylls* 'sparked an Arthurian revival that prompted no less than a literary second coming of Arthur in Victorian times'[25] ignores, for example, Edward Bulwer-Lytton's twelve-volume epic poem *King Arthur* published in 1848. More recent critics discuss Tennyson's earlier Arthurian poems in conjunction with the *Idylls*, as in Inga Bryden's survey of the variety of Victorian Arthurian literature produced between 1830 and 1880, which builds on Roger Simpson's pioneering study of the Arthurian Revival during the first half of the nineteenth century.[26] Specialist Tennyson studies include analyses of chivalry, empire, monarchy, nation and particularly gender, encapsulated in Bryden's conclusion that the figure of Arthur came to embody 'the components of manliness, honour, heroic leadership and liberty which comprised the Teutonic notion of Englishness'.[27] Critics such as Stephen Ahern now recognize that, as Tennyson updates Arthurian romance to reflect the concerns of Victorian England, he 'does not mirror uncritically the sexual politics' – or other aspects – 'of his culture'.[28]

Early Arthurian poems: 'The Lady of Shalott'

Although King Arthur appeared in 'The Palace of Art', written and published in 1832, Tennyson's first complete Arthurian poem was 'The Lady of Shalott'. Written in part by 5–9 October 1831 – thus following the first reviews of *Poems, Chiefly Lyrical* – 'The Lady of Shalott' was completed and published in 1832 and much revised for the 1842 volumes.[29] Its primary source was a medieval Italian novella from the *Cento Novelle Antiche*, dated before 1321, and for the characters of 'The Lady' and 'Sir Lancelot' Tennyson drew on Sir Thomas Malory's romance *Le Morte D'Arthur* (1485), new editions of which were published in 1816 and 1817. Critics also note the general influence of volumes in Somersby's library; Roger Simpson additionally mentions two contemporary English poems – Louisa Stuart Costello's 'The Funeral Boat', dating from 1829,[30] and 'A Legend of Tintagel Castle' by Letitia Elizabeth Landon, which appeared in October 1832.[31]

Tennyson's first Arthurian poems are experiments in form and content; their central characters early studies for the chivalric constructs of *Idylls of the King*. 'The Lady of Shalott' becomes 'Elaine' (1859), 'the lily maid of Astolat', who dies for love of Lancelot (*Lancelot and Elaine*, 1870, 2). Embowered (17) in a remote island castle, 'The Lady of Shalott' is distanced from the rural labour of the toiling 'reapers' (28), with whom she is linked by her ceaseless weaving and echoing 'song' (30), and from 'the knights at Camelot' (167) who share her noble birth. Her ambiguous position is reflected in the poem's form, with the Lady's name recurringly placed in the stanzas' closing refrain:

> Four gray walls, and four gray towers,
> Overlook a space of flowers,
> And the silent isle imbowers
>   The Lady of Shalott.

(15–18)

Her title and single status – she 'hath no loyal knight and true' (62) – suggest the ideals of courtly love prescribed by the chivalric code, which is inseparable from the nineteenth-century Medieval Revival and symbolized by the image of the 'red-cross knight' who 'for ever kneeled | To a lady in [Sir Lancelot's] shield' (78–9). Chivalry – the medieval knightly system and its values – was revived in the Elizabethan era and in the late eighteenth century. Early-nineteenth-century interest in late-eighteenth century studies of chivalry and translations of medieval ballads, chronicles and romances was enhanced by the early poetry and later novels of Sir Walter Scott, particularly *Ivanhoe* (1819). As Richard Barber observes, Scott helped to create 'a distinctly artificial picture of the Middle Ages': like most nineteenth-century writers on chivalry, he turned to idealized literary sources rather than historians for inspiration.[32] Scott in turn inspired Kenelm Digby to write *The Broad Stone of Honour: Rules for the Gentleman of England* – first published in 1822 and expanded and frequently reprinted between 1823 and 1877 – in which he defined two chivalric periods, Homeric and medieval, the latter superior because infused with Christian values. Chivalric idealism survived the rain-soaked farce of the Eglinton Tournament in 1839 and became increasingly focused on the figure of Victoria, encouraged by Albert who 'took chivalry very seriously indeed', by royal events such as the *Bal Costumé* of 1842, and by the many Arthurian projects of the 1850s.[33]

Critics generally agree that in 'The Lady of Shalott', with its medieval sources and setting, Tennyson explores the relationship between 'art' ('Shalott') and 'life' ('Camelot') in early 1830s England. Leonée Ormond sees the poem as 'a questioning of the poet's vocation, whether to live in a tower or to descend into the world of everyday life'.[34] For Britta Martens, 'The Lady of Shalott' and 'The Palace of Art' are 'Tennyson's exercises in solipsism', in which 'contact with the real world brings death to the artist figure'.[35] Critics such as Joseph Chadwick and Carl Plasa,[36] who analyse the poem in greater depth, identify the artist figure as a male poet or as Tennyson himself – a male poet working in a genre perceived as feminine – a view which is supported by the circumstances of the poem's publication and the poet's acute sensitivity to adverse criticism. As discussed in Chapter 2, throughout 1831 and 1832 Tennyson was being urged to publish again, but final preparations for a new volume were delayed by the poet's anguished response to the review of *Poems, Chiefly Lyrical* (1830) by John Wilson ('Christopher North') in the May 1832 edition of *Blackwood's Edinburgh Magazine*.

Joseph Chadwick identifies the artist figure/poet as Tennyson by relating the poem to Arthur Henry Hallam's 1831 review of *Poems, Chiefly Lyrical*. Hallam defined Tennyson as a 'poet of sensation', thus placing him in the mainstream of 'English Romantic aesthetics' which regarded the Romantic artwork or poem as both autonomous and feminine, a view symbolized by the embowered Lady, weaving and singing.[37] Chadwick argues that 'the ideals of femininity and autonomy' central to Hallam's view of the poetry of sensation are challenged within the text when the Lady – 'half sick of shadows' (71) – rejects the autonomy and mimetic art represented by 'Shalott' for the life and expressive art of 'Camelot'. These ideals are also challenged by the text, a published poem which alludes to its nineteenth-century context. The Lady rejects not only an artistically creative space but also the private domestic space appropriate to an 'Angel in the House', whose identity – like that of the Lady – is determined by male voices, initially by 'the reaper' (33–6) and finally by 'Sir Lancelot' (169–71). Ultimately, however, the poem's challenges are qualified, as the Lady's rejection of artistic and domestic autonomy leads to her death.

'The Lady of Shalott' foreshadows the ambivalence towards nineteenth-century patriarchal attitudes reflected in poems such as 'Dedication: To the Prince Consort' (1862), a title encapsulating Albert's ambiguous role. The opening lines of 'The Lady of Shalott' place the medieval characters in a landscape of Lincolnshire wolds (3), suggesting a contemporary English context. As the poem progresses, Lancelot becomes feminized and the Lady acquires masculine characteristics, ultimately appearing to become a male poet/artist figure, a transgression enhanced by intertextual reference to literary sources which further imply the characters' Englishness. Lancelot is accompanied by the clash of phallic symbols and his song has been linked to Shakespearean male licentiousness,[38] yet as Carl Plasa points out, 'tirra lirra' is a feminine rhyme, and in the closing refrain of stanza twelve – 'Sang Sir Lancelot' (108) – he occupies a space which the stanza-structure has defined as feminine.[39] Subverting the allusion to Wordsworth, a male reaper listens to the song of a female poet figure, but the dying Lady acquires the boldness of Lancelot's masculine gaze:

> And down the river's dim expanse
> Like some bold seër in a trance,
> Seeing all his own mischance –
> With a glassy countenance
>   Did she look to Camelot.

> (127–31)

Critical comments on the apparent banality of Lancelot's final words ignore both the religious and metaphysical implications discerned by Edgar F. Shannon,[40] and the religious concerns of the poem's context:

> Who is this? and what is here?
> And in the lighted palace near

> Died the sound of royal cheer;
> And they crossed themselves for fear,
>   All the knights at Camelot:
> But Lancelot mused a little space;
> He said, 'She has a lovely face;
> God in his mercy lend her grace,
>   The Lady of Shalott.'
>
>   (163–71)

Joseph Chadwick, referring to Arthur Hallam's 1831 review, believes that Lancelot's merely appreciative and 'suspiciously . . . casual comment' appropriately 'defines the fate of the poet of sensation in the public realm'.[41] For Kathy Alexis Psomiades, it is 'an inadequate response to the Lady'.[42] However, Shannon argues – with justification – that such a response is itself inadequate. Critics who regard 'Lancelot's meditative tribute to her beauty . . . as an inadequate or even trivial response', he suggests, 'seem conveniently to ignore or belittle the succeeding prayer of intercession'.[43] As Shannon observes, the words of reverence and faith – which recall the Anglican burial service familiar to Tennyson from his Somersby Rectory upbringing – reflect Lancelot's real concern for the Lady's spiritual welfare and are appropriate to the occasion. By invoking God's 'grace' (defined by Shannon as 'God's gift of unmerited spiritual recognition and illumination through divine love') Lancelot, the unknowing cause of the Lady's death, becomes the agent of her redemption.

Lancelot's final words also remind readers that the poem's medieval – therefore Catholic – faith was again a cause for concern in contemporary England. For Edgar F. Shannon, the poem's symbolism is religious rather than chivalric, with 'tirra lirra' echoing the sound of Shelley's heaven-bound skylark and Lancelot's shield image suggesting the cross and the Eucharist.[44] However, religion and chivalry are inseparably embodied by Lancelot, linked by Shannon with 'the Red-Cross Knight of Holiness' in Edmund Spenser's *The Faerie Queen* (1590–96), who foreshadows the exemplary knights of *Idylls of the King* – 'we that fight for our fair father Christ' (*The Coming of Arthur*, 1869, 509). Despite its medieval sources and self-consciously medievalist language – 'and unhailed | The shallop flitteth silken-sailed' (21–2) – 'The Lady of Shalott' is inseparable from its nineteenth-century social, political and religious context. Following the Catholic Emancipation Act of 1829 Catholicism and Englishness were no longer mutually exclusive and the Oxford Movement, which began with John Keble's Assize Sermon of July 1833, determined 'to reassert the

Catholicity of the Anglican Church'.[45] David Newsome argues that the Oxford Movement might have been formed at any time in the 1830s, but its militant form was 'precipitated by the Whig government's intention to place church reform at the top of its legislative agenda' and by the resulting establishment of the Ecclesiastical Commission in 1835.

Early Arthurian poems: 'Sir Launcelot and Queen Guinevere' and 'Sir Galahad'

By 1835, when the Ecclesiastical Commission was established, Tennyson had completed 'Sir Galahad' and written a large part of the *Ballad of Sir Lancelot*. Only brief sections of the *Ballad* survive: a few lines of Lancelot's love-song and a description of Lancelot and Guinevere riding through woodland in spring which, as 'Sir Launcelot and Queen Guinevere: A Fragment', was published with 'Sir Galahad' in 1842. 'Sir Launcelot and Queen Guinevere' (partly written in 1830, but still a work 'in Progress' in June 1833[46]) and 'Sir Galahad' (written by 19 September 1834) are inseparable from the Victorian Medieval Revival. In the poems Tennyson portrays opposing aspects of chivalry, prefiguring 'the world-wide war of Sense and Soul, typified in individuals', which is explored in *Idylls of the King*.[47]

In the strict moral climate of early-Victorian England Tennyson could not appear to condone an adulterous relationship and in 1842 published only Lancelot and Guinevere's ride through the forest. John Mitchell Kemble described the poem as a 'companion to *The Lady of Shalott*'[48] and the connection is suggested by Tennyson's use of a similar stanza form and third person omniscient narrator. '[I]n the Spring, Queen Guinevere and Sir Lancelot ride through the forest green, fayre and amorous:' the youth and innocence of their love is suggested by the season, and the burgeoning and very English natural world discussed in Chapter 3:

> Then, in the boyhood of the year,
> Sir Launcelot and Queen Guinevere
> Rode through the coverts of the deer,
> With blissful treble ringing clear.
>   She seemed a part of joyous Spring:
> A gown of grass-green silk she wore,
> Buckled with golden clasps before;
> A light-green tuft of plumes she bore
>   Closed in a golden ring.

> (19–27)

In 'Sir Launcelot and Queen Guinevere' Tennyson depicts the chivalrous relationship between a man and a married woman which was closely related to medieval courtly love and 'in its purest form . . . was entirely Platonic'.[49] Mark Girouard explains that in continental Europe such relationships had lasted far beyond the Middle Ages 'in the form of *cavalieri serventi*', but first appeared in Victorian England as 'a direct result of the revival of chivalry'. Contemporary English attitudes to adultery are suggested by Kemble's reaction to Lancelot's song from the unfinished *Ballad*, which includes the verse:

> Bathe with me in the fiery flood
> And mingle kisses, tears and sighs
> Life of the Life within my blood,
> Light of the Light within mine eyes.[50]

Kemble warned his friend W.B. Donne, 'for the sake of my future clerical views and Alfred's and Sir L's character, I must request that it be kept as quiet as possible'. It was 'but a loose song', he added, sung as Lancelot took Guinevere 'to live with him at Joyous Gard, having rescued her from being burnt as an adulteress'. Perhaps for that reason Tennyson did not include Lancelot's love-song in the 1842 volumes.

J.M. Kemble's 'sketch' of 'Sir Launcelot and Queen Guinevere' includes an encounter with 'Sir Galahad', the 'type of chastity' and Lancelot's 'own son'.[51] In Thomas Malory's *Le Morte D'Arthur* (1485) Galahad is the illegitimate son of Lancelot and Elaine, 'the lily maid of Astolat', but the relationship is not referred to in 'Sir Galahad'. 'Sir Galahad was intended' by Tennyson 'for something of a male counterpart' to 'St Agnes' (1836)[52] and the poems' shared visionary intensity is heightened by use of first person narration.

'Sir Galahad' – both poem and protagonist – is inseparable from the Victorian Medieval Revival and contemporary religious concerns. He embodies the conflict between 'purity' and 'the severe idea of virginity', which was the subject of intense discussion within the Oxford Movement.[53] 'Sir Launcelot' is represented as 'Queen Guinevere's devoted cavalier'; in 'Sir Galahad', by contrast, Tennyson portrays an ardently chaste Christian knight who – despite his skill in the mock-combat of the 'clanging lists' (9) and delight in the 'ladies' who bestow on him their 'favours' (13–14) – rejects human love to embark on an unceasing quest for divine love. The inexplicable incidents he encounters on his journey – the 'secret shrine' (29), the 'magic bark' (38) and the vision of 'the holy Grail' (42) – represent the Catholic mystery the Oxford Movement intended to reassert:

> A gentle sound, an awful light!
>   Three angels bear the holy Grail:
> With folded feet, in stoles of white,
>   On sleeping wings they sail.
> Ah, blessèd vision! blood of God!
>   My spirit beats her mortal bars,
> As down dark tides the glory slides,
>   And star-like mingles with the stars.

(41–8)

'Sir Galahad' anticipates mid-nineteenth-century and characteristically English 'muscular Christianity', a concept linked with medieval chivalry. The term *muscular Christianity*, first used in 1857, was associated with Thomas Hughes and Charles Kingsley, who in 1861 defined two kinds of medieval Christianity, 'monastic and chivalric'.[54] Monks were regarded as ascetic and asexual, and Tennyson satirized self-sacrificing but ultimately self-indulgent monastic Christianity in 'St Simeon Stylites' – 'Simeon of the pillar' (1842, 158) – who yearns for sainthood. Chivalric Christianity, which evolved in reaction to monasticism, aimed at dedicating 'masculinity to God in all activities of normal life, including the battlefield'. It is therefore closely related to 'muscular Christianity', defined by Thomas Hughes in 1861 as founded on 'the old chivalrous and Christian belief, that a man's body is given to him to be trained and brought into subjection, and then used for the protection of the weak, [and] the advancement of all righteous causes'.[55] This ideal added self-restraint – to become a defining characteristic of the nineteenth-century English gentleman – to Protestantism's 'conviction' that 'true religion . . . strengthened and consecrated a valiant and noble manhood'.[56] 'Sir Galahad' personifies both muscular and chivalric Christianity. First encountered in 'the tide of combat' (10), he is portrayed as actively masculine in his Grail quest and fight to protect vulnerable women – 'For them I battle till the end, | To save from shame and thrall' (15–16) – with the impression of masculine strength enhanced by forceful vocabulary and Anglo-Saxon monosyllables – 'tough lance' (2), 'hard brands' (6) and 'splintered spear-shafts' (7).

The concept of purity was central to muscular and chivalric Christianity. For Thomas Hughes, 'the crown of all real manliness, of all Christian manliness, is purity',[57] which was differentiated from virginity or celibacy, an ideal advocated by Catholics and High Churchmen. Purity, by contrast, was for all men and women, placed the emphasis on love and marriage, and entailed pre-marital chastity and marital fidelity. 'Sir Galahad' glories in his purity, asserting immediately and aggressively that:

> My good blade carves the casques of men,
>   My tough lance thrusteth sure,
> My strength is as the strength of ten,
>   Because my heart is pure.

>   (1–4)

Although accomplished at knightly pursuits, 'Sir Galahad' 'yearn[s] to breathe the airs of heaven' (63). However, his rejection of human love is conflicted. He is both 'pure' (4) and 'virgin' (24), and appears physically torn by his intense longing for holiness:

> But all my heart is drawn above,
>   My knees are bowed in crypt and shrine:
> I never felt the kiss of love,
>   Nor maiden's hand in mine,
> More bounteous aspects on me beam,
>   Me mightier transports move and thrill;
> So keep I fair through faith and prayer
>   A virgin heart in work and will.

>   (17–24)

'Sir Galahad's final vision is of the heaven that awaits him:

> I muse on joy that will not cease,
>   Pure spaces clothed in living beams,
> Pure lilies of eternal peace,
>   Whose odours haunt my dreams;
> And, stricken by an angel's hand,
>   This mortal armour that I wear,
> This weight and size, this heart and eyes,
>   Are touched, are turned to finest air.

>   (65–72)

In muscular and chivalric Christianity, purity is inseparable from love and marriage. However, for 'Sir Galahad' it is associated with transfiguration and the afterlife attained when 'stricken' by angels, an ambiguous term which implies that his decision is misplaced. Ultimately, therefore, in his rejection of 'the warmth of double life' (*The Holy Grail*, 1869, 62) – the domestic ideal essential to the Tennysonian world order – 'Sir Galahad' is a monastic Christian related to his contemporary 'St Simeon Stylites', also written in 1833 and published in 1842.

Early Arthurian poems: 'Morte d'Arthur' and 'The Epic'

Tennyson's preoccupations with medievalism and Englishness became linked with the royal succession and monarchical authority in 'Morte d'Arthur'. 'Morte d'Arthur' was written in 1833–34 and published in 1842 framed by 'The Epic', probably completed between 1837 and 1838. The framing poem's closing vision carried considerable relevance for Tennyson's contemporaries; King Arthur returns, at Christmas and to popular acclaim, reborn as 'a modern gentleman' (294) embodying the qualities of royalty, religious faith and social reform:

> There came a bark that, blowing forward, bore
> King Arthur, like a modern gentleman
> Of stateliest port; and all the people cried,
> 'Arthur is come again: he cannot die.'
> . . .
> And, further inland, voices echoed – 'Come
> With all good things, and war shall be no more.'
> At this a hundred bells began to peal,
> That with the sound I woke, and heard indeed
> The clear church-bells ring in the Christmas-morn.
>
> (293–303)

Written during the winter that followed Arthur Hallam's death, news of which Tennyson received on 1 October 1833, 'Morte d'Arthur' is very different from the early Arthurian verse discussed so far: restrained, elegiac, at times deeply personal, and in the iambic blank verse whose rhythms evoke Shakespeare, it is one of the finest works in the Tennysonian canon. (Marcia C. Culver examines the poem's draft versions to conclude that the 'weary peace' Tennyson achieved in the 'Morte d'Arthur' evolved only 'with time and revision'.[58]) Like many critics, Roger Simpson regards the wounded King Arthur as 'both a type of the dead Arthur Hallam and of the crucified Christ'[59] and the final scene, in which the 'tallest' and 'fairest' of the 'three Queens' cradles the head of the wounded King, resembles a – very English – *pietà*:

> There those three Queens
> Put forth their hands, and took the King, and wept.
> But she, that rose the tallest of them all
> And fairest, laid his head upon her lap,
> And loosed the shattered casque, and chafed his hands,
> And called him by his name, complaining loud,
> And dropping bitter tears against his brow
> Striped with dark blood:
>
> (205–12)

With his 'wide blue eyes' (169) and 'light and lustrous curls' (216) King Arthur is not only 'fair' ('The Epic', 298) but also fair-complexioned; although Arthur's ancestors were 'dark in hair and eyes . . . and dark was Uther too, | Wellnigh to blackness', Tennyson's king 'is fair | Beyond the race of Britons and of men' (*The Coming of Arthur*, 1869, 327–30).

Stephanie L. Barczewski traces the nineteenth-century Saxonization of Arthur to conclude that Tennyson was the most influential nineteenth-century 'promoter of King Arthur's "Saxon" origins'.[60] Dafydd Moore observes that the poet's use of Malory as the definitive source of Arthurian material additionally and more subtly helped to fabricate or reinvent 'the Arthurian tradition as, historically speaking, an English one',[61] a view confirmed by John Forster's 1842 critique of 'Morte d'Arthur', which welcomed the 'epic fragment on the good old English subject of King Arthur'.[62]

Tennyson and his fellow Cambridge Apostles looked to the medieval English literary past for the social and spiritual revival implied by King Arthur's imagined return. 'Morte d'Arthur' and 'The Epic' evolved during a decade of rapid change and were published early in the Hungry Forties. During these years industrialization and urbanization threatened the English landscape discussed in Chapter 3 and symbolized by Avilion's 'Deep-meadowed . . . orchard-lawns | And bowery hollows' ('Morte d'Arthur', 262–3). Civil unrest accompanied the passage of the 1832 Reform Act, which extended the franchise; the Poor Law Amendment Act of 1834 altered the system of parish relief; Chartism developed, and the 'Young England' and Oxford Movements were formed.

Richard Monckton Milnes declared that the 'introduction' to 'Morte d'Arthur' 'succeeds in gracefully linking on the old English story to present English domestic life'.[63] With its contemporary references and conversational tone, 'the Epic' directly alludes to 'the church-commissioners' (15) whose establishment in 1835 to reform Anglicanism intensified the Oxford Movement's militancy. In 'Morte d'Arthur' the decline of religion is represented by the neglected 'chapel' – a 'broken chancel with a broken cross, | That stood on . . . barren land' – to which Bedivere 'bore' the wounded King (8–10). Arthur, by contrast, believes both in the power of prayer, which separates humankind from the animal world, and an indissoluble network of human prayer linking heaven and earth:

> For what are men better than sheep or goats
> That nourish a blind life within the brain,
> If, knowing God, they lift not hands of prayer
> Both for themselves and those who call them friend?
> For so the whole round earth is every way
> Bound by gold chains about the feet of God.

> (250–5)

Arthur's knights not only exemplify chivalry, with their socially ameliorative mission 'To ride abroad redressing human wrongs' (*Guinevere*, 1859, 468), but can also be seen as disciples when – linking the Round Table with Christianity – Bedivere mourns 'the true old times' that 'have been not since the light that led | The holy Elders with the gift of myrrh' (229–33).

'Morte d'Arthur' is also linked to 'present English domestic life' by its concern with the royal succession and monarchical authority. The wounded King Arthur fears that he is dying and is uncertain of his prophesied return:

> I perish by this people which I made, –
> Though Merlin sware that I should come again
> To rule once more –

> (22–4)

In England in the early 1830s the throne was occupied by an ageing monarch who, with his Hanoverian predecessors, was neither respected nor mourned. When William IV died in 1837 the crown passed to the adolescent Victoria, the first female monarch since Queen Anne (1702–14). Victoria's marriage in 1840 and the subsequent births of nine children secured the succession, but her accession had suggested a potential conflict between royal authority and the subordinate role recommended for *The Women of England* (1839) by contemporary writers such as Sarah Stickney Ellis.

Arthur's enduring symbol of kingship is the sword, Excalibur:

> [I] took it, and have worn it, like a king:
> And, wheresoever I am sung or told
> In aftertime, this also shall be known:
>
> (32–5)

Bedivere's initial refusal to 'fling [Excalibur] into the middle mere' (37) as commanded by the King, raises the related questions of royal authority and a subject's duty to obey the sovereign. For Arthur, Bedivere's first failure betrays his chivalric 'fëalty' as 'a noble knight' (75); the second is both 'Unknightly' and 'traitor-hearted' (120), causing the King to rage that:

> Authority forgets a dying king,
> Laid widowed of the power in his eye
> That bowed the will.
>
> (121–3)

In a soliloquy that surveys both the abstract and the personal – a subject's duty to 'a king' and his own loyalty to Arthur, 'the King' – Bedivere ultimately questions the dying King Arthur's judgement:

> What good should follow this, if this were done?
> What harm, undone? deep harm to disobey,
> Seeing obedience is the bond of rule.
> Were it well to obey then, if a king demand
> An act unprofitable, against himself?
> The King is sick, and knows not what he does.
>
> (92–7)

Bedivere's disturbing conclusion – 'The King is sick, and knows not what he does' (97) – would remind contemporary readers of the illness and incapacity of George III, father of the ageing present king, William IV.

As Richard D. Mallen argues, the decades during which Tennyson worked on *Idylls of the King* – from 1842 to 1885 – were important to the evolution of the monarchy in modern England.[64] Mallen refers to Walter Bagehot's assertion, made just before the 1867 Reform Act, that England had become a 'disguised republic' and to Bagehot's view that the country's transition from constitutional monarchy to republic had begun with the 1832 Reform Act, but remained hidden from 'the masses' who mistook royal pageantry for real political authority. Bagehot believed that as 'the masses' were not ready for republican citizenship, the disguise – in effect creating a figurehead-monarch – prevented the increasing possibility of loss of deference and consequent social unrest. Tennyson's recurring fear of social instability, and the growing admiration for Queen Victoria discussed in Chapter 4, support Mallen's suggestion that the poet also recognized the need to maintain monarchy's outward show and in *Idylls of the King* – by ultimately portraying Arthur as a symbolic sovereign – not only explored the loss of monarchical power in post-Reform England but also contributed to the stabilizing disguise. However, the progressive diminution of royal authority and its replacement by a figurehead-monarch is anticipated in 'Morte d'Arthur' – written soon after the 1832 Reform Act – by Bedivere's reluctance to obey the King.

'Morte d'Arthur' and its frame-poem 'The Epic' embody the Victorian critical debate as to whether poetry should reflect the age. With the 'poet Everard Hall's (4) assertion that 'a truth | Looks freshest in the fashion of the day' (31–2) 'The Epic' argues for modern poetry. Edward FitzGerald noted that the introduction to 'Morte d'Arthur' was 'added to anticipate or excuse the "faint Homeric echoes," ... to give a reason for telling an old-world tale';[65] John Sterling similarly observed that the 'miraculous legend of Excalibar [*sic*] does not come very near us, and as reproduced by any modern writer must be a mere ingenious exercise of fancy',[66] views which anticipate *Aurora Leigh*'s 'distrust' of 'the poet who ... trundles back his soul five hundred years, | Past moat and drawbridge, into a castle-court' (1857, V, 189–92).[67] By contrast, 'Morte d'Arthur' anticipates the *Idylls*' 'parabolic drift',[68] exploring in medieval guise contemporary concerns with religion, monarchy and morality. However, the narrator's conclusion that 'Perhaps some modern touches here and there | Redeemed it from the charge of nothingness' ('The Epic', 277–9) does not reflect the generally favourable contemporary reviews nor later critics' belief that 'Morte d'Arthur' is 'among the glories of nineteenth-century English poetry'.[69]

'Godiva'

'Godiva' is an early medievalist poem which was admired by many contemporary reviewers but is unjustly ignored today. Tennyson 'remodels' the eleventh-century English legend of Lady Godiva into a blank verse narrative poem, which illuminates not only medieval and Victorian gender roles and attitudes to class but also the poet's painful reluctance to 'lay the nerve of self | Bare to the slurs of shallow cleverness'[70] by publishing another volume. 'Morte d'Arthur' and 'Godiva' – both published in *Poems* (1842) – are linked by their medieval settings and Leigh Hunt's dislike of the apparent false modesty of their contemporary frames, declaring that the 'mixed tone of contempt and nonchalance' of 'such exordiums as those to "Morte d'Arthur" and "Godiva"' 'looks a little instructive, and is . . . a little perilous'.[71] By contrast, John Forster in the *Examiner* welcomed with 'rapture . . . that lovely and most perfect poem'.[72] The poem is rarely mentioned by modern critics, although Roger Simpson suggests that Tennyson derived the image of Godiva 'shower[ing] the rippled ringlets to her knee' (47) from John Moultrie's 'Godiva', quoted in the *Quarterly Review* in 1821,[73] a copy of which was at Somersby.

Firmly linked to nineteenth-century England by the brief introductory frame (purportedly written as Tennyson 'waited for the train at Coventry' (1) in June 1840), 'Godiva' illustrates and ultimately subverts the neo-feudalist attitudes to class promulgated – in prose and verse – by the contemporary politicians who founded the Young England Movement.[74] Lord John Manners, visiting a Lancashire cotton factory in 1842, noted approvingly that the proprietor was a 'modern lord', with 'absolute dominion' over his workmen, adding there was 'never . . . so complete a feudal system as that of the mills; soul and body are, or might be, at the absolute disposal of one man, and that to my notion is not at all a bad state of society'.[75] The 'absolute dominion' of Tennyson's 'grim Earl, who ruled | In Coventry' (12–13) threatens the 'overtaxed' (9) people he scorns with poverty as relevant to England in the Hungry Forties as to medieval Coventry. Yet the plight of the starving women and children is eased by the altruistic Godiva while acting in complete obedience to her husband, the Earl:

> . . . for when he laid a tax
> Upon his town, and all the mothers brought
> Their children, clamouring, 'If we pay, we starve!'
> . . . She told him of their tears,
> And prayed him, 'If they pay this tax, they starve.'
> Whereat he stared, replying, half-amazed,
> 'You would not let your little finger ache
> For such as *these*?' – 'But I would die,' said she.
> . . . He answered, 'Ride you naked through the town,
> And I repeal it;'
>
> (13–30)

A medieval – and Victorian – husband also had 'absolute dominion' over his wife and Godiva's subservient role is encapsulated in the repeated phrase 'her lord' (16, 78). Godiva's marriage, of dynastic or financial convenience, resembles the fate forecast for Amy in 'Locksley Hall' (written 1837–38) – 'He will hold thee, when his passion shall have spent its novel force, | Something better than his dog, a little dearer than his horse' (49–50). As Tennyson's vividly humorous sketch suggests, the 'grim Earl' (12, 44) is no Lancelot:

> She sought her lord, and found him, where he strode
> About the hall, among his dogs, alone,
> His beard a foot before him, and his hair
> A yard behind.
>
> (16–19)

However, the marriage provides 'the diamond at her ear' (25) and enables Godiva to command the townspeople to 'keep within, door shut, and window barred' (41). 'Godiva' was written when Edward Moxon and Edward FitzGerald were intensifying their pressure on Tennyson to publish a new volume. As a female poet-figure who finds the courage to leave her private domestic space for the public world Lady Godiva resembles the Lady of Shalott, but 'Godiva' contains a more graphic representation of the poet's apprehension at the thought of re-entering public life. Recurring images of sight and sound emphasize the vulnerability of the naked poet-figure as she 'rode forth' (53) and 'rode back, clothed on with [the] chastity' (65) that symbolizes her fidelity to the Earl's patriarchal authority:

> The deep air listened round her as she rode,
> And all the low wind hardly breathed for fear.
> The little wide-mouthed heads upon the spout
> Had cunning eyes to see: the barking cur
> Made her cheek flame: her palfrey's footfall shot
> Light horrors through her pulses: the blind walls
> Were full of chinks and holes; and overhead
> Fantastic gables, crowding, stared:
>
> (54–61)

An early draft of the poem confirms that the Peeping Tom figure (a seventeenth-century addition to the medieval legend[76]) – whose 'eyes, before they had their will, | Were shrivelled into darkness in his head, | And dropt before him' (69–71) – represented the 'modern' critic who, Tennyson feared, '[w]ould turn my verse to scandal'.[77] Lady Godiva 'Not less through all bore up' (62) and with her ride 'she took the tax away | And built herself an everlasting name' (78–9) – as the poem 'Godiva', published in the 1842 volumes, helped to lay the cornerstone of Tennyson's fame. Dorothy Mermin notes that feminist writers such as Harriet Martineau invoked the example of Lady Godiva in their campaign against the Contagious Diseases Acts (1864, 1866 and 1869). When told that 'American ladies were shocked to think of [the] personal exposure' such a campaign entailed, Martineau replied 'English ladies think of the Lady Godiva' and later referred to 'that representative Englishwoman, Godiva of blessed memory'.[78]

Tennyson's chivalric gentlemen: 'Ode on the Death of the Duke of Wellington'

The medieval Lady Godiva personifies the moral example also required of a dutiful Victorian wife. Since the 1980s the characteristics of Victorian womanhood have frequently been analysed by critics concerned with gender theory, who have subsequently and increasingly become interested in the history of masculinity. Marion Shaw, for example, discusses the non-identical but overlapping concepts of mid-Victorian *manliness* and *masculinity*, defining 'masculinity' as 'a set of beliefs about male sexuality . . . inextricably linked to concepts of male self-expression and power', and 'manliness' which came to mean 'the exercise of restraint upon the manifestations of male sexuality'.[79] In his more recent study of nineteenth-century Britain, John Tosh considers *manliness* – summarized as 'fundamentally a set of values by which men judged other men', not necessarily concerned with patriarchal 'control over women'[80] – and *masculinities*, a term coined in the 1970s, arguing that the plural accurately reflects present-day Western society's view that 'masculinity is anything but a monolith'.

As Robin Gilmour observes, of particular importance to mid-nineteenth-century English society was the concept of the English gentleman. With its origins in feudalism and the qualification of birth, 'the idea of the gentleman'[81] was central to the social and political compromise between the landed aristocracy, whose power was declining, and the expanding middle classes, and became inextricably linked with Empire. (The 'imperial mission' is now often seen as 'the export version of the gentlemanly order'.[82]) The idea of the chivalric English gentleman was discussed or defined in a variety of Victorian publications. The final chapter of Samuel Smiles's *Self Help*, published in 1859 to encourage social mobility, strength of character and individuality rather than wealth, has the title 'Character – The True Gentleman'. John Ruskin's 'Of Vulgarity', in Volume V (1860) of *Modern Painters*, regards the true gentleman as a superior being who justifies his position by extending chivalric qualities to 'those beneath him'.[83] The ideal of the morally exemplary Christian gentleman is examined in John Henry Newman's *The Idea of a University*, written in 1852, published in 1873 and originally a series of *Discourses* on the sensitive subject of establishing a Catholic university in Dublin. In Newman's analysis negatives predominate and his ultimate definition of a gentleman, or 'ethical character', is 'one who never inflicts pain'.[84] Modern critics such as J.A. Mangan and James Walvin note that the Victorian ideal of manliness comprises the qualities of 'physical courage, chivalric ideals' and the 'virtuous fortitude' which implies 'military and patriotic virtue'.[85] Norman Vance's similar but earlier definition adds religious principle to the suggestion of heroism and differentiates between the 'heroic acts' of early-nineteenth-century warfare and the 'heroism of peace' defined in Thomas Carlyle's lectures *On Heroes, Hero-Worship, and the Heroic in History* (1844).[86]

The heroism of war and peace, patriotic virtue and religious faith are embodied in Tennyson's poems praising 'Godlike men' ('Wellington Ode', 1852, 266) – the military, naval and political figures whose chivalric qualities and Englishness he celebrated as Laureate. The first of these, 'Ode on the Death of the Duke of Wellington', was published on 16 November 1852. The 'Ode' was Tennyson's first separate publication as Laureate ('To the Queen' (1851) dedicated the seventh edition of *Poems*), written not by royal request but because the poet felt 'it was expected of me to write'.[87] Arthur Wellesley, first Duke of Wellington, died on 14 September 1852: the 'Ode' was written in haste in November and, concerned with both profit and example, Tennyson arranged for ten thousand copies to be printed and sold for two shillings to the crowds at the funeral on 18 November. The poem was then reworked at leisure and the revisions – traced in exhaustive detail by Edgar F. Shannon and Christopher Ricks[88] – answer in the affirmative Tennyson's own question: 'Is it so true that second thoughts are best?' ('Sea Dreams', 1860, 65). By emphasizing Wellington's character and achievements, and moderating the early anti-French sentiments, the revised 'Ode' – reprinted in February–March 1853 and in 1855 – acquires a dignity not present in its early form.

Wellington's English identity – and the 'happy valiance'[89] which characterizes English statesmen – is asserted in the poem's content and implied by its form. Tennyson breaks with the tradition of elegiac verse, which proclaims the name of the deceased; only in the title is Wellington named. He is hailed as 'England's greatest son' (95) and 'our English Duke' (189), an attribution of Englishness Wellington would have approved: although born in Ireland, he rejected any suggestion of Irishness: 'You might as well call a man a horse because he was born in a stable'.[90] The 'Ode' commemorates Wellington's funeral and its measured rhythms and form – a Pindaric ode in nine strophes of differing lengths – are appropriate to the ceremonial occasion whose solemnity Tennyson recreates: 'The last great Englishman is low' (18). Wellington was buried in St Paul's, at the heart of 'streaming London's central roar' (9): 'there to rest by . . . Nelson – the greatest military by the side of the greatest naval chief who ever reflected lustre upon the annals of England'.[91] The burial is anticipated in the 'Ode's fifth and central strophe, suggesting that Wellington is 'central' to England in death as in life:

> And render him to the mould.
> Under the cross of gold
> That shines over city and river,
> There he shall rest for ever
> Among the wise and the bold.
>
> (48–52)

The 'Ode' eulogizes Wellington for embodying England and England for generating the Duke. The poem's resolute refusal to name Wellington enhances the exemplary attributes that define 'the great Duke' (1), the most important of which is Englishness. Wellington is 'our chief state-oracle' (23) and 'statesman-warrior' (25), 'Great in council and great in war' (30). 'Moderate' and 'resolute' (25), he is 'Rich in saving common-sense' (32) and the gentlemanly characteristics for which Tennyson had a high regard and which recur throughout his work, from the patriotic poems of the early 1830s to the tribute 'To the Duke of Argyll' published in 1885. Above all, Wellington is English. In his poems Tennyson often refers to Britain or Britons, particularly when praising the island status he represents as a gift from God – 'Thank Him who isled us here, and roughly set | His Briton in blown seas and storming showers' (154–5). As exemplified by the 'Ode', however, it is England which stirs his deepest feelings. References to England increased in frequency and importance with the poem's revisions and Wellington became 'England's greatest son' (95) who, during the 'long self-sacrifice of [his] life' (41), 'kept us' – the English – 'free'

(91). Accordingly, Tennyson calls for the 'people's voice' (146) to honour Wellington – 'Eternal honour to his name' (150) – and defines the patriot-statesman's future role:

> We have a voice, with which to pay the debt
> Of boundless love and reverence and regret
> To those great men who fought, and kept it ours.
> And keep it ours, O God, from brute control;
> O Statesmen, guard us, guard the eye, the soul
> Of Europe, keep our noble England whole,
> And save the one true seed of freedom sown
> Betwixt a people and their ancient throne,
> That sober freedom out of which there springs
> Our loyal passion for our temperate kings.
>
> (156–65)

Despite its dignity and general restraint, the 'Ode' establishes a myth of monarchy, England and Wellington which resonates with a notion of chivalry composed from Victorian ideas of medieval England. Neither the nation nor the newspapers had mourned the far-from-temperate Hanoverian 'kings', whom Wellington himself had dismissed as 'the damn'dest millstones about the neck of any Government that can be imagined'.[92] In 1837 Tennyson had also attacked Victoria's 'fathers', who 'plagued us in anger or vext us in sport' ('The Queen of the Isles', 5–6). The 'Ode's opening lines command empire- and nation-wide mourning, with England united by rhyme, alliteration and grief:

> Bury the Great Duke
>   With an empire's lamentation,
> Let us bury the Great Duke
>   To the noise of the mourning of a mighty nation,
> Mourning when their leaders fall,
> Warriors carry the warrior's pall,
> And sorrow darkens hamlet and hall.
>
> (1–7)

As the poem's catalogue of victories suggests, Wellington's military career was inseparable from imperial conflict. In 1803 – 'Against the myriads of Assaye' – he 'Clashed with his fiery few and won' (99–100), Indian casualties far outnumbering those of Wellington's forces. His political career included periods as Prime Minister (January 1828 to November 1830) – an appointment he owed to Hanoverian royal favour[93] – and Foreign Secretary (December 1834 to April 1835). He was Prime Minister and resolutely opposed to electoral reform when the 'Swing' riots of 1830–31 were beginning to be savagely repressed. Wholly 'dismissive of the concept of democracy', Wellington once observed that 'it was dangerous to give votes to the "lower orders", because "plunder is everywhere the object; and the lower we go, the stronger we find the desire to plunder".'[94] In 1848 as Lord High Constable he organized the military against the Chartists, a movement whose existence additionally subverts the unity of class and loyal monarchism assumed by Tennyson. England's agricultural labourers and radicals, and many of the Empire's subjects, were therefore unlikely to share the 'universal woe' (14) Tennyson invokes. However, in the 'Ode' 'our English Duke' (189) is portrayed as the embodiment of medievalist chivalric ideals, an enduring 'great example' (220) that – in war and peace – the 'path of duty' is 'the way to glory' (202, 210, 224) and personifying Tennyson's belief that 'On God and Godlike men' such as Wellington 'we build our trust' (266).

Tennyson's chivalric gentlemen: 'The song that nerves a nation's heart'

Three poems written between 1854 and 1885 exemplify Tennyson's enduring preoccupation with chivalric English military and naval heroism and his increasingly 'urgent patriotism of national security'.[95] The word 'duty' resounds throughout the 'Wellington Ode' and is the later poems' unspoken theme; however, for many in the Light and Heavy Brigades, and for Sir Richard Grenville of 'The Revenge', the 'path of duty' was 'the way to' – posthumous – 'glory' ('Ode', 202, 210, 224) rather than a long career in public life. The poems honour heroic death in the Crimea and Azores, but are also inseparable from Tennyson's concern to support soldiers fighting for English interests abroad and those who 'guard' England's 'sacred coasts' ('Ode', 172).

Tennyson's 'ballad on the charge of the Light Brigade at Balaclava'[96] (25 October 1854) was written in haste on 2 December 1854, after reading a *Times* editorial reporting 'some hideous blunder', and published in the *Examiner* on 9 December.[97] The Light Brigade's courage is reflected in their unquestioning obedience – 'Their's not to reason why, | Their's but to do and die' (14–15) – and encapsulated in the poem's central image of chivalric combat, which links the soldiers with the medieval 'Sir Galahad' whose 'good blade carves the casques of men' (1):

> Flashed all their sabres bare,
> Flashed as they turned in air
> Sabring the gunners there,
> Charging an army.
>
> (27–30)

Jerome J. McGann notes that Tennyson's image of the 'Sabring' soldiers Anglicizes a French tradition of military art, in which artists such as Géricault heroized the non-aristocratic *chasseurs* of Napoleon's army.[98] For McGann, therefore, 'The Charge' is 'a patently aristocratic poem', an argument belied by Tennyson's choice of popular 'ballad' form. Tennyson heroizes the Light Brigade, but it is more likely – as Kathryn Ledbetter suggests – that he meant to 'memorialize' the soldiers' 'martyrdom to arrogant, aristocratic blundering' and draw attention to their lack of military training, supplies and support.[99] Byron Farwell confirms that the Crimean War was 'undoubtedly the worst managed war of the [nineteenth] century'; 'logistics, tactics and strategy were all badly handled' and the soldiers were 'as inexperienced as their officers'.[100]

Although differing in form and content, 'The Charge of the Light Brigade' is therefore similar in purpose to the 'National Songs for Englishmen'.[101] These were written during the invasion panic that followed Louis Napoleon's *coup d'état* in December 1851 and in response to the public and parliamentary insistence on retrenchment which followed Wellington's victory at Waterloo and reduced government spending on the army and navy.[102] The House of Lords subsequently rejected a Bill to organize a militia. 'The Charge' is a controlled poem with minimal, precisely used punctuation, repetition and refrain – 'Then they rode back, but not | Not the six hundred' (37–8) – which only in the final stanza invokes 'Honour' for the 'Noble six hundred' (53–5). By contrast, the 'National Songs' are aggressively patriotic popular ballads – exhorting volunteers to take arms, or protesting that soldiers' equipment is obsolete – and poems on behalf of 'The thinking men of England', which urge the press 'To raise the people and chastise the times | With such a heat as lives in great creative rhymes' ('Suggested by Reading', 1852, 5–12), an intention embodied in the image of medieval combat at the heart of 'The Charge'.

'The Charge of the Light Brigade', considered with the 'National Songs for Englishmen', represents an example and a warning 'that the best and purest glow of chivalry is not dead, but vigorously lives among us yet'.[103] A similar dual purpose is reflected in 'The Revenge: A Ballad of the Fleet' and 'The Charge of the Heavy Brigade at Balaclava', whose protagonists are defined by their Englishness and heroized by imagery of chivalric combat. Early in 1877 Tennyson 'rediscovered' Edward Arber's 'English Reprint' on *The Revenge* (1591), published in 1871,[104] which described 'The Revenge's 'great Sea-Fight' against 'the Spanish host' as 'the Balaclava charge of that Spanish War'.[105] 'The Revenge' – published in *Nineteenth Century* in March 1878 during the final Russo-Turkish War (1877–78) and mirroring contemporary jingoistic fervour – is additionally linked to Tennyson's Crimean heroes. The poem was juxtaposed with an article by Sir Garnet Wolseley (a Crimean commander) arguing that although England was militarily stronger than in 1854, its navy should be strengthened to protect the 'great empire . . . built up for us by the military achievements of our forefathers',[106] a cause Tennyson later promoted in 'The Fleet', published in *The Times* on 23 April 1885 with the subtitle 'On its reported insufficiency'.[107] For Samuel Smiles, the 'True Gentleman . . . invariably proves himself such in need and in danger'[108] and Sir Richard Grenville and 'The little Revenge' – like the Light Brigade – 'ran on sheer into the heart of the foe' (33). Throughout the poem Grenville's English virtues are contrasted with Spanish cruelty and Catholicism. He rescues his 'good English men' (29) – by implication Protestant – from 'these Inquisition dogs and the devildoms of Spain' (12), chooses to 'fight' rather than 'fly' (25), even when mortally wounded, and is eulogized for his courage:

> [he] had been so valiant and true,
> And had holden the power and glory of Spain so cheap
> That he dared her with one little ship and his English few.

> (105–7)

Tennyson returned to a military theme with 'The Charge of the Heavy Brigade at Balaclava', written in March 1881 at the request of Alexander William Kinglake (a Crimean War historian and Tennyson's Cambridge contemporary[109]) and published in *Macmillan's Magazine* in March 1882. Hours before the Light Brigade charge, the soldiers of the Heavy Brigade, latter-day Sir Galahads – 'Whirling their sabres in circles of light!' (34) – had routed 'a superior Russian force'[110] and Tennyson invokes 'Glory' (65, 66) for a Brigade whose success had been eclipsed by the later disastrous failure. Kathryn Ledbetter argues that the 1882 'Charge' reflects 'a democratization in Tennyson's perspective' as the Heavy Brigade soldier, unlike the aristocratic Light Brigade, was a 'common man'.[111] However, from the opening stanza the poem is dominated by the Brigade's commander, General Sir James Yorke Scarlett, son of the first Baron Abinger, who – with Tennyson's other 'Godlike men' – is from the upper classes and portrayed as a medievalist knight:

> . . . he dashed up alone
> Through the great gray slope of men,
> Swayed his sabre, and held his own
> Like an Englishman there and then.
>
> (16–19)

The Englishness of the Crimean War heroes became inseparable from the English landscape, the Empire and Tennyson himself when the 'Prologue to General Hamley' and the 'Epilogue' were added to 'The Charge of the Heavy Brigade' in 1885. The 'Prologue' was written in November 1883 after Sir Edward Hamley's visit to Aldworth:

> You came, and looked and loved the view
>   Long-known and loved by me,
> Green Sussex fading into blue
>   With one gray glimpse of sea;
>
> (5–8)

The poem is a dedicatory tribute to an English soldier whose distinguished Crimean war record was widely believed to have overshadowed his victory at 'Tel-el-Kebir' (28) during the 1882 Anglo-Egyptian War. The 'Epilogue', written after September 1883, was 'founded on a conversation' with Laura Tennant[112] and responded to a letter from Mary Brotherton – sent during the Second Anglo-Afghan War (1878–80) – which criticized the poet's 'warlike spirit' and argued that 'war . . . is indefensible from a Christian point of view'.[113] In a dialogue with 'Irene' (the Greek for Peace) the 'Poet' defends himself at length against her charge that:

> You praise when you should blame
>   The barbarism of wars.
> A juster epoch has begun.
>
> (3–5)[114]

Although he rejects 'War, for War's own sake' (29), the 'Poet' believes that even when a nation's cause is wrong the 'patriot-soldier' (31) must be celebrated in verse. Defining his role in terms that recall the

medieval courtier-poets or 'kingly-poets' (19) of the Drexel text and 'To
the Queen' (1851), Tennyson concludes:

> And here the Singer for his Art
>   Not all in vain may plead
> 'The song that nerves a nation's heart,
>   Is in itself a deed'.

(79–80)

They also serve who only write Laureate verse.

'Lofty examples in comprehensive forms'?
Idylls of the King

Tennyson's definition of King Arthur as 'a man who spent himself in
the cause of honour, duty and self-sacrifice'[115] apparently places the
medieval King among the exemplary Englishmen or 'Godlike men' on
whom 'we build our trust' ('Wellington Ode', 266). Although the 'vision
of Arthur as I have drawn him . . . had come upon' Tennyson with his
boyhood discovery of Malory,[116] the first instalment of *Idylls of the King* –
four poems named after Enid, Vivien, Elaine and Guinevere – was not
published until 1859. *The Coming of Arthur*, *The Holy Grail*, *Pelleas and
Ettarre* and *The Passing of Arthur* followed in December 1869, with the
final *Idyll* – *Balin and Balan* – appearing in 1885. Critics such as Linda
K. Hughes remind modern readers that Tennyson's 'original audiences'
encountered the poem 'a part at a time over some four decades'[117] and
studying the poems in their original publication order makes clear that
each *Idyll* reflects the decade in which it was written.

Tennyson uses the 'Arthur' poems to explore the diminution of
monarchical authority. Royal authority is challenged directly in *The
Passing of Arthur* – as in the earlier 'Morte d'Arthur' (written 1833–34)
on which it is based – when the wounded King, angered by Bedivere's
initial refusal to 'fling [Excalibur] far into the middle mere' (205), replies
'much in wrath' that 'Authority forgets a dying king' (286–9). Authority
is challenged more subtly in *The Coming of Arthur* – an *Idyll* of multiple
narratives which became the first poem in the *Idylls'* final order – by
conflicting accounts of Arthur's origins, both natural and supernatural,
and the initial indirect reference to the King's 'great authority' (260),
reported by his half-sister Bellicent, not by the narratorial voice:

> For I was near him when the savage yells
> Of Uther's peerage died, and Arthur sat

Crowned on the daïs, and his warriors cried,
'Be thou the king, and we will work thy will
Who love thee.' Then the King in low deep tones,
And simple words of great authority,
Bound them by so strait vows to his own self.

(255–61)

The 1859 *Idylls* are directly linked to nineteenth-century England by the 'Dedication: To the Prince Consort' added in 1862 and, as with the medievalist poems discussed above, succeeding *Idylls* are also inseparable from their context. *The Coming of Arthur* was written during Victoria's extended withdrawal from public life following Albert's death in December 1861, after the Second Reform Act (1867) had doubled the electorate, and when Walter Bagehot believed that England had become 'a disguised republic',[118] and the *Idyll* reflects contemporary anxiety as to royalty's role in an increasingly democratic age. In the opening lines, King Leodogran debates whether to give his only daughter Guinevere in marriage to Arthur, aware that many 'Lords and Barons of his realm' are questioning 'Who is he | That he should rule us? who hath proven him | King Uther's son?' (64–9) and – foreshadowing Arthur's failure to secure his own succession – conscious that 'A doubtful throne is ice on summer seas' (247). (Images of the natural world are central to *Idylls of the King*.)

With each narration, Arthur's legitimate origins are clouded and further distanced. Appropriately, the first account of Arthur's *Coming* is given by Bedivere, 'the first of all his knights | Knighted by Arthur at his crowning' (173–4). Bedivere relates how the widowed Ygerne was forced to marry Uther,[119] who died believing himself childless; for his safety, Arthur – born 'all before his time' (210) – was delivered first to Merlin, then fostered by 'Sir Anton . . . and his wife' (221–2). Bellicent's 'tale' was told to her by the dying 'Bleys, our Merlin's master' (358–9), who saw the 'naked babe' Arthur – 'an heir for Uther' – carried 'to Merlin's feet' by a giant wave (383–5). At Almesbury, Bellicent's story is narrated in turn to Guinevere by the unquestioning and garrulous young novice, as one of 'the tales | Which my good father taught me' (*Guinevere*, 1859, 314–15). For Leodogran, Arthur's royal lineage is confirmed as if by divine authority, in a dream in which the 'phantom king' (*The Coming of Arthur*, 1869, 429, 435) is finally transformed – and capitalized:

Till with a wink his dream was changed, the haze
Descended, and the solid earth became

> As nothing, but the King stood out in heaven,
> Crowned.

> (440–4)

Reviewing *Idylls of the King* in October 1859, Gladstone attributed the requirement for example to Englishness – 'Lofty examples in comprehensive forms is, without doubt, one of the great standing needs of our race'.[120] Arthur was the first:

> . . . of all the kings who drew
> The knighthood-errant of this realm and all
> The realms together under me, their Head,
> In that fair Order of my Table Round,
> A glorious company, the flower of men,
> To serve as model for the mighty world,
> And be the fair beginning of a time.

> (*Guinevere*, 1859, 457–63)

However, despite the 'momentary likeness of the King' which flashed 'From eye to eye through all their Order' (*The Coming of Arthur*, 1869, 269–70) the knights do not resemble Arthur, the 'blameless King and stainless man' (*Merlin and Vivien*, 1859, 777). Ultimately Arthur's authority fails and Camelot falls. Merlin is ensnared by Vivien, and Lancelot and Guinevere's adulterous relationship becomes known. The knights are 'forsworn', as 'their vows – | First mainly through that sullying of our Queen – | Began to gall the knighthood' (*The Last Tournament*, 1871, 656, 676–8), a view which anticipates Arthur's confrontation with Guinevere at Almesbury and suggests that women's moral authority is central to Camelot as to the Victorian home. The dying Arthur mourns:

> And all whereon I leaned in wife and friend
> Is traitor to my peace, and all my realm
> Reels back into the beast, and is no more.

> (*The Passing of Arthur*, 1869, 24–6)

The young Arthur's authority as king is challenged by Leodogran's courtiers, who question his birth. Although a medieval – and Victorian – husband had 'an absolute dominion' over his wife,[121] Arthur's authority as husband is subverted by rumours spread throughout Camelot concerning his marriage. Christian belief is also central to *Idylls of the King* and Arthur is constructed as a new man for the Victorian age, a chivalrously idealistic 'modern gentleman' ('The Epic', written 1837–38, 294) exemplifying the 'union of tenderness and strength' Tennyson 'called "the man-woman" in Christ'.[122] Echoes of Anglican liturgy underline Bellicent's initial report of Arthur's 'great authority' – 'he spake and cheered his Table Round | With large, divine, and comfortable words' (*The Coming of Arthur*, 1869, 266–7). An 1857 trial run of the first of the *Idylls* was printed as *Enid and Nimuë: The True and the False* (1859) and Arthur's Christ-like androgyny is recognized by true – and 'changed' – characters as 'that gentleness, | Which, when it weds with manhood, makes a man' (*Geraint and Enid*, 1869, 824, 866–7). False characters such as Tristram – also in a triangular relationship, with 'Isolt of Britain' and 'Isolt of Brittany' – scorn the 'eunuch-hearted King' (*The Last Tournament*, 1871, 584–5, 444), while 'base interpreters' (*Merlin and Vivien*, 1869, 793) – notably Vivien – actively undermine Arthur's masculine, marital and monarchical authority:

> Man! is he man at all, who knows and winks?
> Sees what his fair bride is and does, and winks?
> By which the good King means to blind himself,
> And blinds himself and all the Table Round
> To all the foulness that they work.
>
> (779–83)

Arthur confronts Guinevere at Almesbury with the authority of both King and husband and the assumed divine authority associated with Leodogran's acceptance of kingship. As Arthur denounces her for destroying Camelot, Guinevere 'grovelled with her face against the floor' (*Guinevere*, 1859, 412):[123]

> Then came thy shameful sin with Lancelot;
> Then came the sin of Tristram and Isolt;
> Then others, following these my mightiest knights,
> And drawing foul ensample from fair names,
> Sinned also, till the loathsome opposite
> Of all my heart had destined did obtain,
> And all through thee!
>
> (484–90)

In language which chillingly foreshadows the Contagious Diseases Acts of the 1860s, Arthur also attacks the complaisant husband harbouring

a 'false' wife who – 'taken everywhere for pure' – like a 'disease . . . |
Creeps, no precaution used, among the crowd' and 'poisons half the
young' (512–19). However, proclaiming the 'vast pity' that 'almost
makes me die | To see thee' (531–2), Arthur's self-defined Christian com-
passion allows him to 'forgive thee, as Eternal God | Forgives' (541–2).

The Almesbury scene, which is Tennyson's creation and allows us
to hear Guinevere's voice, reflects recent legislation that changed
women's status within marriage and, many believed, altered English
society's moral order. The Matrimonial Causes Act (1857) established
divorce courts and gave women limited access to divorce and increased
access to children after divorce. Guinevere is no Victorian domestic – or
royal – 'Angel'. (As Clare Broome Saunders comments, 'the scale of her
wrongdoing' not only enhances the qualities of the 'perfect king' but
also eliminates 'all possible reference to Victoria'.[124]) Guinevere is child-
less, and the fostered 'Nestling' succumbed to 'mortal cold' and 'Past
from her' (*The Last Tournament*, 1871, 25–8). She is also a sexual being,
symbolically preferring the 'garden rose' and 'wild-wood hyacinth' to
'the spiritual lily' (*Balin and Balan*, 1885, 259–66). Scornfully repelled
by Arthur's 'passionate perfection' and all-absorbing 'fancy of his Table
Round', Guinevere is aware that 'who loves me must have a touch of
earth' and she loves Lancelot – 'I am yours, | Not Arthur's . . . save by
the bond' (*Lancelot and Elaine*, 1869, 122–35). At Almesbury, although
conscious of her 'own too-fearful guilt', her 'repentance' is subverted by
an ambiguous line ending:

> But help me, heaven, for surely I repent.
> For what is true repentance but in thought –
> Not even in inmost thought to think again
> The sins that made the past so pleasant to us:
> And I have sworn never to see [Lancelot] more,
> To see him more.

> (*Guinevere*, 1859, 368–75)

Guinevere's 'memory' (with Tennyson's) immediately returns to the
past. Her reverie of 'the golden days | In which she saw [Lancelot] first'
(376–8) recalls the idyllic springtime vision of 'Sir Launcelot and Queen
Guinevere: A Fragment' (written 1830–33) – 'for the time | Was maytime,
and as yet no sin was dreamed' (*Guinevere*, 1859, 384–5). Guinevere and
Lancelot rode 'under groves that looked a paradise | Of blossom, over
sheets of hyacinth | That seemed the heavens upbreaking through the
earth' (386–8), with the vocabulary echoing the 'sweet talk or lively,

all on love' (383). Guinevere's trance-like immersion in the past ends at 'that point where first she saw the King' and 'thought him cold, | High, self-contained, and passionless' (400–3) and – in the immediate present, as if confirming her impression – when she hears his 'voice | Monotonous and hollow like a Ghost's | Denouncing judgement' (416–18). For Arthur, Guinevere has become a 'foul ensample' (487), destroying his 'model for the mighty world' (462) and 'the golden days' of male companionship and 'high talk of noble deeds' (496–7). His language of forgiveness reflects both lack of understanding and the contemporary commercialism Tennyson deplored – 'I weighed thy heart with one | Too wholly true to dream untruth in thee' (537–8) – and his final farewell is superficial: 'O golden hair . . . | O imperial-moulded form, | And beauty such as never woman wore' (544–6). Guinevere's belatedly remorseful response similarly acknowledges that 'It was my duty' and 'my profit' to have loved the King, but only finally and conditionally 'would [it] have been my pleasure' (652–4).

Guinevere, like *The Coming of Arthur*, is an *Idyll* of multiple and carefully juxtaposed narratives. Before the Queen's self-revelation, the 'prattling' little novice (181) proves herself to be another base interpreter, relating to Guinevere the 'talk at Almesbury | About the good King and his wicked Queen' (206–7), that Camelot's fall is 'all woman's grief' and Guinevere's 'disloyal life | Hath wrought confusion in the Table Round | Which good King Arthur founded, years ago' (216–19). The novice's tale foreshadows and subverts Arthur's accusation, as she is an unreliable witness. '[C]losed about by narrowing nunnery-walls', knowing nothing of the world's 'wealth' and 'woe' (340–2), the novice is both garrulous and credulous, repeating without question her father's tales of Arthur's birth and marriage. The related narratives, separated only by the insight into Guinevere's own consciousness, imply that Arthur's attitudes are also shaped by society and that unquestioning acceptance of the Medieval Revival's prescribed gender roles – authoritarian and idealistic husband, idealized and asexual wife, and Platonically adoring *cavalieri serventi* – is inappropriate to human emotional development and understanding and to Tennyson's belief that 'Upon the sacredness of home life . . . the stability and greatness of a nation largely depend'.[125]

With Tennyson's enduring 'passion for the past', noted by Arthur Henry Hallam as early as July 1831,[126] it was natural for the poet to turn to the Middle Ages to consider nineteenth-century English anxieties. As demonstrated by the poems discussed above, Tennyson's uses of and preoccupation with medievalism changed with time. Through fabrications – imaginative and often idealized representations – of the medieval past he explored contemporary concern with religion and monarchy, examined gender roles, relations and conduct, and celebrated 'Godlike men' of past and present distinguished by their courage and Englishness. Medievalist poems reflect the poet's public role, and his personal loss, and are inseparable from the upper-classes: 'churls' feature in Tennyson's Arthurian poems only to 'Pass onward from Shalott' ('The Lady of Shalott', 1832, 52–4) or to enhance Arthur's Christian compassion – 'My churl, for whom Christ died' (*The Last Tournament*, 1871, 62). In *Idylls of the King*, written and published from the 1830s until the 1880s, Tennyson re-imagined medieval literature and ideals to create a not wholly exemplary 'model for the mighty world'. And from the earliest poems, Tennyson fulfilled *Aurora Leigh*'s demand – that poets' 'sole work is to represent the age, | Their age, not Charlemagne's, – this live, throbbing age' (1857, V. 202–3).[127] Despite their medieval guise, Tennyson's medieval protagonists were nineteenth-century English men and women.

6
'Ever-broadening England': Tennyson and Empire

The years 1815 to 1902 were 'pre-eminently Britain's Imperial century'.[1] By 1902 the British Empire had expanded to cover a fifth of the world's land surface and exercise authority over a quarter of its population and during the century English national identity had been increasingly defined in opposition to the Empire's Others. Tennyson's life spanned almost eight decades of the imperial century and questions of empire recur throughout his work. Contributions to *Poems by Two Brothers* (1827) narrate the destruction of ancient empires and the speaker of *Timbuctoo* (1829) gazes on the fabled city's 'Imperial height' (162). Poems of the early 1830s reflect an ambivalent attitude towards more recent empires, particularly the British Empire administered from England's capital city. (As Robert MacDonald remarks, '[t]he Empire was the colonised world overseas, but its centre and reason for being was London.'[2]) By contrast, in the later poems of monarchy Laureate Tennyson attacks the Empire's critics and vehemently defends 'ever-broadening England, and her throne | In our vast Orient' (To the Queen', 1873, 30–1) thus exemplifying, in more than one sense, Francis Palgrave's comment that Tennyson came to occupy an 'imperial position in Poetry'.[3]

In this chapter I examine Tennyson's poetic representations of and written and verbal references to empire, predominantly the British Empire, its peoples, and critical historic moments such as the uprising known to contemporaries as the 'Indian Mutiny' of 1857 and the Morant Bay Rebellion in Jamaica in 1865. (Although Tennyson did not mark the Jamaican uprising in verse, he was involved in the controversy that followed.) As in Chapters 4 and 5, the content and form of Tennyson's poems are examined in generally chronological order, in their changing historical context and with reference to critical arguments and to the poet's letters, to consider whether the poems of empire, written throughout his career, represent a smoothly untroubled linear progression towards Tennyson's later pro-imperial position, or whether – in poems such as 'The Defence of Lucknow' (1879) – Tennyson 'was willing to question, if not condemn, the Victorian status quo he had come to represent'.[4]

Changing terminologies

Britain's expanding Empire brought enhanced awareness of national identity, both English and Other. Catherine Hall argues that 'being a coloniser' became an inseparable part of nineteenth-century 'Englishness'.[5] In this chapter therefore I also examine Tennyson and his contemporaries' views of and confrontations with Otherness, together with the related development of Anglo-Saxonism and 'race science' and touching on contentious terms such as *Indian Mutiny* and *race*. Many critics follow the example of Don Randall, who places 'Mutiny' in quotation marks throughout his text 'to recall that such a naming of the 1857 rebellion is already an interpretation, and one that has been cogently questioned',[6] while Catherine Hall refers to 'the "Indian Mutiny"/Sepoy Rebellion of 1857'.[7] Douglas A. Lorimer points out that the Victorians themselves 'were often uncertain about what meaning they assigned to "race"' and 'their meanings changed during the course of the long nineteenth century'.[8]

Analyses of the establishment, working and rhetoric of the British Empire, and of Tennyson's empire poems, have changed since the nineteenth century. The bibliography of studies of the nineteenth-century Empire and imperialism is immense and Andrew Porter noted in 1999 that historians 'now acknowledge both its complexity and its place in the broader history of indigenous societies outside Europe' and 'are much more alive to the varied processes of interaction, adaptation, and exchange which shaped the Imperial and colonial past'.[9] Consequently, their 'assessments of Empire' are 'more cautious but also more sophisticated'. A similar argument can be applied to postcolonial criticism in general and to assessments of Tennyson's empire poems in particular. The latter critics analyse *Idylls of the King* or discuss single or several poems rather than, as in this chapter, surveying the poems throughout Tennyson's career. This has tended to obscure the change in Tennyson's attitude to empire. Colin Graham observes that whereas postcolonial criticism's founding texts 'imply an utter distinction between coloniser and colonised', the 'revisionings' of recent years have led to an understanding of imperialism as a cultural 'two-way flow'.[10] Graham cites as example subaltern studies, the writings of Homi K. Bhabha, and Mary

Louise Pratt's concept of transculturation, arguing that although individual critics' ideas and strategies may differ, collectively they emphasize that 'the underlying movement in recent post-colonialism has been into the complexities of cultural exchange and interface in the context of empire' and away from 'the essence of absolute oppositions'.

The revisionings of recent years are also reflected in critiques of Tennyson's empire poems. Earlier critics argued that Tennyson's view of the Empire was linear and progressive; since the 1990s a more questioning approach has been discerned in his work. Patrick Brantlinger, representing the 'linear, progressive' argument, defines imperialism as 'an evolving but pervasive set of attitudes towards the rest of the world' which 'influenced all aspects of Victorian and Edwardian culture' and regards Tennyson as an obvious example of a writer whose early and often unconscious imperialist attitudes 'crystallize into more consciously articulated positions' in later work.[11] However, Lynne O'Brien challenges Brantlinger's assessment of Tennyson as 'the imperialist poet', declaring that 'Tennyson's commitment to extolling his nation's imperialist activity is more complex than Brantlinger and others suggest'.[12] Robin L. Inboden views the poet's 'musings on colonial and imperial politics' as 'conflicted',[13] while Marion Shaw believes that critics in a postcolonial, deconstructive age are more interested in Tennyson's 'less assured scriptings of the imperial theme'.[14]

The terminology of the Empire has also changed. The unifying definition British Empire became 'standard usage throughout the nineteenth century'[15] and the term both recognizes the significance of Scottish and Irish emigration to 'Imperial expansion'[16] and suggests the role of governmental authority. Critics now refer variously and interchangeably to 'the British Empire' and 'English imperialist conquest',[17] or to 'Britain and its colonies' and 'England and her colonies'.[18] Catherine Hall uses English rather than British, not only because England and the English form the object of her study but also because 'English was constituted as a hegemonic cultural identity' in the period 1830–67.[19] Hall's terminology accords with Tennyson's own sentiments. In the poems of empire Tennyson refers both to 'Britain' and 'England' but, as with the poems of monarchy, it is 'England' and 'our English Empire' ('Hands All Round, 1882, 14) which evoke his deepest emotions.

The early poems: 'Anacaona'

Tennyson's over-riding concern in the early poems of empire is the British – or English – Empire. He refers unfavourably to the Russian and

Spanish Empires, suggesting that his interest is nationalist. 'Hail Briton!' (1831–33) contrasts English freedom of speech with the 'iron sceptre of the Czar' (196), which in November 1830 suppressed the Polish uprising. *Poems by Two Brothers* (1827) include 'Lamentation of the Peruvians', whose 'state' and 'strength' (2) were destroyed by Francisco Pizarro, the discoverer and conqueror of Peru. Tennyson alludes to the destructive power of Spanish colonial conquest in less Byronic terms in 'Anacaona' (1830). Catherine Hall argues that the Caribbean 'has had a special place in the English imagination' because of 'its primacy in the encounter between Europe and the new world' and the poem's setting is Haiti, which was discovered and claimed for the Spanish Crown by Columbus in 1492 and renamed *La Isla Española* or Hispaniola, thus symbolically inaugurating Europe's 'colonising epoch'.[20] Written during Tennyson's Cambridge years, 'Anacaona' was recited in October 1830 as 'one of the poems he has lately written',[21] but not printed until Hallam Tennyson's *Memoir* of his father was published in 1897.

'Anacaona' is a young poet's escapist fantasy. She is the 'queen' (15, 28) of Xaraguay, Haiti's western province, immediately defined by her colour and Otherness as 'A dark Indian maiden' (1) and portrayed as living in harmony with the luxuriant and colourfully un-English natural world – 'crimson-eyed anana' (4), 'orange groves' (5), 'scarlet crane' (31, 32) – of an Edenic island 'paradise' (19, 20) which, like many of Tennyson's contributions to the 1827 volume, reflects both the influence of travel books in Somersby's extensive library and the poet's own yearning for 'the purple seas' and 'palms . . . of the South' ('You ask me, why', written *c*.1833, 4, 28). Antonio de Ulloa's *Voyage to South America* (1772), in Dr Tennyson's collection, was the source of the island's natural history, while the historic figure of Anacaona was drawn from the poet's own copy of Washington Irving's *Life and Voyages of Christopher Columbus* (1828).[22]

For critics such as David G. Riede, writing after Edward Said, 'Anacaona' and other Tennyson poems betray 'the dominant Orientalist discourse of his age'.[23] Even discourse about the West is obviously Orientalist in its use of 'the word "Indians" to represent Native Americans' – or indigenous Haitians. The term *orientalism*, like the British Empire, has an extensive critical history, summarized with particular clarity by Alexander Lyon Macfie.[24] In the eighteenth and nineteenth centuries, orientalism was principally used to refer to the work of orientalist scholars, 'versed in the languages and literatures of the orient', a meaning it retained until the decolonizing decades which followed World War II when scholarly revisionings turned 'orientalism into one of the most highly charged words in modern scholarship'. Of the 'four principal assaults' on traditional orientalism, Edward Said's critique proved to be 'by far the most effective' and *Orientalism* (1978) became a founding text of postcolonial criticism. Said argues that the orientalist creates – and apparently genders – the orient: 'his' stereotypical images oppose an 'essentially rational, developed, superior . . . masculine Europe (the West, the self)' and an 'irrational, backward . . . inferior . . . feminine and sexually corrupt' orient '(the East, the other)' which, with other orientalist fantasies, contribute – consciously or unconsciously – to the construction of a 'saturating hegemonic system'. In Said's own defini-tion, Orientalism is 'a Western style for dominating, restructuring, and having authority over the Orient'.[25] The debate which followed the publication of *Orientalism* continued during the 1980s and 1990s, to be followed in turn by the revisions of later critics which Colin Graham believes have moved away from 'absolute oppositions'.[26] Julie F. Codell and Dianne Sachko Macleod argue that 'colonial discourse was avail-able to all parties in the Empire' and was often inverted, with such transpositions becoming 'more openly resistant as colonialism entered the twentieth century'.[27] Mary Louise Pratt explores the use of the term *transculturation* to describe 'how subordinated or marginal groups select and invent from materials transmitted to them by a dominant or met-ropolitan culture'.[28]

David G. Riede believes that in terms of Tennyson's poetic development the most important characteristic of Orientalism is the 'eroticism that was unsuitable in speaking of the chaste English', but completely natural in descriptions of 'the Orient or Oriental women'.[29] For Riede, the con-trast is particularly exemplified by 'Mariana' (1830) and 'Fatima' (1832). The women await lovers who have abandoned them, but Mariana's sup-pressed yearnings are narrated by a male speaker and her state of mind is suggested by her desolate and predominantly dark surroundings, while Fatima articulates an explicit longing for erotic fulfilment:

> My whole soul waiting silently,
> All naked in a sultry sky,
> Droops blinded with his shining eye:
> I *will* possess him or will die.
> > I will grow round him in his place,
> > Grow, live, die looking on his face,
> > Die, dying clasped in his embrace.

> (36–42)

In his well-known critique of *Poems, Chiefly Lyrical* (1830), which included 'Mariana', William Johnson Fox remarked that Tennyson 'can cast his own spirit into any living thing, real or imaginary' – the poet 'has the secret of the transmigration of the soul'.[30] Riede regards Tennyson's ability to enter into the feelings and appropriate the consciousness of the female figures 'who are generally thought to represent his own poetic sensibility' – and erotic yearnings – as a form of 'imaginative imperialism', a term which refers to ideas of 'the Romantic imagination as an imperial selfhood'[31] rather than imperialism in its political and cultural sense. However, Riede's definition raises the question of the difference between imperialism (in its political and cultural sense) and what might be termed the imaginative Orientalism of 'Fatima', which are linked by their association with authority. Robert Johnson concludes that '[a]bove all, imperialism is a concept of power and influence';[32] Edward Said argues that Orientalism has 'authority over the Orient',[33] and Tennyson uses his poetic power to create the Orient by entering into and appropriating the consciousness of Fatima. As Johnson points out, the term *imperialism* has 'a tortured historiography': it might describe 'political domination, economic exploitation and military subjugation'; it could include territorial expansion by settlement or invasion, or refer to ways in which an empire maintains itself or influences others. Ultimately, therefore, power that often involved 'the violent dispossession of indigenous peoples'[34] is not comparable with the power and influence of poetic representation.

Tennyson's representation of Anacaona is concerned with the body rather than the soul. He does not appropriate her consciousness but foregrounds her physical appearance, and Orientalist eroticism allows the omniscient narrator's male gaze to linger over the naked Anacaona:

> Wantoning in orange groves
>   Naked, and dark-limbed, and gay,
> Bathing in the slumbrous coves,
> In the cocoa-shadowed coves,
>   Of sunbright Xaraguay.

(5–9)

Washington Irving's *Life and Voyages of Christopher Columbus,* Tennyson's source for the historic Anacaona, records that she was celebrated as much for her intelligence as her beauty – 'She possessed a genius superior to the generality of her race' – and, as a widow, wore 'an apron of various-coloured cotton'.[35] Tennyson, however, accentuates the poetic

Anacaona's youth, nakedness and colour, by repetition and by punctuation of the generally unbroken lines – 'A dark Indian maiden' (1), 'Naked, and dark-limbed, and gay' (6). Susan Shatto observes that the 'native inhabitants' portrayed in empire poems with an historical or imaginative origin are 'types of the Romantic "Noble Savage", who are invariably naked and brown and live on islands in a state of happy innocence'.[36] Anacaona is additionally defined by her carefree nature – 'Happy, happy was Anacaona' (34, 46) – heightened by the poem's lilting rhythms and frequent use of her musical name. She sings and dances 'All day long' (17) and throughout the island, 'Naked, without fear, moving | To her Areyto's mellow ditty' (61–2), the legendary ballads through which the islanders preserved their 'earliest history'.[37] 'Anacaona', written soon after the publication of *Poems, Chiefly Lyrical* in June 1830, with few reviews received, can also be seen as representing the unconstrained poetic spirit, safely distanced from 'pitiless Reviewers' ('I dare not write an Ode', *c.*1827, 12) and the need to earn a living from poetry, which confronted Tennyson when his father died in March 1831.

In her study of Tennyson and Matthew Arnold's 'poetic depictions of the wealth of the East',[38] Emily Haddad shows how poetry and commerce are linked in Tennyson's early empire poems. She argues that poems such as 'Recollections of the Arabian Nights' (1830) exemplify a classic Orientalism, influenced by Romanticism: they portray 'the East' – and Caribbean Xaraguay – as a world set apart, in time and distance, one of natural wealth in which gold predominates, either metaphorically or as an architectural or natural feature, but not as money. 'Recollections' is set 'in the golden prime | Of good Haroun Alraschid'; Anacaona is defined in the refrain as 'The golden flower of Hayti', and in its economic innocence Anacaona's 'paradise' (19, 20) represents a refuge from the commercial and industrial pressures of Victorian England. Haddad points out, however, that 'the implied rejection of modernity' has a less positive aspect. Citing Adam Smith's assertion that 'money has become in all civilized nations the universal instrument of commerce', she concludes that 'the absence of money implies the absence of civilization'. By representing eastern – and Caribbean – economies as pre-capitalist, Tennyson is identifying such economies as 'backward' and 'primitive', with their backward economic systems unable to manage their natural wealth, and their correspondingly primitive forms of government – invariably, as in Xaraguay, a 'simple form of monarchy' with Anacaona an 'Indian queen' (28) – unable effectively to resist 'imperial subjugation'.

Anacaona and her people were subjugated, and she was later killed, by 'the white men' she 'welcome[d]' with gifts to 'happy Hayti' (64–5). The slaughter and destruction of ancient empires recur throughout Tennyson's early poems, but in 'Anacaona', as Alan Sinfield remarks, Tennyson 'disturbs by understatement';[39] he merely alludes to her fate, which is presaged by 'The shadow of the Albatross | Floating down the sea' (44–5):

> But never more upon the shore
>   Dancing at the break of day,
> In the deep wood no more, –
> By the deep sea no more, –
>   No more in Xaraguay
> Wandered happy Anacaona,
>   The beauty of Espagnola,
>   The golden flower of Hayti!

(77–84)

Hallam Tennyson's *Memoir* records that Tennyson liked but did not publish the poem because he was dissatisfied with 'the natural history and the rhymes'; he 'evidently chose words which sounded well, and gave a tropical air to the whole, and he did not then care . . . for absolute accuracy'.[40] However, Tennyson's apparent sympathy for Anacaona is revealingly qualified by his unguarded and objectionable comment in a letter to Richard Monckton Milnes, when Milnes suggested publication in *The Tribute* in 1837: 'See now . . . whether you had any occasion to threaten me with that black b— Anacaona and her cocoa-shadowed *coves* of niggers – I cannot have her strolling about the land in this way – it is neither good for her reputation nor mine'.[41] Although Tennyson had been prepared for his transmigration into Fatima's soul to be published in *Poems* (1832), he clearly thought it inappropriate for his Orientalist fantasy of the naked Anacaona to appear in *The Tribute* (1837), an anthology proposed by Lord Northampton to raise money for 'the indigent and deserving Reverend Edward Smedley'.[42]

Anacaona's fate implies that in 1830 Tennyson was ambivalent or even hostile to 'imperial/colonial claims'[43] – at least to those of Spain. What is alluded to in 'Anacaona' becomes painfully explicit in the extended dramatic monologue 'Columbus' (1880), to be discussed later in the chapter and which suggests that Tennyson's aversion to the Spanish Empire intensified with time. Echoing the vocabulary of 'Anacaona', the imprisoned explorer acknowledges:

> . . . what a door for scoundrel scum
> I opened to the West, through which the lust,

> Villany [*sic*], violence, avarice, of your Spain
> Poured in on all those happy naked isles –.
>
> (166–9)

'Anacaona' was written soon after the 1829 Relief Act granted Catholic Emancipation in Britain and Tennyson's apparent hostility to Spanish colonialism can also be interpreted as the anti-Catholicism which recurs throughout his poems, most markedly in the 'National Songs for Englishmen' written during the invasion panic that followed Louis Napoleon's *coup d'état* in December 1851. ('Suggested by Reading an Article in a Newspaper' (1852), for example, refers to the Catholic Church as 'that half-pagan harlot kept by France!' (70).) As Columbus acknowledges, Hispaniola was claimed for 'our great Catholic Queen' in order that:

> This creedless people will be brought to Christ
> And own the holy governance of Rome.
>
> (183–6)

The early poems: 'Hail Briton!'

Elements of 'Hail Briton!', the longest and most diffuse of the political poems of the early 1830s, suggest that at this stage of his career Tennyson was also ambivalent towards the British Empire. Although 'Hail Briton!' remained unpublished until 1949 its ideas and images reappear throughout Tennyson's work and the poem echoes the measured *In Memoriam* stanza form and the concerns of 'Love thou thy land' (written 1833–34) and 'You ask me, why' (written *c*.1833), particularly the freedom of speech defined in the early political poems as an English characteristic:

> But thou mayst speak thy mind aloud,
> And in the streets, or sitting still
> Art free to blame or praise at will
> The throne, the senate, and the crowd.
>
> ('Hail Briton!', 13–16)

Written between 1831 and 1833, during the turbulent passage of the Reform Bill through Parliament when many believed 'The land is filled with crying wrongs, | . . . Law speaks unheeded' (117–19), 'Hail Briton!' warns against the proximity and potentially revolutionary influence of the 'unstable' (19) Celtic temperament (a lifelong Other for Tennyson), fears the abuse of power which follows when people – individually, collectively and at all social levels – leave the 'middle road of sober thought' (112), and defines the patriot-statesman's gradualist role: 'To shape, to settle, to repair | With seasonable changes fair | And innovation grade by grade' (150–2). As Patrick Brantlinger remarks, Tennyson might have written 'Hail Briton!' at any time from the early 1830s on.[44]

In the third stanza Tennyson declares that his symbolic Briton should be acclaimed for free speech:

> Not for a power, that knows not check,
>   To spread and float an ermined pall
>   Of Empire, from the ruined wall
> Of royal Delhi to Quebec –
>
> (9–12)

Directly and by allusion, the imagery associates the British Empire with death and destruction. 'To spread and float' suggests that the Empire's expansion is a gentle, even organic movement, rather than an inexorable process of annexation and occupation, and 'pall' can be defined as a cloth covering a coffin, hearse or tomb, with the adjectival 'ermined' evoking the 'power' and privilege of Parliament and throne. Anacaona's subjugation and later destruction by Spanish colonizers were similarly foreshadowed by the shadowy albatross 'Floating down the sea' and the 'white man's white sail' which 'Floated in the silent summer' ('Anacaona', 45, 49–52). Delhi's 'wall' – linked by rhyme with the funereal 'pall' – was 'ruined' during the 'wars against the Marathas in 1803–4, when Delhi came under British administration',[45] critical historic moments symbolized by the clashing 'golden keys of East and West' (23–4) which not only orphaned the speaker of 'Locksley Hall' (1842, 155–6) but also established the 'power' of the East India Company's 'arms over the [Indian] subcontinent'.[46]

Tennyson appears to value freedom of speech more than Empire. However, in the opening stanzas he assumes that his Briton has a permanent and powerful presence in the world:

> Hail Briton! in whatever zone
>   Binds the broad earth beneath the blue,
>   In ancient seasons or in new,
> No bolder front than thine is shown:
>
> (1–4)

He similarly takes for granted the naval strength represented by: 'The many ships of war that blow | The battle from their oaken sides' (7–8) and which are inseparable from English popular culture and maritime history. An apparently ambivalent view of Empire is countered by the chauvinism which recurs throughout Tennyson's poems, overtly or subtly echoing the sentiments of the patriotic ballads of the late 1820s: 'There are no men like Englishmen, | So tall and bold as they be' ('National Song', 1828–29, 7–8). In 'Hail Briton!', Tennyson also assumes Britons' uniquely beneficent role – 'this great people, . . . | This people that hath finisht more | Than any other for mankind' (37–40) – citing the 'venerable names' (77) of 'Hampden' (57) and his successors – 'men of Saxon pith and nerve' (68) – who, by defying the absolutist and pro-Catholic Stuarts and helping to establish parliamentary monarchy in 1688, became an enduring national example:

> They wrought a work which time reveres,
> A precedent to all the lands,
> And an example reaching hands
> For ever into coming years.

> (81–4)

Tennyson's symbolic Briton, with his characteristic free speech (although poetic diction is firmly controlled by the *In Memoriam* stanza form) is hailed as a similar exemplar of 'Freedom' (85), but the initial juxtaposition of Britons' worldwide presence and the strength of 'the world's largest navy'[47] suggests that freedom, when associated with 'Empire' (11), is underpinned by force.

'To ransom them from wrong': 'O mother Britain lift thou up'

Freedom dominated the political agenda in England in the late 1820s and early 1830s. The 1829 Catholic Relief Act completed the process of Catholic Emancipation, the Reform Act of 1832 extended the freedom to vote further down the social scale, and the 'immensely popular' anti-slavery movement was 'at its height'.[48] 'O mother Britain lift thou up' was written between 1833 and 1834 to celebrate 'the abolition of slavery in the British West Indies' in August 1833.[49] Although slave trading – the trade in and capture and shipment of slaves – had been abolished within the British Empire in 1807, it was not until 1833 that the Act abolishing slavery itself 'throughout the British colonies' was passed as one of the earliest actions of the reformed Parliament.[50] Even then, as a concession won by the planters, slaves in agriculture were to remain 'apprenticed to their former masters until 1840', although the apprenticeship system was ended in August 1838. 'O mother Britain' was not published in Tennyson's lifetime, but like other of his early, minor poems it remains of critical interest by anticipating the concerns of later, canonic works. The chauvinism revealed in 'Hail Briton!' is heightened and simplified in 'O mother Britain' as, apostrophizing 'mother Britain', the poet celebrates 'thy good deed' (22) and incomparable greatness in extending freedom to 'the far-off shores' (5):

> O mother Britain lift thou up,
>   Lift up a joyful brow,
> There lies not in the circled seas
> A land so great as thou.
>
> O let the far-off shores be glad,
>   The isles break out in song,
> For thou didst buy them with a price
> To ransom them from wrong.
>
>   (1–8)

Echoing the *abcb* rhyme scheme and the preoccupations of 'I loving Freedom for herself' (1832–34), 'O mother Britain' is an affirmative response to the political poem's rhetorical question – 'What nobler than an ancient land | That passing an august decree | Makes wider in a settled peace | The lists of liberty?' ('I loving Freedom', 25–8) – and intensifies the self-congratulatory tone of a contemporary newspaper report praising 'the benevolent spirit' in which 'the emancipation of all our slave population . . . was decreed'.[51]

The British West Indies, like Xaraguay, are located in the Caribbean. However, Tennyson's imagined 'isles' (6) represent the enduring moral example of 'mother Britain', embodiment of an Empire far removed from Catholic Spain's malign influence on Anacaona and her people – 'But never shall this world forget | Who taught the peoples right' (11–12). In the 1830s the British West Indies 'consisted of a large number of islands and territories acquired over two centuries', which were 'characterized by different forms of colonial government' and significantly different 'levels of economic development'.[52] Jamaica had been an increasingly important producer of sugar from the early seventeenth century. By 1900 the island was supplying 'nearly one-fifth of the calories in the

English diet' and, as Catherine Hall observes, 'sugar became a part of the English self'.[53] Tennyson's isles, by contrast, are geographically imprecise and undifferentiated, superficially sketched as 'hills of canes' and 'palmy valleys' (13–14). The islanders are absent, suggesting that the abstract and English concept of freedom is more important to Tennyson than the newly-liberated slaves, who have neither presence nor voice, and the isles' celebratory 'song' (6) is sung by the poet. The poem's viewpoint is London, with the only named geographical feature the 'Thames' (17), and Tennyson's metropolitan vision – both chauvinist and Orientalist – distorts colonial history by asserting that the islands were acquired in an act of apparent altruism: 'For thou didst buy them with a price | To ransom them from wrong' (7–8). 'O mother Britain' not only justifies the 'power political' of colonial possession but also – in its assumption of moral superiority – exemplifies the 'power moral', which Edward Said regards as an integral part of 'the third meaning of Orientalism'.[54]

'O mother Britain' represents both a moral and a maternal exemplar. The poem's title encapsulates critical views that nineteenth-century representations of the relationship between the British Empire and its colonies were 'wrapped in the warm language of family ties'.[55] The personification of 'mother Britain' also reflects the change from early abolitionists' concern with the male sibling relationship (the 'brotherhood of man') to the parental role within the family of man which, Catherine Hall believes, 'has always been constituted through hierarchy and inequalities of power'.[56] Metaphors of the Empire as family implicitly confer authority on the parents and assume the legitimacy, dependent status and obedience of the children. In the idealized Victorian family ultimate authority was conferred on the father, while the mother (occupying the moral high ground as the 'Angel in the House') 'taught' the children and, by extension, 'the peoples right' (12).

Ansgar Nünning argues that the 'ideologically charged metaphor of the empire as a family' became 'the foremost unifying device' in discursively constructing the 'imperial idea'.[57] The metaphor domesticates and therefore naturalizes the relationship between Britain and its colonies, enhancing loyalty. Tennyson's 'mother Britain' and the assumed altruism of the islands' acquisition – a foretaste of the late-nineteenth century's 'imperial discourse of benevolence'[58] – anticipate the imperialist elements of later, laureate verse. 'Opening of the Indian and Colonial Exhibition by the Queen' (1886), for example, demands that Britain's 'Sons, be welded each and all, | Into one imperial whole' (36–7). By approvingly attributing authority to 'mother Britain', Tennyson also implies a less hierarchical view of marriage – the relationship 'Nor equal, nor unequal' (*The Princess*, 1847, VII, 285). Written several years before Victoria's accession in 1837, 'O mother Britain' bridges the divide between the political and economic 'world of men' (9) and women's domestic sphere and foreshadows the multiple roles of Victoria, celebrated by Laureate Tennyson as 'Mother, Wife, and Queen' ('To the Queen', 1851, 28).

Seeking 'Summer isles of Eden': 'The Lotos-Eaters', 'Ulysses' and 'Locksley Hall'

The imaginary 'isles' (6) of 'O mother Britain' represent moral example; the 'far-off shores' (5) encountered in three contemporary poems offer a refuge from England in the Hungry Forties and portray the protagonists' confrontations with Otherness. 'The Lotos-Eaters' (written in 1830–32, first published in 1832 and extensively revised for the 1842 volumes) was influenced by classical mythology's 'sunset-flushed' (17) 'Islands of the Blest' and, as with 'Anacaona', Washington Irving's description of 'the idyllic life on Haiti'.[59] Apparently without volition – rolled 'shore-ward' by the 'mounting wave' – the mariners reach 'the land' (1–2), an Orientalist island set apart in time and distance, its natural wealth suggested by 'yellow sand' (37) rather than gold. Wearied by years of exploration and the relentless 'toil' (60, 61, 69) – 'ever climbing up the climbing wave' (95) – that resembles the exhausting monotony of mechanized labour, they succumb to the enervating atmosphere, the subliminal 'sweet music' (46) which evokes *The Tempest* and the 'enchanted' lotos borne by the 'Dark-face[d]' islanders (26–8).

The mariners reject the opening call for 'Courage' (1), their dreams 'Of child and wife' (40) and of return to the 'wasted lands' of 'Blight and famine' (159–60) which, although distanced by allusion to 'Gods' (155), suggest the depressed condition of England in the 1840s. They resolve to remain in 'Lotos-land' (154), prefiguring the European colonizers who, it was feared, would yield to the temptation of 'going native' and become assimilated into the customs and cultures of indigenous peoples. But the mariners' island paradise is illusory. The 'long rest' (98) they seek becomes a drug-induced stupor paradoxically replicating the sensation of exhaustion that creates the need for oblivion (and as Isobel Armstrong points out, nineteenth-century English industrial workers often became similarly addicted to opium[60]) and the mariners are caught in a self-perpetuating cycle which mirrors the circular movement – enhanced by visual and aural repetition – as 'Round and round the spicy downs the yellow Lotos-dust is blown' (149). 'The Lotos-Eaters' is thus critical of the mariners' abdication of responsibility, their addiction and the conditions which caused it, and of the indigenous islanders, 'mild-eyed melancholy Lotos-eaters' (27) who, unable to manage their abundant natural resources, allow the island's fruit and flowers to ripen and fall, unpicked:

> The full-juiced apple, waxing over-mellow,
> Drops in a silent autumn night.
> All its allotted length of days,
> The flower ripens in its place,
> Ripens and fades, and falls, and hath no toil,
> Fast-rooted in fruitful soil.
>
> (78–83)

The call for courage in 'The Lotos-Eaters' is countered by the mariners' lotos-induced inertia. 'Ulysses', also published in 1842, was written in October 1833, soon after Tennyson learned of Arthur Hallam's death and 'gave my feeling about the need of going forward, and braving the struggle of life perhaps more simply than anything in "In Memoriam"'.[61] Discontented with idleness, Ulysses resolves to roam – 'I cannot rest from travel' (6) – but his need to go forward is qualified by age and world-weariness. He leaves on his final voyage late in the day and in life, and the diminished energies of age – and grief – are suggested by the measured rhythm and extended vowel sounds:

> The long day wanes: the slow moon climbs: the deep
> Moans round with many voices.
>
> (55–6)

However, by departing, Ulysses abdicates both domestic and royal responsibility. He acknowledges his son's admirable qualities only in a formal farewell speech and is contemptuous of his wife and people:

> It little profits that an idle king,
> By this still hearth, among these barren crags,
> Matched with an agèd wife, I mete and dole
> Unequal laws unto a savage race,
> That hoard, and sleep, and feed, and know not me.
>
> (1–5)

Ulysses, both protagonist and poem, is inseparable from colonialism – and Englishness. For Alan Sinfield, Tennyson's Homeric hero is a 'colonizer' who 'requires ever more remote margins to sustain his enter-prise'.[62] Matthew Rowlinson remarks that, on relinquishing authority to Telemachus, Ulysses resembles 'a colonial administrator turning over the reins to a successor'.[63] Famed for 'always roaming with a hungry heart' (12), he imposes his influence on the people and places he encounters – 'I am a part of all that I have met' (18). Ulysses' legacy includes language, and analysis of his speech again reveals Tennyson's 'use of English – in preference to words derived from French and Latin'.[64] Monosyllables and words of Old or Middle English origin predominate, suggesting that Ulysses is etymologically related to the Anglo-Saxon Miller of Chapter 2, and the opening lines – in which the '<u>idle</u> <u>king</u>' complains that '<u>matched</u> <u>with</u> <u>an</u> agèd <u>wife</u>, <u>I</u> <u>mete</u> <u>and</u> <u>dole</u>/Unequal <u>laws</u> <u>unto</u> a savage race' (1–4) – immediately identify Rowlinson's departing official as a specifically English colonial administrator.

The publication history makes clear that the poem also travelled widely. As Edgar F. Shannon notes, in January 1844 'Ulysses' – 'one of the most exquisite . . . poems in this or any other language' – was reprinted in the *Foreign and Colonial Quarterly Review*, published in London but 'designed for the colonies'.[65] In later decades, 'Ulysses' was regularly reprinted in anthologies intended for 'the classroom',[66] thus becoming an intrinsic part of the establishment of English literary study in secondary, higher and adult education, for men and women. English poetry appeared on the Indian curriculum before it became the subject of formal instruction in England, when the English Education Act (1835) 'officially required the natives of India to submit to the study of that literature'.[67] The legislation had been encouraged by Thomas Babington Macaulay who, speaking on 'The Government of India' in 1833, argued that '[t]o trade with civilised men is infinitely more profitable than to govern savages'.[68] Under the 1853 India Act English language and literature became required examination subjects for admission to the Indian Civil Service. 'Ulysses' is therefore also an inherent part of the process by which India was 'Conquered and annexed and Englished!' (Robert Browning, 'Clive', 1880, 17). Tennyson encouraged Francis Palgrave to publish *The Golden Treasury* (1861), whose Preface concludes with the words: 'wherever the Poets of England are honoured, wherever the dominant language of the world is spoken, it is hoped that they will find fit audience',[69] which implies the poet's approval of the colonizing spread of English poetry and its values.

Although 'Ulysses' was later used for ideological purposes, the poem dates from the prehistory of British imperialism. In England in 1833 the phrase 'British Empire' referred only to the British Isles.[70] The term *imperialism* entered the English language in the 1840s, used to describe the aims of the French *parti impérialiste* and from 1852 to refer critically to Louis Napoleon (Napoleon III).[71] The earliest articulation of an imperialist policy dates from 1868, with the *Spectator*'s view – thirty years before Kipling exhorted America and Britain to 'Take up the White Man's burden' (1898) – that imperialism 'in its best sense' might involve 'a binding duty to perform highly irksome or offensive tasks'.[72] The term formed part of the acrimonious debate on the Royal Titles Bill, which created Victoria 'Empress of India' in 1876 and, *The Times* complained, 'threaten[ed] the Crown with the degradation of a tawdry Imperialism'.[73]

'The Lotos-Eaters' and 'Ulysses' anticipate elements of the imperialist attitudes of later decades. The implied disapproval of indigenous inhabitants was articulated by English colonial administrators such as Henry Lushington, author of *The Double Government, the Civil Service, and the India Reform Agitation* (1853), who vehemently disputed 'the contention . . . that Indians in general were equal in ability and morality with Europeans'.[74] Ulysses' closing reference to 'my mariners' (45) as 'One equal temper of heroic hearts' (68) echoes the funeral prayer by John Donne – familiar from Tennyson's Anglican rectory childhood and recalling Arthur Hallam's recent death – which suggests the colonizing mission of 'Ulysses', both protagonist and poem, has divine approval. That Anglican liturgy and English literature were turned to ideological purpose was confirmed by Earl Grey, writing in 1853: 'The authority of the British Crown is at this moment the most powerful instrument, under Providence, of maintaining peace and order in many extensive regions of the earth, and thereby assists in diffusing amongst millions of the human race, the blessings of Christianity and civilization.'[75]

'Locksley Hall' (written in 1837–38 and published in 1842) contains a violent Orientalist fantasy which foreshadows certain racist attitudes developing in mid-nineteenth-century England. The speaker – a child of, and orphaned by, the Empire – is now a soldier, returned to say 'a long farewell to Locksley Hall' (189). Disillusioned by the commercial values of contemporary English society, which prevented his marriage to Amy, and aware that 'I myself must mix with action, lest I wither by despair' (98), he imagines escaping to 'some retreat | Deep in yonder shining Orient, where my life began to beat' (153–4), an island 'Paradise' (160) again characterized by natural abundance and a pre-capitalist economy:

> Or to burst all links of habit – there to wander far away,
> On from island unto island at the gateways of the day.

Larger constellations burning, mellow moons and happy skies,
Breadths of tropic shade and palms in cluster, knots of Paradise.

Never comes the trader, never floats an European flag,
Slides the bird o'er lustrous woodland, swings the trailer from the crag;

Droops the heavy-blossomed bower, hangs the heavy-fruited tree –
Summer isles of Eden lying in dark-purple spheres of sea.

                                                    (157–64)

The speaker dwells on the imagined sexual freedom of his island retreat. 'There', he rages, in a racist and misogynistic fantasy from which the reader, as intended, recoils and which the speaker soon – but not wholly – disowns:

. . . the passions cramped no longer shall have scope and breathing space;
I will take some savage woman, she shall rear my dusky race.

Iron jointed, supple-sinewed, they shall dive, and they shall run,
Catch the wild goat by the hair, and hurl their lances in the sun;

Whistle back the parrot's call, and leap the rainbows of the brooks,
Not with blinded eyesight poring over miserable books –

Fool, again the dream, the fancy! but I *know* my words are wild,
But I count the gray barbarian lower than the Christian child.

                                                    (167–74)

His imagined violation of an indigenous island woman, which mir-rors the forced sexual encounters of colonial conquest and the slav-ery whose abolition Tennyson had celebrated in 'O mother Britain' (1833–34), has been interpreted in differing ways. For Susan Shatto, the rapid rejection of the speaker's fantasy merely illustrates 'how hatred can be the reaction against envy'.[76] Lynne O'Brien's more considered view – that '[f]or Tennyson, sexual passion seems to be among those primitive characteristics that man will rise above in his spiritual evolu-tion'[77] – is reflected in 'Locksley Hall' by the speaker's fear of 'herd[ing] with narrow foreheads . . . | Like a beast with lower pleasures, like a beast with lower pains!' (175–6) and in 'Locksley Hall Sixty Years After' (1886), with its 'sounding watchword, "Evolution"' (198), by the mature love he shared with Edith which replaced his youthful passion for Amy. (The self-control this implies became a defining characteristic of the English gentleman discussed in Chapter 5.) David Riede also links the imagined scene with Englishness, arguing that the speaker's 'transgressive, imperialist fantasy' is rejected 'because the English and their age of progress are immeasurably superior to the lower races at the far end of empire'.[78]

Isobel Armstrong is disturbed by the uncertainty of tone which makes it unclear whether 'Locksley Hall' is 'a dramatic poem or whether the virulent bluster has a deconstructive moment', adding that 'if it is parody it is bad parody'.[79] 'Locksley Hall' is a dramatic monologue, elements of which prefigure Tennyson's extended 'monodrama' *Maud* (1855), and the rapid rejection of his fantasy exemplifies the violent mood swings of the protagonist, a man of 'deep' but unstable 'emotion' (108) and yearning for 'large excitement' (111). Portrayed as self-obsessed and self-dramatizing from his childhood as 'a trampled orphan' (156), the speaker is later scorned by 'comrades' for his 'foolish passion' (145–6) and finally 'shamed through all my nature to have loved so slight a thing' (148). However, and as Seamus Perry argues, it is questionable whether the poem's dramatic context provides sufficient sanction for the speaker's 'sexual aggression, imperialist race-hatred, and deep self-loathing'.[80] The formal control imposed by the poem's regular, end-rhymed and often end-stopped couplets also counters the words' excused wildness.

The speaker's 'wild' words (173) carry a disturbing echo of Tennyson's own virulent bluster when Richard Monckton Milnes suggested publishing 'Anacaona' in January 1837. Despite welcoming the abolition of slavery, Tennyson was clearly not immune to 'the Victorian concept of "colour prejudice"', an expression which 'originated in abolitionist discourse in the 1820s and 1830s'.[81] The second half of the nineteenth century saw a heightening of racial consciousness in England, exemplified by the changing title of Thomas Carlyle's essay: published in *Fraser's Magazine* in February 1848 as 'Occasional Discourse on the Negro Question', when reprinted as a pamphlet in 1853 the title contained the derogatory term 'Nigger'. By the end of the century the terminology of colour prejudice had been replaced by 'the new language of race instinct' which developed with the discipline of psychology and 'naturalized' prejudice. Tennyson could not have regarded his views as racialist or racist, words which date respectively from 1901 and 1926, and throughout his work uses 'race' in the sense of a group of persons, animals or plants, connected by common descent or origin. In

1837 he celebrated the future 'race of the Queen of the Isles' (40) and in 1885 mourned that 'Many a planet by many a sun may roll with the dust of a vanished race' ('Vastness', 2).

'Race in human affairs is everything'

The publication of *Poems* (1842) – which included 'The Lotos-Eaters', 'Ulysses' and 'Locksley Hall' – established Tennyson's poetic reputation in the 1840s. In 1850 he achieved personal happiness and public recognition with his marriage to Emily Sellwood and appointment as Poet Laureate, when he became part of an English literary tradition reaching back beyond John Dryden, the first official Poet Laureate, to Ben Jonson, who was granted a court pension by James I in 1616. And during the Hungry Forties, with abolition achieved, attention turned away from the distant Empire to the condition of England – described by Thomas Carlyle in 1843 as 'dying of inanition'[82] – and the political campaigns of Chartism and the Anti-Corn Law League.

By 1850, as Reginald Horsman argues, earlier emphasis on 'Anglo-Saxon liberties' had been 'transformed into a racist doctrine'.[83] Horsman – whose sphere of study is racial Anglo-Saxonism in Britain and America – defines Anglo-Saxonism as 'the concept of a distinct, superior Anglo-Saxon race, with innate endowments enabling it to achieve a perfection of governmental institutions and world dominance'.[84] Although an inseparable part of English thought in the first half of the nineteenth century, its origins were in the sixteenth-century English Reformation and contained multiple strands. The 'religious myth of a pure English Anglo-Saxon church', used to justify Henry VIII's break with Rome, was succeeded in the seventeenth century by a more powerful secular myth of 'a free Anglo-Saxon government' on which parliamentarians based their opposition to increasing Stuart pretensions. Conflicting interpretations of English history followed the 'Glorious Revolution' of 1688, dominated by the Whig view of the past which resounds throughout Tennyson's political poems and regarded England as:

> A land of settled government,
>   A land of just and old renown,
>   Where Freedom slowly broadens down
> From precedent to precedent:
>
> ('You ask me, why', written *c*.1833, 9–12)

The Whig theory of history was rejected by 'anti-Whigs' (who had a more realistic view of Anglo-Saxon society) and by 'Real Whigs' or English radicals – enthusiastic Anglo-Saxons – who, while accepting the continuous history of English political institutions, believed that seventeenth-century struggles had not wholly restored England's pre-Conquest liberties. However, Whigs and English radicals shared the developing interest in Anglo-Saxons' Germanic or Teutonic ancestors.

Reginald Horsman believes that while sixteenth- and seventeenth-century Anglo-Saxonism was largely nonracial, the mid-eighteenth century saw a change in emphasis from 'the continuity of free institutions to the inherent racial traits which supposedly explained them'.[85] This was influenced by factors such as expanding British power, increasing interest in the English language – as 'comparative philologists linked language to race and nation' – and particularly by the work of early-nineteenth-century ethnologists, which 'was decisive in giving a definite racial cast to Anglo-Saxonism'. The writings and influence of James Cowles Prichard, William Lawrence and their successors are examined in Nancy Stepan's exhaustive study of 'the main stages in the history of the idea of race in the natural sciences in Britain' between 1800 and 1960.[86] Horsman regards the 1840s as 'a watershed in the surging growth of Anglo-Saxonism', when continuing belief in Anglo-Saxon freedom merged with comparative philologists' ideals of 'Teutonic greatness and destiny' and ethnologists' developing views on innate 'Caucasian superiority'. While Tennyson – like 'Ulysses' – was becoming 'a name' (11), 'new racial ideas' began to appear in English publications, reflected in the views of 'Carlyle, Thomas Arnold, Disraeli, and Charles Kingsley'. However, Douglas A. Lorimer – concerned with 'historical continuities and discontinuities' in race, science and culture in the second half of the nineteenth century – warns against attributing the origins of racist ideas to particular writers as the 'Victorian use of race was so pervasive'.[87]

The Races of Men: A Fragment, by the discredited Edinburgh anatomist Robert Knox, was published in London in 1850 – Tennyson's laureate year.[88] Despite Douglas A. Lorimer's injunction not to emphasize the work of individual authors, Knox is 'a pivotal figure' in mid-nineteenth-century racial Anglo-Saxonism; his influence was both immediate and, through his 'disciple' James Hunt, enduring.[89] Lorimer himself observes that Knox is 'often identified as the British equivalent to Gobineau as a founding father of modern racism'.[90] *The Races of Men* was designated *A Fragment* because it contained the outlines of lectures delivered by Knox throughout England in 1845, whose object was 'to show that in human history race is everything'.[91] As Reginald Horsman asserts, the lectures represent 'a passionate espousal of racial doctrines'[92] and Knox's use of the word 'race' can be understood in both its nineteenth- and twentieth-century sense. Considering his 'native country, Britain', Knox notes the enduring existence of three 'distinct races of men' – 'Celtic, Saxon, and Belgian or Flemish'.[93] He declares an overriding interest in the 'Saxon', which is 'about to be the dominant race on the earth' (9–10), and demonstrates a ferocious hatred of 'the Celtic character', contemplating with equanimity 'the quiet and gradual extinction of the Celtic race in Ireland' and 'Caledonia' (26–7). 'Look[ing] all over the globe', Knox chillingly concludes that 'the dark races' are physically and psychologically incapable of progress: 'it is always the same; the dark races stand still, the fair progress' (222–4). Foreseeing the 'sure extinction' of 'Mexicans, Peruvians, and Chilians' [*sic*], Knox observes that 'we have cleared Van Diemen's Land of every *human* aboriginal; Australia, of course, follows, and New Zealand next' (229–30). For Knox, the 'ultimate expulsion' of 'the dark races' from 'all lands which the fair races can colonize seems almost certain' (314), a genocidal dispossession of indigenous peoples Tennyson had implicitly condemned in 'Anacaona' (1830) when carried out by 'the white men . . . fair-faced and tall' (65–8) of the Catholic Spanish Empire.

'Martyrs of Empire': 'Havelock' and 'The Defence of Lucknow'

Tennyson's – and public – interest in the British Empire was reignited in the 1850s and 1860s. Some historians regard this period as the end of the 'informal empire', associated with Britain's expanding world market, and the growth of a 'formal empire' of annexations, protectorates and spheres of influence,[94] although others question the adequacy of such terms to cover the 'complexity of Britain's relationship with the extra-European world'.[95] Attention was captured by two key events of imperial history, the uprising known to Tennyson and his contemporaries as the 'Indian Mutiny' (1857–59) and the Morant Bay Rebellion in Jamaica (1865), which received extensive and often inaccurate coverage in the English press and subsequently generated a large body of literature and critical writing. Patrick Brantlinger, for example, examines literary representations of the 'Indian Mutiny' in his attempt to trace the development of 'imperialist ideology . . . from 1830 to the 1880s', while Don Randall considers the sermons preached on 7 October 1857, 'a Public Day of Fast, Humiliation, and Prayer' commanded by Queen Victoria.[96] Laura Callanan examines the context of the 1865 Morant Bay Rebellion, reaction to the news in England, and the transcript of the Royal Commission's Inquiry in 1866.[97]

Tennyson responded to the 'Indian Mutiny' with two poems, very different in content and form. 'Havelock – Nov. 25th, 1857', printed in the *Memoir*,[98] was written in rapid response to the news of Havelock's death which reached England on 7 January 1858, a delay demonstrating the difficulty of receiving accurate and detailed information from India. Taking at least six weeks to arrive, and 'notoriously spare in detail', news generated by the recently developed telegraph system was susceptible to delay by 'intercontinental relays' and local sabotage.[99] 'Havelock' is an unexceptional popular ballad or marching song, but its four short verses encapsulate Tennyson's ideal of masculine military courage and self-sacrifice and a chivalric view of war:

> Bold Havelock march'd,
> Charged with his gallant few,
> Ten men fought a thousand,
> Slew them and overthrew.

> (5–8)

The poet declares that 'Bold Havelock march'd, | . . . March'd and fought himself dead' (9–12), thus earning a Tennysonian tribute – 'Tender and great and good' (14) – which, by suggesting both feminine and masculine qualities, enhances the Christian associations. In fact, Havelock died of dysentery some days after the relief of Lucknow,[100] but with his heroic death in battle he joins the ranks of Tennyson's 'Godlike men' ('Wellington Ode', 1852, 266) – the military, naval and political figures whose chivalric qualities and Englishness he celebrated as Laureate. The historic Sir Henry Havelock attracted widespread national interest: in his extended epic poem *Havelock's March* (1860), the Chartist poet Gerald Massey (1828–1907) also celebrated Havelock's death as 'one of the martyrs of Empire'.[101]

Tennyson's friend Benjamin Jowett suggested the subject of an '"In Memoriam" for the dead in India' after the death of his brother, the second to die in India, in December 1858.[102] However, Tennyson's more considered response to the 'Indian Mutiny' – which 'had stirred him to the depths'[103] – was not written until March 1879, published the following month in *Nineteenth Century* and later included in *Ballads and Other Poems* (1880). 'The Defence of Lucknow' is formed of seven

stanzas of differing lengths, whose densely packed hexameters resemble
experimental poems such as 'Boädicea' (1864) which aim to re-echo the
pandemonium of revolt and suggest the rapid heartbeat and staccato
questions and answers produced by intense fear – 'What have they
done? where is it? Out yonder. Guard the Redan!' (36) – but the stanzas are controlled by the necessary mid-line pause in reading and the
rhyme scheme in which couplets predominate, perhaps implying that
the English will prevail.

'The Defence of Lucknow' is Tennyson's 'Dedicatory' 'ballad of the
deeds | Of England, and her banner in the East', laid at the 'pale feet' of
Princess Alice ('Dedicatory Poem to the Princess Alice', 19–21). Queen
Victoria's second daughter, and by marriage the Grand Duchess of Hesse-
Darmstadt, Alice died on 14 December 1878 'of kissing her child, who
was ill with diphtheria'[104] and (as discussed in Chapter 4) was mourned
by Tennyson as 'England's England-loving daughter' (15) for her dying
request that an English flag should cover her coffin. The phrase 'Banner
of England' begins 'The Defence of Lucknow' and is the poem's recurring symbol of Englishness, five of the seven stanzas ending with the
refrain 'And ever upon the topmost roof our banner of England blew'.
The reality of the flag was also important to Tennyson and he later confirmed its exact location with Joseph Fayrer, Lucknow's civil surgeon.[105]
Dorothy Jones observes that flags 'are particularly interesting signifiers
of empire' as they are both 'fabric and fabrication',[106] able to subsume
the countries in which they 'blew' under the rule of another, however
distant. Tennyson's dedicatory 'banner of England', flying over the
Lucknow Residency, links monarchy and empire as firmly as Victoria's
contested title Empress of India, assumed in 1876.

Gautam Chakravarty confirms that the 'siege of the Lucknow
Residency fired popular imagination in Anglo-India and in Britain': it
lasted from June to November 1857 and two military campaigns were
required to rescue the garrison.[107] Chakravarty argues that by isolating
the events at Lucknow from their causes, the poetry of the siege – unlike
historiography or the novel – produced 'an uncomplicated story of
heroism, hardship and sacrifice, embellished with figures of xenophobia
and national pride', and he regards 'the Poet Laureate's commemora-
tion' as both 'simplistic' and 'characteristic'. 'The Defence of Lucknow'
is certainly a story of heroism, hardship and sacrifice, with characteristically Tennysonian elements, but it cannot be regarded as simplistic,
particularly when considered in relation to Tennyson's poems in general and not in isolation. 'The Defence of Lucknow' is inseparable from
Tennyson's view of women and the family, from its 'Dedicatory Poem'

and from his relationship with the Royal Family, which had become closer following the Prince Consort's death in 1861. The dying Albert had been nursed by Princess Alice, with whom Tennyson later corresponded on the 'Dedication' to *Idylls of the King*,[108] and his sadness at her death was deepened by the coincidence of dates (Alice died on the anniversary of Albert's death).

'The Defence of Lucknow' is also inseparable from its context – and Tennyson's national pride. Written as dissenting voices began to question the cost of Empire, and during the Second Anglo-Afghan War (1878–80) which, like the First (1839–42), attempted to secure India's western border, the poem would remind readers of the human cost involved in maintaining Victoria's Empire. As the repeated pronoun 'we' makes clear, the narrative voice is that of a survivor of the siege and the poem portrays the actions, reactions and heightened emotions of the 'soldiers and men' (41) rather than praising their gentlemanly commander as in 'Havelock'. However, the poem's most intense moment of national pride – placed for emphasis at the beginning of the central stanza – echoes Tennyson's recurring celebrations of English military courage in the face of overwhelming odds:

Handful of men as we were, we were English in heart and in limb,
Strong with the strength of the race to command, to obey, to endure,
Each of us fought as if hope for the garrison hung but on him;

(46–8)

The Lucknow garrison contained 'children and wives' (8, 51) which, as Robin L. Inboden notes, intensifies the pathos and 'undermines the idea that Britain's interest in India is purely military and mercenary'.[109] The exemplary English family is also inseparable from empire, but 'The Defence of Lucknow' undermines the conventional Victorian view of female weakness, foregrounded as the second stanza opens by placing the words 'Frail' and 'Women' at the beginning of successive lines, to be countered by the women's later actions:

Frail were the works that defended the hold that we held with our lives –
Women and children among us, God help them, our children and wives!

(7–8)

For many in England, the 'Indian Mutiny' was defined by sensationalist news reports of the fate – real or imagined – of women and children, suggested in 'The Defence of Lucknow' by the men's plan, if the garrison fell, to kill the women and children themselves: 'Better to fall by the hands that they love, than to fall into theirs!' (53). (Christina Rossetti's poem 'In the Round Tower at Jhansi, June 8, 1857' dramatizes a reported incident of this kind.) The women of the Lucknow garrison are heroized, their 'valour' emphasized as, enduring hardship and sacrifice, they fulfil the traditional roles of nurturing and giving life which link them with Princess Alice:

> Valour of delicate women, who tended the hospital bed,
> Horror of women in travail among the dying and dead.

> (87–8)

Tennyson's portrayal of the events at Lucknow subverts the idea of conflict as a chivalric pastime. Earlier imagery of cavalry charge and sword is replaced by the reality of siege warfare. The outnumbered English soldiers are heroized for defending the garrison against an onslaught of modern weaponry – 'rifle-bullets' and 'cannon-balls' (14), mines (24), revolvers (26) and pickaxes (27), 'cannon-shot, musket-shot' (34) and 'grape[shot]' (42), rifles (56) and 'hand-grenades' (59) – and the human consequences of battle are graphically represented:

> Ever the day with its traitorous death from the loop-holes around,
> Ever the night with its coffinless corpse to be laid in the ground,
> Heat like the mouth of a hell, or a deluge of cataract skies,
> Stench of old offal decaying, and infinite torment of flies,
> Thoughts of the breezes of May blowing over an English field,
> Cholera, scurvy, and fever, the wound that *would* not be healed,
> Lopping away of the limb by the pitiful-pitiless knife, –
> Torture and trouble in vain, – for it never could save us a life.

> (79–86)

The briefly intervening vision of England's temperate climate and green landscape echoes Gerald Massey's use of similar imagery in *Havelock's March* (1860)[110] and, as Richard A. Sylvia notes, suggests that 'on Indian soil' the English soldiers are 'dangerously out of place'.[111] However, while warning of the danger associated with Empire campaigns, by heroizing the soldiers Tennyson also upholds an ideal of national strength, unity and sacrifice, necessary to ensure 'That ever upon the topmost roof our banner in India blew' (72).

The most contentious aspect of 'The Defence of Lucknow' is Tennyson's conflicting characterizations of Indian soldiers. Robin L. Inboden rightly states that the poem reflects the worst elements of 'Victorian racism and condescension'.[112] He argues that Tennyson's attitude is complicated by his reference to the besieging Bengal army as 'traitors' (66), a term which implies belonging: for Tennyson, 'those who rejected British domination were not nationalists or even enemies' but 'traitors by virtue of having been presumed Englishmen'. Tennyson's portrayal of Indian soldiers is inseparable from his view of the Empire as a family, with 'mother Britain' at its head (and from December 1878 his awareness that a child may cause the death of the mother). 'Opening of the Indian and Colonial Exhibition by the Queen' (1886), for example, welcomes 'sons and brothers' (3) and refers to 'the mother' (12), 'fathers' (15) and 'kin' (23). In 'The Defence of Lucknow' Tennyson welcomes Indian soldiers who 'fought' under the symbolic 'banner of England':

Praise to our Indian brothers, and let the dark face have his due!
Thanks to the kindly dark faces who fought with us, faithful and few,
Fought with the bravest among us, and drove them, and smote them, and slew,

(69–71)

Robin L. Inboden argues that while readers 'must wince at the condescending consciousness of race in this passage', Tennyson's 'characterization of sympathetic Indians' can be seen as 'sincere, if misguided'.[113] However, Tennyson's attitude is further complicated by his reference to the besieging army as 'tigers' (51), echoing his notorious views on the Morant Bay Rebellion in Jamaica which took place on 11 October 1865. The uprising was suppressed with extreme brutality: in the month-long period of martial law declared by Governor Edward Eyre 'British forces killed 439 people, . . . flogged 600 men and women and destroyed upwards of 1,000 homes'.[114] The case became a *cause célèbre* in England, dividing opinion. An increasingly immoderate editorial in *The Times* on 18 November 1865, also drawing on the language of empire as family, complained: 'Though a fleabite compared with the Indian Mutiny [the Rebellion] touches our pride more and is more in the nature of a disappointment. . . . Jamaica is our pet institution, and its inhabitants are our spoilt children. Alas for . . . the improvement of races.'[115] In October 1866 Tennyson contributed to 'Governor Eyre's Defence Committee' as 'a tribute to the nobleness of the man' and 'a protest against the spirit in which a servant of the State, who had saved to us one of the Islands of the Empire, and many English lives, seems to be hunted down'.[116] But he declined to join the Committee, unable to declare 'that I approve all the measures of Governor Eyre'.

Tennyson's more immediate response to the Jamaica Rebellion is reported by John Addington Symonds, a fellow dinner guest in December 1865. While Gladstone deplored 'the slaughter', Tennyson reiterated that 'We are too tender to savages, we are more tender to a black than ourselves', varying the repetitions with an occasional *obbligato* of 'Niggers are tigers, niggers are tigers'.[117] In Western poetry and art 'the tiger has consistently symbolized bloodthirsty cruelty'[118] and Tennyson's racist comments can also be interpreted as relating to temperament, akin to recurring references to 'The blind hysterics of the Celt' (*In Memoriam*, CIX, 16). However, whether 'traitors' (66) – choosing to reject the 'banner of England' – or 'tigers' (51), apparently turbulent by nature, the majority of Indian soldiers remain outside the symbolic garrison, defined despite Robin L. Inboden's comment as 'our myriad enemy' (35). Only the 'faithful and few' (70) suppress their perceived revolutionary tendencies to fight with the iconic 'English' (46) soldiers. Repeatedly defined as 'dark' (29, 33, 69, 70), the Indian soldiers are ultimately contrasted with 'the wholesome white faces' of 'Havelock's good fusiliers' (101), a discriminatory comparison which, like the uprising itself, reveals that the unity of the Empire is a fabrication or fantasy inseparable from Tennyson's imperial vision.

'To keep our English Empire whole!'

Tennyson's letter to the Eyre Defence Committee in October 1866 concluded that 'the outbreak of our Indian Mutiny remains as a warning to all but madmen against want of vigour and swift decisiveness'.[119] The final poems of empire to be discussed reveal the poet's increasing concern to preserve the unity of the Empire, with England as its exemplary centre. Tennyson was aware that imperial unity could be threatened by the 'little wars, military expeditions, rebellions [and] mutinies' that recurred throughout Victoria's reign and by questioning 'the price of empire'[120] which resulted from the uneasy socio-political condition of England in the 1870s. Demonstrations and fears of Fenianism had accompanied the 1867 Reform Act, the divisive Home Rule Movement began in 1870, and the onset of the Great Depression in 1873 brought agricultural and industrial decline, in contrast to the increasing industrial, military and imperial strength of Russia, newly unified Germany (1871) and, following the Civil War (1861–65), the recently United States. Challenges to expenditure on the Empire were countered by assertions of loyalty[121] and by the debate on imperial federation which continued throughout the 1870s and 1880s. In 1870 Tennyson observed that England's 'true policy lies in a close union with our colonies'[122] and when the Imperial Federation League was formed in July 1884 the poet and his son Hallam became members, clearly approving the League's specific aim – 'the political federation of the British Empire' into a single entity, with 'an Imperial Parliament responsible for common foreign and defence policy'.[123]

Tennyson's indignant response to suggestions of separatism is recorded in letters and verse. A leader in *The Times* of 30 October 1872 commenting on the San Juan Island boundary dispute between the United States and 'Canada', recently named by the British North America Act of 1867, concluded that 'Canadians' should 'look after your own business yourselves; . . . Take up your freedom; your days of apprenticeship are over.'[124] Tennyson interpreted this as advocating secession on grounds of cost, a view he rejected as 'Villa[i]nous'[125] and, in the epilogue to *Idylls of the King*, contrasts with the exemplary loyalty of Queen Victoria:

> And that true North, whereof we lately heard
> A strain to shame us 'keep you to yourselves;
> So loyal is too costly! friends – your love
> Is but a burthen: loose the bond, and go.'
> Is this the tone of empire? here the faith
> That made us rulers?

> (14–19)

'To the Queen' (1873) demonstrates the Laureate's increasingly intense and inseparable allegiance to Victoria and the Empire. The early ambivalence of 'Hail Briton!' (1831–33) is no longer apparent and Tennyson strongly defends the Empire:

> . . . The loyal to their crown
> Are loyal to their own far sons, who love
> Our ocean-empire with her boundless homes
> For ever-broadening England, and her throne
> In our vast Orient,

> (27–31)

The image of 'ever-broadening England' encapsulates Tennyson's vision of the Empire. By 1873 Tennyson hoped to 'live to see England and her Colonies absolutely one, with as complete a reciprocity of the free gifts of God, as there is between one county and another in the mother-country'.[126] The image also foreshadows the views of J.R. Seeley – 'the founding father of British imperial history'[127] – who in 1883 published his widely read lecture series as *The Expansion of England* and similarly regarded the colonies as 'our own blood, a mere extension of the English nationality into new lands'.[128] Seeley's vision, which was intended to challenge insular thinking and encourage an imperial frame of mind, both influenced and epitomized 'the moment of high imperialism', which in Catherine Hall's view began in 'the late nineteenth century'.[129] Patrick Brantlinger, by contrast, argues that 'a militantly expansionist New Imperialism' began developing in 1870 and involved Germany, Belgium and the United States, with Russia and France representing 'an older, more continuous threat to Britain's imperial hegemony'.[130]

The threat to British imperial unity intensified during the 1870s and 1880s and poems of this period reflect both Tennyson's vision and his anxiety. In 'Hands All Round' (1882) and 'Opening of the Indian and Colonial Exhibition by the Queen' (1886) Tennyson reworks two of the 'National Songs for Englishmen', written during the early 1850s, into ballads respectively celebrating a royal birthday and an imperial exhibition. 'Hands All Round' (1882), with music by Emily Tennyson, was published in March 1882 for Victoria's birthday, the traditional occasion for a court ode. The 1882 poem recasts 'Hands All Round' (1852), transforming a bellicose attack on Louis Napoleon into a patriotic drinking song in praise of 'the great name of England' (12, 23, 36). In three regularly rhyming stanzas the poet pledges in turn 'our Queen' (1), 'England' (2) – symbolized by 'freedom's oak' (5) and linked in refrain with 'Freedom' (11, 35) and 'all her glorious empire' (24) – and:

> . . . all the loyal hearts who long
> To keep our English Empire whole!
>
> (13–14)

However, imperial unity is subverted by the allusion to 'Canada' (19), the recurring wish to confound 'the traitor's hope' (10, 22, 34) and the discriminatory pledge to the Empire's peoples. The poet drinks first to 'all our noble sons, the strong | New England of the Southern Pole!' (15–16), then to 'those dark millions of her realm!' (18); the pronominal opposition – 'our' and those' – betrays an innate racism which segregates its subjects according to skin colour and suggests the superiority of 'our sons' by the attribution of nobility. The final pledge, reminding 'all our statesmen' (25) to look beyond 'borough' and 'shire' (28) to the empire, is undermined by a prayer which implies the existence of 'fears':

> We sailed wherever ship could sail,
> We founded many a mighty state;
> Pray God our greatness may not fail
> Through craven fears of being great.

> (29–32)

Anxiety for the family of empire underlies 'Opening of the Indian and Colonial Exhibition by the Queen' (1886). Recast from 'Britons, Guard Your Own' (1852), 'Opening' was set to music by Sir Arthur Sullivan, sung at the opening ceremony in London on 4 May 1886 and published in *The Times* the following day. Appropriately for a laureate poem on a public occasion (the subtitle is 'Written at the Request of the Prince of Wales') Tennyson refers throughout to 'Britain' and 'British'. Four stanzas of rhyming couplets, with frequent alliteration, suggest the control urged in the refrain – 'Britons, hold your own!' Welcoming 'Sons and brothers' (3) and their 'Gifts' (9), the poet wishes 'the son' also to exhibit the 'strength and constancy' that 'made your fathers great | In our ancient island State' (12–16), whose 'flag . . . | Glorying between sea and sky' (17–18) not only symbolizes the trading relationship between metropole and colony but also 'Makes the might of Britain known' (19). However, past paternal vigour is immediately countered by the acknowledgement that 'Britain failed' (22). In 1872, revising a poem written between 1832 and 1834, Tennyson had turned the loss of American colonies into a triumph of Englishness – the strong sons' independent spirit 'sprang from English blood' ('England and America in 1782', 4, 10). For the poet in 1886, urgently aware of America's growing strength, the loss is a national failure and 'our fathers' sin' (24). Tennyson's closing plea for future family unity is underlined by imagery implying that for colonies to be subsumed under 'the banner of England' requires considerable force:

> Sons, be welded each and all,
> Into one imperial whole,
> One with Britain, heart and soul!
> One life, one flag, one fleet, one Throne!

> (36–9)

'All new-old revolutions of Empire . . . what is all of it worth?'

Tennyson's concern with past failure and future conduct had intensified in 'Columbus' (1880) and 'Vastness' (1885). 'Columbus' draws
on Washington Irving's *Life and Voyages of Christopher Columbus*
(1828), Tennyson's source for 'Anacaona' (1830) completed soon after
Catholic Emancipation was granted in Britain. 'Columbus' was written in the context of anti-Catholic feeling accompanying the Home
Rule movement of the 1870s and the Vatican Council's declaration
of papal infallibility on 18 July 1870 – satirized by Tennyson in
'The Christ of Ammergau' (1870): 'They made the old Pope God – |
Which God, if He will, may pardon' (1–2) – and the poet's recurring anti-Catholicism, implied in 'Anacaona', is bitterly articulated
in 'Columbus'. Although written to 'commemorate the discovery of
America in verse',[131] the blank verse dramatic monologue is not a celebration but a denunciation of the death and destruction caused by
the Catholic Spanish Empire. Dishonoured and imprisoned – 'handled
worse than had I been a Moor' (106) – Columbus recalls long years in
the service of:

> Spain once the most chivalric race on earth,
> Spain then the mightiest, wealthiest realm on earth,
> So made by me.

> (200–2)

The explorer, now in chains, had 'unchained' (211) the Atlantic and
his discoveries 'Gave glory and more empire to the kings | Of Spain
than all their battles!' (22–3). The linguistic colonialism of his first
voyage foreshadows Spanish imperial subjugation – 'Guanahani! but
I changed the name; | San Salvador I called it' (74–5) – and Columbus
acknowledges:

> . . . what a door for scoundrel scum
> I opened to the West, through which the lust,
> Villany [*sic*], violence, avarice, of your Spain
> Poured in on all those happy naked isles –
> Their kindly native princes slain or slaved,
> Their wives and children Spanish concubines,
> Their innocent hospitalities quenched in blood,

> . . . And I myself, myself not blameless, I
> Could sometimes wish I had never led the way.
>
> (166–82)

Ultimately, however, Columbus is 'loyal' (223) to the Spanish king and not wholly repentant. Although old and 'wrenched with pains', he is 'ready to sail forth on one last voyage' and a 'last crusade' to 'save the Holy Sepulchre from thrall' (231–6).

'Columbus' embodies the tyranny of imperial Spain, contrasting with Tennyson's vision of 'mother Britain' and its beneficent role to teach '[other] peoples right' (1833–34, 12). 'Vastness' mirrors the poet's concern at the moral decline of contemporary London, exemplary centre of the British Empire. Cecily Devereux argues that Tennyson's manuscript note – 'What matters anything in this world without full faith in the Immortality of the Soul and of Love?'[132] – obscures the 'considerable cultural specificity' of 'Vastness', published in *Macmillan's Magazine* in November 1885 during the trial of W.T. Stead, editor of the *Pall Mall Gazette*.[133] Stead was prosecuted for publishing in July 1885 'The Maiden Tribute of Modern Babylon', a series of articles on child prostitution in London, which he argued was a class issue, and for 'purchasing' a thirteen-year-old girl with her mother's consent. Stead's intention was to draw attention to the scandal of 'white slavery' and to the Criminal Law Amendment Bill, stalled in Parliament, which proposed to raise the age of female consent from thirteen to sixteen and provide greater protection for young girls. 'The Maiden Tribute' became an Empire-wide *cause célèbre*, 'Vastness' was widely circulated and admired, with the contemporary allusions recognized, and – as editor and poet intended – the articles and poem exposed the corruption that jeopardized the Empire's 'civilizing mission'. In April 1885 Tennyson had responded to Stead's alarmist articles on the navy by publishing 'The Fleet (On Its Reported Insufficiency)' and the anxiously compressed imagery of 'Vastness' implies that Tennyson shared Stead's sense of what he defined as 'the Imperialism of responsibility' rather than 'Jingoism'.[134] An immediate and influential response to 'The Maiden Tribute' was Charles Haddon Spurgeon's sermon, also circulated throughout the Empire, warning 'how justice has dealt with empire after empire, when they become corrupt'.[135] As Tennyson observes:

> Many a hearth upon our dark globe sighs after many
>   a vanished face,

> Many a planet by many a sun may roll with the dust
>   of a vanished race.

(1–2)

At the heart of 'Vastness', as the manuscript note implies, are the lines on 'Love', Tennyson's view of the idealized Victorian family – and imperial – relationship of mother and children:

> Love for the maiden, crowned with marriage,
>   no regrets for aught that has been,
> Household happiness, gracious children,
>   debtless competence, golden mean;

(23–4)

This central vision is framed by stanzas whose contradictory images negate the poet's English ideals. In 'Vastness', the prized English attribute of 'Freedom' allows the English gentleman and patriot-statesman to abuse young working-class girls, with the thirteen-year-old 'Maiden Tribute' of Stead's title exemplifying the corruption that threatens 'ever-broadening England':

> Innocence seethed in her mother's milk, and Charity
>   setting the martyr aflame;
> Thraldom who walks with the banner of Freedom,
>   and recks not to ruin a realm in her name.

(9–10)

Family, national and imperial unity is threatened by 'National hatreds of whole generations, and pigmy spites of the village spire' (25) and the imperial connection is made explicit in Tennyson's anxious question:

> Spring and Summer and Autumn and Winter,
>   and all these old revolutions of earth;
> All new-old revolutions of Empire – change of the tide –
>   what is all of it worth?

(29–30)

Why continue with his poetry's recurring themes – 'politics' (3), 'valour in battle, glorious annals of army and fleet' (7) – or the empire's 'Trade flying over a thousand seas' (13) if 'All that is noblest' continues to be negated by 'all that is basest' (32) and ultimately we become 'the dust of a vanished race' (2). But in the closing line, which echoes the manuscript note, Tennyson finds consolation in the memory of Arthur Hallam:

> Peace, let it be! for I loved him, and love him for ever:
> the dead are not dead but alive.

> (36)

'From out the sunset poured an alien race'

'Vastness' achieves a sense of resolution in the memory of human love. In 'Akbar's Dream', resolution is attained by the British restoration of Akbar's 'sacred fane' (167). Written in 1891–92 and published in 1892, 'Akbar's Dream' is one of Tennyson's final poems: he died in October 1892 at the age of eighty-three. As with 'The Defence of Lucknow' the subject was suggested by Benjamin Jowett, who had long wanted Tennyson to 'write on . . . the idea that "All religions are one"'[136] and sent the poet 'books relating to Akbar'.[137] 'Akbar's Dream' is a blank verse dramatic monologue, comprehensively annotated by Tennyson. Paul Stevens and Rahul Sapra point out that 'the poem is so carefully researched that its extensive notes constitute an integral part of its overall design as a political speech act'.[138] The Moghul Emperor Akbar (1542–1605) relates his creed of religious toleration, creation of a unifying 'syncretic "Divine Faith" (*Din-e-Elahi*)'[139] and prophetic vision to his minister, friend and counsellor, Abul Fazl:

> I let men worship as they will, I reap
> No revenue from the field of unbelief.
> I cull from every faith and race the best
> And bravest soul for counsellor and friend.

> (63–6)

Aware that religious 'forms | Are needful', Akbar believes 'the hand that rules' should – like an English monarch or statesman – 'With politic care, with utter gentleness, | Mould them for all his people' (119–22). With imagery that carries echoes of empire violence, Akbar uses his 'power':

> . . . to fuse
> My myriads into union under one;
> To hunt the tiger of oppression out

>   From office; and to spread the Divine Faith
>   Like calming oil on all their stormy creeds.
>
>   (148–52)

But Akbar is troubled by 'The shadow of a dream' (5):

>   That stone by stone I reared a sacred fane,
>   A temple, neither Pagod, Mosque, nor Church,
>   But loftier, simpler, always open-doored
>   To every breath from heaven, and Truth and Peace
>   And Love and Justice came and dwelt therein.
>
>   (167–71)

The structure – symbol of the Moghul Empire – is destroyed by Akbar's 'wild and wayward' son 'Saleem, mine heir' (162–3)[140] and violent religious fundamentalism returns. Akbar is an historic figure, but his 'fane' is Tennyson's creation and in the final restorative vision:

>   From out the sunset poured an alien race,
>   Who fitted stone to stone again, and Truth,
>   Peace, Love and Justice came and dwelt therein,
>   Nor in the field without were seen or heard
>   Fires of Súttee, nor wail of baby-wife,
>   Or Indian widow.
>
>   (182–7)

   With the rebuilding of Akbar's 'fane', the Moghul Empire is subsumed under the 'banner of England'. Although Tennyson's extensive annotations convey his admiration for Akbar's 'new eclectic religion' and legislation 'remarkable for vigour, justice, and humanity',[141] in 'Akbar's Dream' Christianity and the British Empire prevail. Made aware of the Biblical injunction to 'Love' and '"bless" | . . . even "your persecutors"' Akbar finds:

>   The cloud was rifted by a purer gleam
>   Than glances from the sun of our Islâm.
>
>   (73–6)

This moment of enlightenment exemplifies Tennyson's belief that 'the highest good of Akbar's code of morals was . . . quite within the Christian ideal'.[142] For the Laureate's readers in post-Darwinian England, with religious certainties challenged and aware of other belief systems, Akbar's 'Divine Faith' (151) would appear reassuringly Anglican and reflect the ageing poet's personal spiritual concerns.[143] By reconstructing and incorporating the symbolic fane into the Christian family of the British Empire – a beneficent contrast to recurring echoes of empire violence – Tennyson promises the lasting unity that Akbar failed to achieve.

The restorative vision of 'Akbar's Dream' – Tennyson's final poem of empire – is both Orientalist and imperialist. It exemplifies the West's 'power political'[144] over India and privileges the British Empire's history, beliefs and values over those of the Moghul Empire. Tennyson's view of the ruined walls of Akbar's 'fane' is very different from his ambivalent attitude towards 'the ruined wall | Of royal Delhi', linked with 'an ermined pall | Of Empire' in 'Hail Briton!' (1831–33, 10–12) written sixty years earlier. Laureate Tennyson has come to occupy an 'imperial position in Poetry'[145] as he both supports and exhorts a vision of 'ever-broadening England'. However, as demonstrated by the poems examined in this chapter, this altered viewpoint does not represent the smoothly untroubled linear progression that critics such as Patrick Brantlinger suggest.[146] Tennyson's attitude to 'our English Empire' ('Hands All Round', 1882, 14) is both complex and conflicted (as Lynne O'Brien and Robin L. Inboden respectively argue),[147] inseparable from the poet's view of women and the family, the monarchy, masculine courage and English freedom, and from the changing historical context in which the poems were written. The poems discussed incorporate the imaginative imperialism of 'Fatima' (1832), the unquestioning assumption of 'O mother Britain's altruistic and beneficent role (1833–34), the realization in 'Vastness' (1885) that London is no longer the Empire's morally exemplary centre, and in 1892 Tennyson's recognition – in prose, but not in verse – of Moghul history. Ultimately, therefore, and to recast Richard A. Sylvia's critical comment, the poems of empire reveal that Tennyson 'was willing to question' but not to 'condemn the Victorian status quo he had come to represent'.[148]

Conclusion: Fabricating Englishness

The nineteenth century's preoccupation with the meaning of Englishness began with the origin of the term in 1804. By 1884, the third and final recorded nineteenth-century use of the term cited in the *Oxford English Dictionary* reveals a rich set of established meanings and ideologies. In the intervening decades – surveyed in this Conclusion – an ideology of Englishness had been established which was both reflected in and shaped by cultural forms and emerging myths in general and Tennyson's poetry in particular. Historians and critics who continue to debate the nature and history of Englishness, past and present, discern in the nineteenth century defining 'moment[s] of Englishness'[1] when national identity was shaped by crisis or change. The Reform Acts of 1832, 1867 and 1884 defined inclusion and exclusion for the nation. The turbulent period of the First Reform Act was a particular defining moment for England – and for Tennyson. Movements for reform and the abolition of slavery led to increasing interest in national character and awareness of the Empire's Others. Tennyson's first independent volumes – *Poems, Chiefly Lyrical* (1830) and *Poems* (1832) – were published and reviewed by periodical critics. Concerned for the unifying and 'sympathetic' nature of poetry, and for the poetic succession, reviewers attempted to shape Tennyson's language and define his national role.

Nineteenth-century Englishness was gendered. The 1832 Reform Act formally defined the English political citizen as masculine. Developing interest in national character was also defined in terms of gender. Sarah Stickney Ellis, for example, directed the social duties and domestic habits of English women to form the moral centre of the English home as a microcosm of society. Contrasting attributes of manliness differed depending on class and religion and became inseparable from the idea of the classically educated English gentleman and the development of 'muscular Christianity' associated with Thomas Hughes and Charles Kingsley. Tennyson's poetry mirrored, confirmed and at times subverted the gendered nature of national identity. Morality and manliness remained defining characteristics of Tennyson's ideal Englishmen throughout his career. The early domestic idyl/ls define daughters by their father's profession. Under English law, a married woman's legal existence was subsumed into that of her husband, and the Victorian wife – like the medieval 'Godiva' – was subject to 'her lord' (1842, 16, 78). Victorian domestic ideology, and the related fear of the 'fallen' woman, became encapsulated in the temples and floral imagery of John Ruskin's *Of Queens' Gardens* (1864), published as contemporary legislation began to change women's status within marriage and, for many, appeared to alter English society's moral order.

Tennyson's Arthurian poems reveal that emerging gendered moralities were mythologized and both qualified and supported by the revived interest in medievalism. 'The Lady of Shalott' (1832, revised 1842) and 'Godiva' (1842) portray the poet's anguish – a masculine figure working in a feminine genre – as he enters, and re-enters, the public world. In 1850 Tennyson became Poet Laureate, a defining moment for English poetry. The Crimean War poems (1854 and 1882) written as Laureate idealize the 'Godlike' Englishmen – latter-day Sir Galahads – who fight and die for England. *Idylls of the King*, written and published from the 1830s to the 1880s, reflect the decades in which they were written. The 'prone' figure of Guinevere (*Guinevere*, 1859, 411) symbolizes Victorian wives' subservient position, the failure of the Queen's moral role and thus – for Arthur – the failure of his 'model for the mighty world' (462).

Englishness was redefined with the accession of 'Victoria, Queen of England' in 1837. Domestic ideology intensified with royal marriage and motherhood. Tennyson's increasing and unqualified admiration for Victoria as 'Mother, Wife, and Queen' ('To the Queen', 1851, 28) – and his often unsuccessful attempts to attribute Victoria and Albert's chivalric virtues to their descendants – are mirrored in the poems of monarchy written throughout her reign. The transformation in poetic form and tone between 'The Queen of the Isles' (1837), a rapidly written popular ballad to welcome the accession, and the consciously classical 'Ode' to celebrate the 'Jubilee' (1887), exemplifies the linear progression of Tennyson's allegiance to the monarchy. The transformation both mirrors and enhances the public veneration of monarchy which increased during Victoria's long reign, but does not acknowledge the continuing co-existence of radical and republican sentiment.

Landscape became an inseparable element of nineteenth-century Englishness. Rural England was increasingly idealized in response to the changes wrought on the country and its predominantly rural society by the Industrial Revolution. The landscape was transformed by canals, roads, railways and expanding industrial towns. Rural England recovered from 'Swing' riots and the Hungry Forties to endure the Great Depression of the late nineteenth century. Accordingly, poets turned to an idealized pre-industrial past to create an alternative 'land of lost content', more imaginary than real. The local rural scene came to represent England as a whole, transformed into 'portable icons'[2] of Englishness for those leaving the country for town or empire. Tennyson's poetry reveals an enduring love of English nature and landscape. Closely observed elements of the 'language of Englishness'[3] unify *Idylls of the King*. He turned to the rural English scene for the settings of many poems published in 1842. The idyllic setting of 'The Gardener's Daughter' (1842) represents in microcosm Tennyson's ideally ordered world. However, poetic imagery suggests a qualified commitment to the developing ideology of rural England. The 'English Idyls' betray the unstable conditions in which they were written, and the Edenic landscape essential to create 'The Poet's Song' conceals a serpent (10).

Nineteenth-century ideas of Englishness were increasingly shaped by the imperial project and related questions of race. Movements for abolition and reform, and awareness of the expanding Empire, defined the English in opposition to the Other. The Act abolishing slavery was passed in 1833 as one of the earliest actions of the reformed Parliament, and Tennyson's 'O Mother Britain' (written 1833–34) echoes the self-congratulatory tone of the contemporary press. However, the domesticating metaphor of the Empire as family, which conferred moral authority on the parent and assumed the obedience of dependent colonial children, was shaken by mid-nineteenth-century uprisings in India (1857–59) and Jamaica (1865). As historians observe, 'nations and national identities are not only gendered – they are also raced'.[4] During the 1840s and 1850s publications such as Robert Knox's *The Races of Men* (1850) transformed the rapid growth of Anglo-Saxonism into a racist doctrine. Tennyson's recurring hostility to Spain's imperial project was shaped by aversion to Catholicism and the Celtic temperament. His attitude to 'our English Empire' ('Hands All Round [1882]', 14) changed from the ambivalence of the early political poems to resounding defence of 'ever-broadening England' as the Great Depression led many to question the Empire's increasing cost. Tennyson's final empire poem, 'Akbar's Dream', was written and published only months before his death in 1892. Although the poet's extensive annotations convey his appreciation of Akbar's tolerance and humanity, with the reconstruction of the symbolic 'fane' Christianity and the Raj finally prevail. Ultimately, therefore, Laureate Tennyson attained an 'imperial position in Poetry'[5] in both senses of the term.

Examination of Tennyson's 'domestic poetry' – his portrayals of English nature and landscape, monarchy, medievalism and the 'English Empire' – written throughout his career and in their changing nineteenth-century context, confirms that many representations of England and the English were more idealized than real, hence fabrications. However, Tennyson's representations of Englishness are complex and often conflicting fabrications, betraying ideological and personal faultlines. The idyllic, microcosmic garden of Rose, 'The Gardener's Daughter' is neither 'wholly in the busy world, nor quite | Beyond it' (1842, 33–4). The Jubilee Ode's 'one full voice of allegiance' (1887, 22) silences the radicals and republicans whose anti-monarchism persisted throughout Victoria's reign. Camelot proves an inappropriate model for the nineteenth-century world. The Laureate's call for the family of Empire to be 'welded each and all, | Into one imperial whole' ('Opening of the Indian and Colonial Exhibition', 1886, 36–7) implies awareness that imperial unity requires force.

Englishness past and present is of continuing interest to historians and critics, and Tennyson's 'domestic poetry' offers a unique insight into emergent ideas of Englishness in the nineteenth century. His life and work spanned much of the nineteenth century. As Poet Laureate for over forty years he was the authoritative public voice of English poetry, and one of the 'thinking men of England' ('Suggested by Reading', 1852, 12). In addition, he established an unparalleled relationship with the monarchy. As a popular and much-published poet, Tennyson both reflected and shaped changing connotations of Englishness. He responded to the changing English countryside, the expanding 'English Empire', and the Victorian Medieval Revival which allowed him to explore contemporary concern with gender roles, relationships and moral conduct. He fulfilled the early critics' requirement for poets to represent 'the age': despite their medieval guise, Tennyson's Arthurian protagonists are nineteenth-century English men and women. This study confirms Tennyson's enduring concern with England and the English; a particular defining moment of nineteenth-century Englishness was the birth of Alfred Tennyson in August 1809.

Notes

Introduction: The Enigma of Englishness

1 Unsigned review, '*Poems, Chiefly Lyrical*', *Atlas*, 27 June 1830, p. 411.
2 [Richard Monckton Milnes], '*Timbuctoo*', *Athenaeum*, 22 July 1829, p. 456. (Keats, Shelley and Byron had died in 1821, 1822 and 1824.)
3 [William Johnson Fox], '*Poems, Chiefly Lyrical*', *Westminster Review*, 14 (1831), 210–24 (p. 224).
4 Unsigned review, '*Poems by Two Brothers*', *Gentleman's Magazine*, 97 (1827), p. 609.
5 'Hands All Round [1882]', 14.
6 'Suggested by Reading' (1852), 12.
7 'Suggested by Reading' (1852), 5.
8 T.S. Eliot, 'In Memoriam', *Essays Ancient and Modern* (London: Faber and Faber, 1936), pp. 175–90 (p. 189).
9 Richard A. Sylvia, 'Reading Tennyson's *Ballads and Other Poems* in Context', *Journal of the Midwest Modern Language Association*, 23 (1990), 27–44 (p. 27).
10 *Tennyson Among the Poets*, ed. Robert Douglas-Fairhurst and Seamus Perry (Oxford: Oxford University Press, 2009); John Batchelor, *Tennyson: To Strive, To Seek, To Find* (London: Chatto & Windus, 2012.)
11 Simon Jenkins, *A Short History of England* (London: Profile, 2011); Peter Ackroyd, *The History of England: Volume 1, Foundation* (London: Macmillan, 2011); Jeremy Paxman, *Empire: What Ruling the World Did to the British* (London: Viking, 2011); Roy Strong, *Visions of England* (London: Bodley Head, 2011).
12 Edward W. Said, *Orientalism: Western Conceptions of the Orient*, 4th edn (London: Penguin, 1995), p. 13.
13 Hallam Tennyson, *Alfred Lord Tennyson: A Memoir, By His Son*, 2 vols (London: Macmillan, 1897), II, p. 127. Hereafter *Memoir*, 1897.
14 In an unsigned review of *Poems* (1842) John Sterling described Tennyson as 'the most genial poet of English rural life that we know', *Quarterly Review*, 70 (1842), 385–416 (p. 416).
15 *Oxford English Dictionary Online*, http://dictionary.oed.com [accessed 28 April 2010].
16 *A Memoir of the Life and Writings of the late William Taylor of Norwich*, ed. J.W. Robberds, 2 vols (London: Murray, 1843), I, p. 512. Taylor also appears to coin the term 'Dutchness', II, p. 252.
17 *Oxford English Dictionary Online*, http://dictionary.oed.com [accessed 23 August 2010]. The historian Edwin Jones uses 'Englishry' throughout *The English Nation: The Great Myth*, 2nd edn (Stroud: Sutton, 2000), for example referring to Alfred the Great as 'a fine example of Englishry at its best' (p. 3).
18 'The Decencies', *New Monthly Magazine and Humorist*, 53 (1838), 118–24 (p. 118).

19 'The Grosvenor Exhibition (Third Notice)', *Athenaeum*, 19 January 1884, p. 93. Hereafter the term Englishness is not italicized unless it forms part of a book title.

20 Reviewing *Idylls of the King* in October 1859, Gladstone commented: 'Lofty examples in comprehensive forms is, without doubt, one of the great standing needs of our race', [W.E. Gladstone], '*Idylls of the King* [1859] and Earlier Works', *Quarterly Review*, 106 (1859), 454–85 (p. 465).

21 *The Letters of Alfred Lord Tennyson*, ed. Cecil Y. Lang and Edgar F. Shannon, Jr, 3 vols (Oxford: Clarendon Press, 1982–90), I, p. 270 ([20 December 1846]). Hereafter *AT Letters*.

22 Richard Chenevix Trench, *On the Study of Words*, 2nd edn (London: Parker, 1852); *English: Past and Present: Five Lectures* (London: Parker, 1855).

23 *Memoir*, 1897, II, p. 133, n. 1.

24 Edward Bulwer-Lytton, *England and the English*, 2nd edn, 2 vols (London: Bentley, 1833).

25 [Nassau Senior], 'France, America, and Britain', *Edinburgh Review*, 75 (1842), 1–48 (p. 17).

26 Washington Irving, *The Sketch Book of Geoffrey Crayon, Gent.* (New York: Heritage, 1939).

27 Ralph Waldo Emerson, *English Traits* (London: Routledge, 1856); Emerson's observations were made during his first visit to England in 1833.

28 Emerson, p. 309.

29 *New Monthly Magazine and Humorist*, 53 (1838), 118–24 (p. 118).

30 Sarah Stickney Ellis, *The Women of England: Their Social Duties, and Domestic Habits* (London: Fisher, 1839), p. 10.

31 Walter Bagehot, *The English Constitution*, ed. Miles Taylor (New York: Oxford University Press, 2001), p. 35.

32 Norman Davies, *The Isles: A History*, 2nd edn (Basingstoke: Macmillan – now Palgrave Macmillan, 2000), p. 863. George Orwell, 'The Lion and the Unicorn: Socialism and the English Genius' (1941) and 'The English People' (1947).

33 Peter Mandler, *The English National Character: The History of an Idea from Edmund Burke to Tony Blair* (London: Yale University Press, 2006), p. 4.

34 Robert Colls, *Identity of England* (Oxford: Oxford University Press, 2002), p. 8.

35 Krishan Kumar, *The Making of English National Identity* (Cambridge: Cambridge University Press, 2003), pp. x–xi.

36 Kumar, p. xii.

37 Catherine Hall, 'The Rule of Difference: Gender, Class and Empire in the Making of the 1832 Reform Act', in *Gendered Nations: Nationalisms and Gender Order in the Long Nineteenth Century*, ed. Ida Blom, Karen Hagemann and Catherine Hall (Oxford: Berg, 2000), pp. 107–35 (p. 107).

38 Jane Rendall traces the long history of the struggle for the parliamentary vote for all women, 'The citizenship of women and the Reform Act of 1867', in *Defining the Victorian Nation: Class, Race, Gender and the Reform Act of 1867*, ed. Catherine Hall, Keith McClelland and Jane Rendall (Cambridge: Cambridge University Press, 2000), pp. 119–78 (p. 119).

39 The phrase 'Victoria, Queen of England' recurs in the refrain of the street ballad 'Queen Victoria', reproduced in John Lucas, 'Love of England: The Victorians and Patriotism', *Browning Society Notes*, 17 (1987–88), 63–76 (fig. 3).

40 Lucas, 1987–88, p. 64.
41 Richard Williams, *The Contentious Crown: Public Discussion of the British Monarchy in the Reign of Queen Victoria* (Aldershot: Ashgate, 1997).
42 Kumar, pp. xi–xii.
43 'To the Queen' (1873), 30–1.
44 *Spectator*, 4 June 1842, cited in Edgar F. Shannon, Jr, *Tennyson and the Reviewers* (Cambridge, MA: Harvard University Press, 1952), p. 60.
45 'Ode on the Death of the Duke of Wellington' (1852), IX, 266.
46 *Guinevere* (1859), 462.
47 Francis Palgrave cited in Hallam Tennyson, *Alfred Lord Tennyson: A Memoir, By His Son* (London: Macmillan, 1899), p. 837.

1 'A Poet in the Truest and Highest Sense': The Early Poems and their Reception

1 [John Forster], *'Poems'*, *True Sun*, 19 January 1833, p. 3.
2 Isobel Armstrong, *Victorian Scrutinies: Reviews of Poetry 1830–1870* (London: Athlone Press, 1972), p. 14.
3 *The Letters of Alfred Lord Tennyson*, ed. Cecil Y. Lang and Edgar F. Shannon, Jr, 3 vols (Oxford: Clarendon Press, 1982–90), I, p. 13 ([March? 1827]). Hereafter *AT Letters*.
4 June Steffensen Hagen, *Tennyson and his Publishers* (London: Macmillan, 1979), p. 2.
5 Hallam Tennyson, *Alfred Lord Tennyson: A Memoir, By His Son*, 2 vols (London: Macmillan, 1897), I, p. 7.
6 *Lincoln, Rutland, and Stamford Mercury* 20 April 1827 and *Sunday Mercury* 22 April 1827, cited in Edgar F. Shannon, Jr, *Tennyson and the Reviewers* (Cambridge, MA: Harvard University Press, 1952), p. 183, n. 1 and n. 2; *Journal de littérature étrangère*, 7 (1827); Marjorie Bowden, *Tennyson in France* (Manchester: Manchester University Press, 1930), p. 8.
7 The 2005 equivalent of £20 is £989.00 *The National Archives Currency Converter*, http://www.nationalarchives.gov.uk/currency [accessed 1 June 2012].
8 Robert Bernard Martin, for example, refers to 'two perfunctory notices', *Tennyson: The Unquiet Heart*, 2nd edn (London: Faber and Faber, 1983), p. 45.
9 Unsigned review, *'Poems by Two Brothers'*, *Literary Chronicle and Weekly Review*, 19 May 1827, p. 308.
10 Kathy Chater and Simon Fowler, 'A Storehouse of Knowledge', *Ancestors*, September 2005, p. 58.
11 John Nichols edited the *Magazine* from 1792 until his death in 1826, when his son, John Bowyer Nichols, became part editor. His son, in turn, John Gough Nichols, was assistant editor, then editor, between 1828 and 1856. Walter Graham, *English Literary Periodicals* (New York: Nelson, 1930), p. 158.
12 Richard D. Altick, *The English Common Reader*, 2nd edn (Columbus: Ohio State University Press, 1968), p. 319.
13 Altick, pp. 47 and 392.
14 Armstrong, 1972, p. 6. Italics in the original.
15 Unsigned review, *'Poems by Two Brothers'*, *Gentleman's Magazine*, 97 (1827), p. 609.

16 Charles Tennyson, *Alfred Tennyson* (London: Macmillan, 1949), p. 50.
17 [Arthur Henry Hallam], 'On Some of the Characteristics of Modern Poetry, and on the Lyrical Poems of Alfred Tennyson', in Armstrong, 1972, pp. 84–101 (p. 89).
18 *AT Letters*, I, p. 7 (30 October [1825]).
19 *Memoir*, 1897, I, p. 22.
20 Charles Tennyson, 1949, p. 49.
21 Christopher Ricks, 'Two Early Poems by Tennyson', *Victorian Poetry*, 3 (1965), 55–7.
22 James Knowles, 'Aspects of Tennyson: A Personal Reminiscence', *Nineteenth Century*, 33 (1893), 164–88 (p. 173).
23 Charles Tennyson, 1949, p. 50.
24 Robin Gilmour, *The Victorian Period: The Intellectual and Cultural Context of English Literature 1830–1890* (London: Longman, 1993), p. 42.
25 Translation in *AT Letters*, I, p. 12, n. 5.
26 '"I have pass'd the Rubicon" and must stand or fall by the "cast of the die"'. Preface to *Hours of Idleness* (1806), in *Lord Byron: The Complete Poetical Works*, ed. Jerome J. McGann, 7 vols (Oxford: Clarendon Press, 1980–93), I (1983), 32.
27 *AT Letters*, I, p. 3 [1824?].
28 The poet's grandson (Charles Tennyson, 1949, p. 48) describes the effect on Tennyson of his father's deteriorating mental and physical health and increasing violence.
29 For example, 'Translation of the Famous Greek War Song' (undated), *Byron: Poetical Works*, ed. Frederick Page (London: Oxford University Press, 1970), pp. 60–1; 'Modern Greece, A Poem' (1817), *Felicia Hemans: Selected Poems, Letters, Reception Materials*, ed. Susan J. Wolfson (Princeton, NJ: Princeton University Press, 2000), pp. 34–69.
30 *Memoir*, 1897, I, p. 81. Later in the *Memoir*, the poet is quoted as referring to 'The passion of the past, the abiding in the transient, [which] was expressed in "Tears, idle Tears"', I, p. 253.
31 Peter Allen, *The Cambridge Apostles: The Early Years* (Cambridge: Cambridge University Press, 1978), pp. 11–13.
32 Martin, p. 52.
33 See also *AT Letters*, I, pp. 22–3 (18 April [1828]).
34 John Mitchell Kemble, cited in Allen, p. 8.
35 W.D. Paden, *Tennyson in Egypt: A Study of the Imagery in his Earlier Works* (Lawrence: University of Kansas Publications, 1942), p. 139, n. 158. Shannon omits *Classical Journal* and places *Prolusiones Academicae* 'later in the year', p. 2.
36 *AT Letters*, I, pp. 47–8 ([? January 1831]).
37 *Memoir*, 1897, I, p. 47.
38 *The Letters of Arthur Henry Hallam*, ed. Jack Kolb (Columbus: Ohio State University Press, 1981), p. 319 ([14 September 1829]). Hereafter *AHH Letters*.
39 Aidan Day, 'The Spirit of Fable: Arthur Hallam and Romantic Values in Tennyson's "Timbuctoo"', *Tennyson Research Bulletin*, 4 (1983), 59–71 (p. 60).
40 *The Writings of Arthur Hallam*, ed. T.H. Vail Motter (New York: Modern Language Association of America, 1943), p. 37.
41 *Memoir*, 1897, I, p. 46
42 Cited in Shannon, 1952, p. 2.

43 Charles Tennyson (pp. 91–2) attributes the review to Milnes rather than to the editor, John Sterling.

44 *Peacock's Four Ages of Poetry, Shelley's Defence of Poetry, Browning's Essay on Poetry*, ed. H.F.B. Brett-Smith (Oxford: Blackwell, 1921), p. viii; 'Essay on Milton', in *Essays, by Lord Macaulay: Reprinted from the Edinburgh Review, Complete Edition* (London: Routledge, 1887), pp. 1–30 (p. 3); [Thomas Carlyle], 'Signs of the Times', *Edinburgh Review*, 49 (1829), 439–59 (p. 446).

45 *English Verse 1830–1890*, ed. Bernard Richards, 5th edn (London: Longman, 1994), p. xviii.

46 [Richard Monckton Milnes], '*Timbuctoo*', *Athenaeum*, 22 July 1829, p. 456.

47 *Memoir*, 1897, I, pp. 45–6.

48 *Memoir*, 1897, II, p. 355.

49 Mary Louise Pratt, *Imperial Eyes: Travel Writing and Transculturation*, 2nd edn (New York: Routledge, 2008), p. 5.

50 Pratt, p. 201.

51 Pratt, pp. 204–5. Discussing later African explorations, Marion Shaw similarly refers to Stanley's 'outsider's unifying and portentous gaze', in 'Tennyson's Dark Continent', *Victorian Poetry*, 32 (1994), 157–69 (p. 157).

52 Hallman B. Bryant, 'The African Genesis of Tennyson's "Timbuctoo"', *Tennyson Research Bulletin*, 3 (1981), 196–202 (pp. 196–8).

53 Unsigned review, '*Journal d'un Voyage à Temboctou et à Jenné, dans l'Afrique Centrale, &c., 1824–1828*', *Quarterly Review*, 42 (1830), 450–75 (p. 452). The 2005 equivalent of £720,000 is approximately £35,632,800; *The National Archives Currency Converter*, http://www.nationalarchives.gov.uk/currency [accessed 1 June 2012].

54 *Quarterly Review*, 1830, p. 460. *The Narrative of Robert Adams* (London: Murray, 1816), which inspired Tahir Shah's novel *Timbuctoo* (July 2012), claims that Adams was an earlier, albeit involuntary, traveller to Timbuctoo. Between 1810 and 1815 Adams, an African-American seaman, was shipwrecked, sold into slavery, and eventually ransomed to the British consul. However, the *Narrative*'s most recent editor casts doubt on Adams's identity and claims, particularly 'where Timbuctoo is concerned'; Preface, *The Narrative of Robert Adams, A Barbary Captive: A Critical Edition*, ed. Charles Hansford Adams (Cambridge: Cambridge University Press, 2005), pp. ix–lvi (p. xiv).

55 Armstrong, 1972, p. 2.

56 *AT Letters*, I, p. 44 (18 June [1830]).

57 Shannon, 1952, p. 184, n. 13.

58 *AHH Letters*, p. 721 ([6 February] 1833). The 2005 equivalent of £11 is £544, http://www.nationalarchives.gov.uk/currency [accessed 1 June 2012].

59 *AHH Letters*, p. 365 ([20–30 June 1830]).

60 The 'Apostolic activity' is detailed in Shannon, 1952, pp. 10–12.

61 Royal A. Gettmann, *A Victorian Publisher: A Study of the Bentley Papers* (Cambridge: Cambridge University Press, 1960), pp. 9–12.

62 Contemporary press and public attitudes to the monarchy are discussed in Chapter 4.

63 Unsigned review, '*Poems, Chiefly Lyrical*', *Atlas*, 27 June 1830, p. 411. As Anna Barton explains, anonymity remained the rule for journalists and critics

writing for daily, weekly, monthly and quarterly newspapers and reviews until the late 1850s. *Tennyson's Name: Identity and Responsibility in the Poetry of Alfred Lord Tennyson* (Aldershot: Ashgate, 2008), p. 82.

64 Cited in Shannon, 1952, p. 4.
65 *The Oxford Companion to English Literature*, ed. Margaret Drabble (Oxford: Oxford University Press, 1985), p. 926.
66 Cited in Shannon, 1952, p. 4.
67 [William Johnson Fox], *'Poems, Chiefly Lyrical'*, *Westminster Review*, 14 (1831), 210–24.
68 Armstrong, 1972, p. 16.
69 Elizabeth Barrett Browning, *Aurora Leigh and Other Poems*, ed. Cora Kaplan, 5th edn (London: Women's Press, 1993), p. 201.
70 Armstrong, 1972, pp. 17–18.
71 *AHH Letters*, p. 396 (18 January [1831]).
72 Cited in Shannon, 1952, p. 6.
73 [Arthur Henry Hallam], 'On Some of the Characteristics of Modern Poetry', in Armstrong, 1972, pp. 84–101.
74 'Our Principles', *Englishman's Magazine*, 1 (1831), 1–4 (p. 1). Succeeding references in this paragraph are taken from pp. 1–3.
75 Victorian medievalism is discussed in Chapter 5.
76 *AHH Letters*, p. 467 (23 August [1831]).
77 Carol T. Christ, *Victorian and Modern Poetics* (Chicago: University of Chicago Press, 1984), p. 56.
78 *AHH Letters*, p. 467 (23 August [1831]).
79 In the early nineteenth century the ballad form had been popularized by Scott, described by Macaulay as 'the great restorer of our ballad poetry', W.W. Robson, 'Tennyson and Victorian Balladry', in *Tennyson: Seven Essays*, ed. Philip Collins (Basingstoke: Macmillan – now Palgrave Macmillan, 1992), pp. 160–82 (p. 166).
80 *Noctes Ambrosianae* was 'a series of more or less imaginary debates' between 'the Ettrick Shepherd' (James Hogg) and 'Christopher North' (John Wilson), who discussed politics, letters, and Scottish and British affairs. Karl Miller, 'Star of the Borders', *Guardian*, 9 August 2003, section G2, p. 4.
81 Cited in Shannon, 1952, p. 7.
82 Patricia Fara, *Newton: The Making of Genius* (New York: Columbia University Press, 2002), pp. 14–15.
83 [John Wilson], 'Tennyson's Poems', *Blackwood's Edinburgh Magazine*, 31 (1832), 721–41.
84 Elizabeth Longford, *Victoria R.I.*, 2nd edn (London: Weidenfeld & Nicolson, 1987), pp. 40–1.
85 The 'Cockney School of Poetry' was a term first used in *Blackwood's* in October 1817, when the editor John Lockhart and his associates began a series of sustained and virulent attacks on Leigh Hunt, Hazlitt and Keats, all Londoners 'of humble origin'. Drabble, p. 209.
86 Tennyson's recognition of the importance of the Lincolnshire landscape is a theme of Chapter 3.
87 With *Of Kings' Treasuries*, published as *Sesame and Lilies* in 1865.
88 *AT Letters*, I, pp. 109–10 ([26 April 1834]).
89 *AHH Letters*, p. 562 ([30 April–6 May 1832]).

90 Cited in Shannon, 1952, p. 9.
91 *AHH Letters*, p. 577, n. 2.

2 'Mr. Tennyson's Singular Genius': The Reception of *Poems* (1832)

1 *The Letters of Arthur Henry Hallam*, ed. Jack Kolb (Columbus: Ohio State University Press, 1981), p. 460 ([14 August 1831]). Hereafter *AHH Letters*.
2 *AHH Letters*, p. 539 (20 March 1832).
3 *The Letters of Alfred Lord Tennyson*, ed. Cecil Y. Lang and Edgar F. Shannon, Jr, 3 vols (Oxford: Clarendon Press, 1982–90), I, p. 73 (20 June 1832). Hereafter *AT Letters*.
4 *AHH Letters*, p. 646 (13 September 1832).
5 *AHH Letters*, p. 652 (24 September 1832).
6 *AT Letters*, I, p. 80 ([13 October 1832]).
7 *AHH Letters*, p. 688 ([20 November 1832]).
8 *AT Letters*, I, p. 84 ([20 November 1832]).
9 Tennyson had asked Moxon, 'don't let the printers squire me', *AT Letters*, I, p. 84 ([20 November 1832]).
10 June Steffensen Hagen, *Tennyson and his Publishers* (London: Macmillan, 1979), p. 37.
11 *AHH Letters*, p. 701 (12 December [1832]). Italics in the original.
12 Charles Tennyson, for example, comments that no reviewer 'treated the volume as being of any real importance'. *Alfred Tennyson* (London: Macmillan, 1949), p. 135.
13 John H. Fisher, *The Emergence of Standard English* (Lexington: University Press of Kentucky, 1996), pp. 9–14.
14 Samuel Johnson, *The Plan of a Dictionary of the English Language* (London: Knapton, 1747), p. 12.
15 John Walker, *Critical Pronouncing Dictionary and Expositor of the English Language* (London: Robinson, 1791), p. xiii. In 1570 John Hart had referred to 'London, where the flower of the English tongue is used', 'The Preface', *A Methode . . . to read English* (London: Denham, 1570), p. 4.
16 Cited in Lynda Mugglestone, 'The Rise of Received Pronunciation', in *A Companion to The History of the English Language*, ed. Haruko Momma and Michael Matto (Malden, MA: Blackwell, 2008), pp. 243–50 (p. 246).
17 Unsigned review, '*Poems*', *Athenaeum*, 1 December 1832, 770–2 (p. 770).
18 Arthur Hallam, 'The Influence of Italian upon English Literature', in *The Writings of Arthur Hallam*, ed. T.H. Vail Motter (New York: Modern Language Association of America, 1943), pp. 213–34 (pp. 214–15).
19 Richard Chenevix Trench, *English: Past and Present: Five Lectures* (London: Parker, 1855), p. 2.
20 Trench, 1855, p. 16.
21 Trench, 1855, pp. 27–8. In a footnote, Trench adds that he is quoting from Jacob Grimm, *Ueber den Ursprung der Sprache* (p. 135) published in Berlin in 1851.
22 Robert Browning, 'Clive', 1880, 9; *The Poetical Works of Robert Browning* (London: Oxford University Press, 1940), p. 603.

23 Gauri Viswanathan, 'Currying Favor: The Politics of British Educational and Cultural Policy in India, 1813–54', in *Dangerous Liaisons: Gender, Nation, and Postcolonial Perspectives*, ed. Anne McClintock, Aamir Mufti and Ella Shohat (Minneapolis: University of Minnesota Press, 1997), pp. 113–29 (pp. 114 and 119).

24 Trench, 1855, p. 21.

25 Hallam Tennyson, *Alfred Lord Tennyson: A Memoir, By His son*, 2 vols (London: Macmillan, 1897), II, p. 133, n. 1. Hereafter *Memoir*, 1897.

26 *Athenaeum*, 1 December 1832, p. 770.

27 *Athenaeum*, 1 December 1832, p. 772.

28 Cited in Edgar F. Shannon, Jr, *Tennyson and the Reviewers* (Cambridge, MA: Harvard University Press, 1952), pp. 14–15.

29 Cited in Shannon, 1952, p. 15.

30 [Robert Bell?], 'Poems', *Atlas*, 16 December 1832, p. 842.

31 Isobel Armstrong, *Victorian Scrutinies: Reviews of Poetry 1830–1870* (London: Athlone Press, 1972), p. 26.

32 Armstrong, 1972, p. 6.

33 Charles Tennyson, 1949, p. 50.

34 [John Forster], 'Poems', *True Sun*, 19 January 1833, p. 3.

35 *Gentleman's Magazine*, 97 (1827), p. 609.

36 Cited in Shannon, 1952, p. 16.

37 Cited in Shannon, 1952, p. 17.

38 Cited in Shannon, 1952, p. 17,

39 Coventry Patmore's sequence of narrative poems celebrating married love, *The Angel in the House* (1854–63), inspired by his first wife Emily, became immensely popular with the Victorian public. Ian Anstruther notes that 40,000 copies of the cheap 1887 edition were sold 'in the first fortnight'. *Coventry Patmore's Angel* (London: Haggerston, 1992), p. 98.

40 Catherine Hall, 'The Rule of Difference: Gender, Class and Empire in the Making of the 1832 Reform Act', in *Gendered Nations: Nationalisms and Gender Order in the Long Nineteenth Century*, ed. Ida Blom, Karen Hagemann and Catherine Hall (Oxford: Berg, 2000), pp. 107–35 (p. 107).

41 David Thomson, *England in the Nineteenth Century, 1815–1914*, 3rd edn, The Pelican History of England, 8 (London: Penguin, 1991), p. 74. See also Alan Sinfield, *Alfred Tennyson* (Oxford: Blackwell, 1986).

42 Edward Bulwer-Lytton, *England and the English*, 2nd edn, 2 vols (London: Bentley, 1833), I, p. 27.

43 Matthew Reynolds, *The Realms of Verse 1830–1870: English Poetry in a Time of Nation-Building* (Oxford: Oxford University Press, 2001), p. 211.

44 Bulwer-Lytton, 1833, I, p. 11.

45 'Of old sat Freedom on the heights', 'You ask me, why, though ill at ease' and 'Love thou thy land, with love far-brought', which were published in *Poems* (1842); 'I loving Freedom', of which lines 1–8 were printed in the *Memoir*, 1897 (I, p. 41); 'Hail Briton!', first printed in 1931.

46 *The Complete Poetical Works of Percy Bysshe Shelley*, ed. Thomas Hutchinson (London: Oxford University Press, 1952), pp. 338–45.

47 [William Johnson Fox], 'Poems', *Monthly Repository*, 73 (1833), 30–41.

48 Cited in Shannon, 1952, p. 19.

49 *AT Letters*, I, p. 109, n. 2 ([26 April 1834]).

50   Washington Irving, *The Sketch Book*, ed. T. Balston (London: Oxford University Press, 1912), p. 298. The *Sketch Book* was published in serial form in the US in 1818 and 1819 and in book form in England in 1820.
51   [John Wilson Croker], 'Poems', *Quarterly Review*, 49 (1833), 81–96.
52   *Memoir*, 1897, I, p. 94.
53   Myron F. Brightfield, *John Wilson Croker* (Berkeley, CA: University of California Press, 1940), p. 350.
54   *AHH Letters*, p. 245 (8 November [1828]).
55   Shannon, 1952, pp. 22–3.
56   Effingham Wilson, 'The Moral and Political Evils of the Taxes on Knowledge . . . the continuance of Stamp Duty on Newspapers, the Duties on Advertisements, and on Printing-Paper', *Westminster Review*, 15 (1831), 238–67.
57   *AHH Letters*, p. 449 ([27 July 1831]).
58   Cited in Shannon, 1952, p. 24. Succeeding references to periodicals in this paragraph are taken from Shannon, pp. 24–6.
59   Brightfield, p. 350.
60   Brightfield, p. 350.
61   *AHH Letters*, p. 754 ([May 1833]).
62   *AHH Letters*, p. 755, n. 1.
63   Harold G. Merriam, *Edward Moxon: Publisher of Poets* (New York: Columbia University Press, 1939), p. 78.
64   Harold Nicolson, *Tennyson: Aspects of his Life, Character and Poetry* (London: Constable, 1923), p. 111.
65   Charles Tennyson, 1949, p. 137.
66   *AT Letters*, I, p. 130 ([Early March 1835]).
67   Cited in Shannon, 1952, p. 20.
68   'Our Weekly Gossip on Literature and Art', *Athenaeum*, 13 April 1833, p. 234.
69   *AHH Letters*, p. 754 ([May 1833]).
70   Cited in Shannon, 1952, p. 20
71   [John Stuart Mill], 'Poems, Chiefly Lyrical [1830], Poems [1833]', in *Tennyson: The Critical Heritage*, ed. John D. Jump (London: Routledge & Kegan Paul, 1967), pp. 84–97.
72   Armstrong, 1972, p. 23.
73   Christopher Ricks points out that Leigh Hunt similarly held '"National Song" to be naught'. The poems were never reprinted; 'National Song' was adapted for Act II of *The Foresters*, completed in 1881 and published in 1892. Headnote to 'National Song', *The Poems of Tennyson*, ed. Christopher Ricks, 2nd edn, 3 vols (London: Longman, 1987), I, p. 275. Hereafter *Poems*.
74   Bulwer-Lytton, 1833, I, p. 7.
75   [Thomas Carlyle], 'Signs of the Times', *Edinburgh Review*, 49 (1829), 439–59, (pp. 442 and 447).

3   'Mr. Tennyson's Truly English Spirit': Landscape and Nature in *Poems* (1842)

1   *Spectator*, 4 June 1842, cited in Edgar F. Shannon, Jr, *Tennyson and the Reviewers* (Cambridge, MA: Harvard University Press, 1952), p. 64.

2 Charles Tennyson, *Alfred Tennyson* (London: Macmillan, 1949), p. 152. Shannon (p. 34) also comments that 'the accepted hypothesis . . . seems correct'.

3 James Knowles, 'Aspects of Tennyson: A Personal Reminiscence', *Nineteenth Century*, 33 (1893), 164–88 (p. 174). Italics in the original.

4 Christopher Ricks, *Tennyson*, 2nd edn (Basingstoke: Macmillan – now Palgrave Macmillan, 1989), p. 147.

5 *The Letters of Edward FitzGerald*, ed. Alfred McKinley Terhune and Annabelle Burdick Terhune, 4 vols (Princeton, NJ: Princeton University Press, 1980), I, p. 239 ([23, 25 November 1839]). Hereafter *EFG Letters*.

6 Ricks, 1989, pp. 148–9.

7 John Olin Eidson, *Tennyson in America: His Reputation and Influence from 1827 to 1858* (Athens, GA: University of Georgia Press, 1943) believes that Ralph Waldo Emerson 'did more than any other single person to make Tennyson known in America' (p. 6).

8 *The Letters of Alfred Lord Tennyson*, ed. Cecil Y. Lang and Edgar F. Shannon, Jr, 3 vols (Oxford: Clarendon Press, 1982–90), I, p. 187 (22 February [1841]). Hereafter *AT Letters*.

9 'I have bought A. Tennyson's poems. How good "Mariana" is.' *EFG Letters*, I, p. 97 ([*c*.15 April 1831]).

10 *EFG Letters*, I, p. 160.

11 *AT Letters*, I, p. 188 ([*c*.22 February 1841]).

12 *EFG Letters*, I, p. 288 ([*c*.15 September 1841]).

13 *EFG Letters*, I, p. 312 (2 March 1842).

14 Tennyson received $150 for the copyright, which Charles Tennyson (p. 192) believes to be 'the first copyright payment by an American publisher to a British author'.

15 *EFG Letters*, I, p. 332 (16 August 1842).

16 1843 1000 copies, 1845 1500 copies, 1846 2000 copies; an illustrated fifth edition followed in 1848. June Steffensen Hagen (p. 202, n. 33) points out that nineteenth-century publishers used the term 'edition' to indicate reissues of a book, using unaltered stereoplates but with title-page labels of 'second' edition, etc. Hagen (p. 66) also details Tennyson's share of the profits, which he received from Moxon in regular instalments. *Tennyson and his Publishers* (London: Macmillan, 1979).

17 'The Sleeping Beauty' had been published in 1830; 'St Agnes' Eve' had been published as 'St Agnes' in 1836 in *The Keepsake* for 1837.

18 *EFG Letters*, I, pp. 326–7 ([June 1842]).

19 Ricks, 1989, p. 163.

20 Shannon, 1952, pp. 170–1.

21 *EFG Letters*, I, p. 315 (17 March 1842).

22 *Spectator*, 4 June 1842, cited in Shannon, 1952, p. 64. [John Sterling], *'Poems'*, *Quarterly Review*, 70 (1842), 385–416 (p. 407).

23 *AT Letters*, I, p. 166 ([October or November 1838]).

24 Alun Howkins, *Reshaping Rural England: A Social History 1850–1925* (London: HarperCollins, 1991), p. 9.

25 Eric Hobsbawm and George Rudé, *Captain Swing*, 2nd edn (London: Phoenix, 2001), pp. 16–19.

26 [Sterling], 1842, p. 387.

27 Quoted in Alun Howkins, 'Deserters from the Plough', *History Today*, 43 (1993), 32–8 (p. 32).
28 See *The Letters of Arthur Henry Hallam*, ed. Jack Kolb (Columbus: Ohio State University Press, 1981), pp. 387–9 for Hallam and Merivale's views on the disturbances.
29 Hallam Tennyson cited in headnote to 'Ode to Memory', *The Poems of Tennyson*, ed. Christopher Ricks, 2nd edn, 3 vols (London: Longman, 1987), I, p. 231. Hereafter *Poems*.
30 [James Spedding], '*Poems*', *Edinburgh Review*, 77 (1843), 373–91 (p. 376).
31 [Sterling], 1842, p. 398.
32 Pauline Fletcher, *Gardens and Grim Ravines: The Language of Landscape in Victorian Poetry* (Princeton, NJ: Princeton University Press, 1983), p. 50.
33 *English Verse 1830–1890*, ed. Bernard Richards, 5th edn (London: Longman, 1994), p. 452.
34 Knowles, 1893, p. 170.
35 Ricks, 1989, p. 94.
36 Tennyson cited in headnote to 'The Gardener's Daughter', *Poems*, I, p. 552.
37 [Sterling], 1842, p. 407.
38 Leonée Ormond, 'Tennyson and Pastoral: Love in a Landscape', *Browning Society Notes*, 15–17 (1985–88), 24–31 (p. 29).
39 John Ruskin, *Sesame and Lilies*, ed. Deborah Epstein Nord (New Haven, CT: Yale University Press, 2002), p. 78.
40 Michael Timko, '"The Central Wish": Human Passion and Cosmic Love in Tennyson's Idyls', *Victorian Poetry*, 16 (1978), 1–15 (p. 5).
41 Cited in Shannon, 1952, p. 63.
42 'Leigh Hunt on *Poems* [1842]', in *Tennyson: The Critical Heritage*, ed. John D. Jump (London: Routledge & Kegan Paul, 1967), pp. 126–36 (p. 129).
43 [Charles Kingsley], 'Tennyson', *Fraser's Magazine*, 42 (1850), 245–55 (p. 247).
44 Cited in Shannon, 1952, p. 67.
45 Tennyson cited in the headnote to 'Mariana', *Tennyson: A Selected Edition*, ed. Christopher Ricks, 2nd edn (London: Longman, 1989), p. 3; italics in the original. Hereafter *Selected Edition*.
46 Leigh Hunt cited in Jump, p. 128.
47 Robert Pattison, *Tennyson and Tradition* (Cambridge, MA: Harvard University Press, 1979), p. 14. Succeeding references in this paragraph are taken from pp. 16–18.
48 Hallam Tennyson, *Alfred Lord Tennyson: A Memoir By His Son*, 2 vols (London: Macmillan, 1897), I, p. 508, n. 1. Hereafter *Memoir*, 1897.
49 Pattison notes (p. 16) Walter Savage Landor's *Fiesolan Idyl* (1831), but points out that Landor's most characteristic experiments in the form came after Tennyson had begun his own variations on the idyl/l theme.
50 Pattison, p. 19. Succeeding references in this paragraph are taken from pp. 18–20.
51 Angela O'Donnell, 'Tennyson's "English Idyls": Studies in Poetic Decorum', *Studies in Philology*, 85 (1988), 125–44 (p. 137). Succeeding references in this paragraph are taken from pp. 131–3.
52 O'Donnell, p. 126.
53 *Memoir*, 1987, I, p. 189. 'The Reception of the Early Poems, by Aubrey de Vere', *Memoir*, 1897, I, pp. 501–11.

54 [Sterling], 1842, p. 406. Jonathan Padley traces the critical confusions from their origin in 1842 and attributes the term 'English Idyls' to Hallam Tennyson. 'No Idyl(l) Matter: The Orthographic and Titular History of Alfred Tennyson's *English Idyls'*, *Tennyson Research Bulletin*, 9 (2007), 97–110.
55 O'Donnell, p. 135.
56 William E. Fredeman, '"The Sphere of Common Duties": The Domestic Solution in Tennyson's Poetry', *Bulletin of the John Rylands Library*, 54 (1972), 357–83 (p. 365). Succeeding references in this paragraph are taken from pp. 369 and 376.
57 *Memoir*, 1897, I, p. 189.
58 Timko, p. 10.
59 Herbert F. Tucker, *Tennyson and the Doom of Romanticism* (Cambridge, MA: Harvard University Press, 1988), p. 274. Succeeding references in this paragraph are taken from pp. 274–6.
60 Elizabeth K. Helsinger, *Rural Scenes and National Representations: Britain, 1815–1850* (Princeton, NJ: Princeton University Press, 1997), p. 67. Succeeding references in this paragraph are taken from p. 86.
61 Roger Ebbatson, *An Imaginary England: Nation, Landscape and Literature, 1840–1920* (Aldershot: Ashgate, 2005), p. 19. Ebbatson alludes to the ideas of Fredric Jameson, who argues 'the priority of the political interpretation of literary texts', *The Political Unconscious: Narrative as a Socially Symbolic Act*, 4th edn (London: Routledge, 1996), p. 17. Succeeding references to Ebbatson in this paragraph are taken from pp. 19–20.
62 Helsinger (p. 241, n. 18) cites George Eliot, *The Mill on the Floss* (1860).
63 A. Dwight Culler, 'The English Idyls', in *Tennyson: A Collection of Critical Essays*, ed. Elizabeth A. Francis (Eaglewood Cliffs, NJ: Prentice-Hall, 1980), pp. 70–94 (p. 80).
64 *Memoir*, 1897, I, p. 196.
65 *EFG Letters*, I, p. 315 (17 March 1842).
66 Cited in Shannon, 1952, p. 62.
67 Helsinger, pp. 77–8.
68 [Sterling], 1842, p. 406.
69 [Kingsley], 1850, p. 250.
70 Cited in Shannon, 1952, p. 75.
71 Tennyson later clarified the allusion by citing '*Cymbeline* II ii 39, *Poems*, I, p. 239, n. 62.
72 [Kingsley], 1850, p. 247. Succeeding references in this paragraph are taken from pp. 245–8.
73 Cited in the headnote to 'Sir Launcelot and Queen Guinevere', *Selected Edition*, p. 97.
74 John Forster cited in Roger Simpson, *Camelot Regained: The Arthurian Revival and Tennyson* (Cambridge: Brewer, 1990), p. 231.
75 *EFG Letters*, I, pp. 323–4 (22 May 1842).
76 Cited in Shannon, 1952, pp. 74 and 61.
77 [Sterling], 1842, p. 399.
78 Isobel Armstrong, *Victorian Poetry: Poetry, Poetics and Politics*, 2nd edn (London: Routledge, 1996), p. 56.
79 Cited in J.F.C. Harrison, *Early Victorian Britain 1832–51*, 2nd edn (London: Fontana, 1979), p. 112.

80 Paul Turner, *Tennyson* (London: Routledge & Kegan Paul, 1976), p. 75.
81 W.W. Robson, 'Tennyson and Victorian Balladry', in *Tennyson: Seven Essays*, ed. Philip Collins (Basingstoke: Macmillan – now Palgrave Macmillan, 1992), pp. 160–82 (pp. 161–5). Succeeding references in this paragraph are taken from pp. 174–6.
82 Cited in Shannon, 1952, p. 74. Italics in the original.
83 *AT Letters*, I, p. 124 ([early October 1834]).
84 Tennyson cited in the headnote to 'The Talking Oak', *Poems*, II, p. 105.
85 John Forster cited in Shannon, 1952, p. 62. [Richard Monckton Milnes], '*Poems*', *Westminster Review*, 38 (1842), 371–90 (p. 389).
86 Turner, p. 86.
87 Headnote to 'The Talking Oak', *Poems*, II, p. 105.
88 [Sterling], 1842, p. 411.
89 *Brewer's Dictionary of Phrase and Fable*, ed. Ivor H. Evans, 9th edn (London: Cassell, 1981), p. 539.
90 Hugh Prince, 'Victorian Rural Landscapes' in *The Victorian Countryside*, ed. G.E. Mingay, 2 vols (London: Routledge & Kegan Paul, 1981), pp. 17–29 (p. 25).
91 Ricks, 1989, p. 148.
92 *Memoir*, 1897, II, p. 127.
93 [Richard Monckton Milnes], '*Timbuctoo*', *Athenaeum*, 22 July 1829, p. 456.
94 Cited in Shannon, 1952, pp. 61–2.
95 Cited in Shannon, 1952, p. 68.
96 [Sterling], 1842, p. 395.
97 Cited in Shannon, 1952, pp. 62–3.
98 Cited in Shannon, 1952, pp. 61–2.
99 Cited in Shannon, 1952, pp. 63–4.
100 Cited in Shannon, 1952, p. 64.
101 Cited in Shannon, 1952, pp. 65–6.
102 Cited in Shannon, 1952, pp. 68–9.
103 Cited in Shannon, 1952, p. 69.
104 Thaïs E. Morgan, 'The Poetry of Victorian Masculinities' in *The Cambridge Companion to Victorian Poetry*, ed. Joseph Bristow (Cambridge: Cambridge University Press, 2000), pp. 203–27 (p. 204).
105 Cited in Shannon, 1952, p. 67.
106 Cited in Shannon 1952, p. 62.
107 Cited in Jump, p. 135.
108 Isobel Armstrong, *Victorian Scrutinies: Reviews of Poetry 1830–1870* (London: Athlone Press, 1972), p. 29.
109 Myron F. Brightfield, *John Wilson Croker* (Berkeley, CA: University of California Press, 1940), p. 426.
110 [Sterling], 1842, p. 402.
111 'Walking to the Mail', written c.1837–38, 67–8. 'Wherefore, in these dark ages of the Press', Ricks, 1989, p. 148.

4 'Fair Victoria's Golden Age': Tennyson and Monarchy

1 John Lucas, 'Love of England: The Victorians and Patriotism', *Browning Society Notes*, 17 (1987–88), 63–76 (p. 64).

2 Elizabeth Langland, 'Nation and Nationality: Queen Victoria in the Developing Narrative of Englishness', in *Remaking Queen Victoria*, ed. Margaret Homans and Adrienne Munich (Cambridge: Cambridge University Press, 1997), pp. 13–32 (p. 14).

3 Richard Williams, *The Contentious Crown: Public Discussion of the British Monarchy in the Reign of Queen Victoria* (Aldershot: Ashgate, 1997), p. 4.

4 Lucas, p. 64. Succeeding references in this paragraph are taken from pp. 64–7.

5 Langland, pp. 14–16.

6 Langland, pp. 23–7.

7 Richard Williams, p. 2. Succeeding references in this paragraph are taken from pp. 3–5.

8 Kingsley Martin, *The Crown and the Establishment* (London: Hutchinson, 1962), pp. 20–1.

9 *Republicanism in Victorian Society*, ed. David Nash and Antony Taylor (Stroud: Sutton, 2000), p. ix. Succeeding references in this paragraph are taken from pp. x–xiii.

10 Frank Prochaska, *The Republic of Britain 1760–2000* (London: Allen Lane, 2000), p. xv. Succeeding references in this paragraph are taken from pp. xvi–xviii.

11 *The Letters of Alfred Lord Tennyson*, ed. Cecil Y. Lang and Edgar F. Shannon, Jr, 3 vols (Oxford: Clarendon Press, 1982–90), I, p. 153 ([c.20 June 1837]). Hereafter *AT Letters*.

12 Contemporary ballad 'Queen Victoria', cited in Lucas, 1987/88, fig. 3.

13 Cited in Elizabeth Longford, *Victoria R.I.*, 2nd edn (London: Weidenfeld & Nicolson, 1987), p. 62.

14 David Thomson, *England in the Nineteenth Century: 1815–1914*, 3rd edn, The Pelican History of England, 8 (London: Penguin, 1991), p. 170.

15 Cited in Richard Williams, p. 193.

16 John Plunkett, *Queen Victoria: First Media Monarch* (Oxford: Oxford University Press, 2003), p. 70.

17 *Dictionary of Subjects and Symbols in Art*, ed. James Hall, 9th edn (London: Murray, 1987), p. 268.

18 Lynne Vallone, *Becoming Victoria* (New Haven, CT: Yale University Press, 2001), pp. 169–70.

19 For discussion of this turbulent period see, for example, Alan Sinfield, *Alfred Tennyson* (Oxford: Blackwell, 1986), Malcolm Chase, *Chartism: A New History* (Manchester: Manchester University Press, 2007).

20 Richard Williams, pp. 10–11.

21 Thomas Carlyle, *On Heroes, Hero-Worship, and the Heroic in History*, ed. Michael K. Goldberg (Berkeley, CA: University of California Press, 1993), p. lxviii.

22 Christopher Ricks, 'The Princess and the Queen', *Victorian Poetry*, 25 (1987), 133–9 (p. 134).

23 Ricks, 'The Princess and the Queen', p. 139.

24 In a letter (15 September 1845) recommending to Victoria that a 'sum of £200 should be offered to Mr. Tennyson', Sir Robert Peel had confirmed that Tennyson's 'pecuniary circumstances are far from being prosperous'. *Queen Victoria's Early Letters*, ed. John Raymond (London: Batsford, 1963), p. 108.

25 For example, in May 1847, *AT Letters*, I, p. 274 (22 May [1847]).

26   *AT Letters*, I, pp. 272–3 (5 March [1847]).

27   *AT Letters*, I, p. 273 (16 April 1847).

28   Robert Bernard Martin, *Tennyson: The Unquiet Heart*, 2nd edn (London: Faber and Faber, 1983), p. 309.

29   Hallam Tennyson, *Alfred Lord Tennyson: A Memoir By His Son*, 2 vols (London: Macmillan, 1897), I, p. 334. Hereafter *Memoir*, 1897.

30   *Tennyson: A Selected Edition*, ed. Christopher Ricks, 2nd edn (London: Longman, 1989), pp. 986–7. Hereafter *Selected Edition*. The poem was published in 1895 from the MS at the Drexel Institute, Philadelphia.

31   Headnote to 'To the Queen', Ricks, *Selected Edition*, p. 485.

32   Charles Tennyson, *Alfred Tennyson* (London: Macmillan, 1949), pp. 334 and 338.

33   Ricks, 'The Princess and the Queen', p. 137.

34   Mark Girouard, *The Return to Camelot: Chivalry and the English Gentleman*, 2nd edn (New Haven, CT: Yale University Press, 1981), p. 198.

35   Dorothy Marshall, *The Life and Times of Victoria*, 2nd edn (London: Weidenfeld and Nicolson, 1992), p. 131.

36   *The Poetical Works of Elizabeth Barrett Browning*, The Oxford Edition (London: Frowde, 1910), pp. 315–16. Italics in the original.

37   For example, at her first Privy Council; see Plunkett, fig. 16, p. 89.

38   Plunkett, p. 2.

39   Plunkett, p. 144.

40   Plunkett, p. 8.

41   Richard Williams, p. 195.

42   Plunkett, pp. 29–30 and 33.

43   *Spectator* (November 1841) cited in Richard Williams, p. 201.

44   W.S. Lilly, 'British Monarchy and Modern Democracy', *Nineteenth Century*, 41 (1897), 853–64 (p. 859).

45   Richard Williams, pp. 17–18.

46   The appalling statistics of nineteenth-century infant morality are detailed in David Newsome, *The Victorian World Picture* (London: Fontana, 1998), pp. 83–4.

47   Prochaska, p. 91.

48   Richard Williams, p. 107.

49   Prochaska, pp. 83 and 73–4.

50   Prochaska, p. 96.

51   *Memoir*, 1897, I, p. 455.

52   Headnote to 'Dedication', *Selected Edition*, p. 675.

53   *AT Letters*, II, p. 294 (23 January 1862).

54   Lytton Strachey observes that 'high-born ladies and gentlemen' thought the young Albert 'was more like a foreign tenor than anything else', *Queen Victoria*, 6th edn (London: Chatto and Windus, 1922), pp. 111–12.

55   *AT Letters*, II, p. 291 ([13 January 1862]).

56   Lines 461–74 of *Guinevere* (1859) are paraphrased in lines 7–10 of 'Dedication'.

57   Richard Williams, p. 105.

58   During the American Civil War a Northern naval officer forcibly removed two Southern envoys from the British steamship 'Trent'; the Prince Consort intervened to modify the Foreign Secretary, Lord John Russell's, strongly worded despatch. Thomson, p. 159.

59 Richard Williams, p. 106.
60 Marshall, p. 120.
61 Robert Bernard Martin, pp. 25, 237 and 280.
62 *AT Letters*, II, p. 292 ([13 January 1862]).
63 Princess Alice to Tennyson, cited in *Dear and Honoured Lady: The Correspondence between Queen Victoria and Alfred Tennyson*, ed. Hope Dyson and Charles Tennyson (London: Macmillan, 1969), p. 65.
64 *AT Letters*, II, p. 329 (13 May 1863).
65 Richard Williams, pp. 49–50.
66 Helen Rappaport, *Magnificent Obsession: Victoria, Albert and the Death that Changed the Monarchy*, 2nd edn (Bath: Windsor-Paragon, 2012), pp. 382–400, details contemporary and more recent challenges to the diagnosis of typhoid by Albert's doctors.
67 Margaret Homans, *Royal Representations: Queen Victoria and British Culture, 1837–1876* (Chicago: University of Chicago Press, 1998), p. 157.
68 Cited in Richard Williams, p. 34.
69 Richard Williams, pp. 31–2.
70 Richard Williams, pp. 47–8.
71 *AT Letters*, III, p. 41 (8 November 1872).
72 Tennyson wrote on 13 March 1872: 'As to writing Odes on the Prince's recovery was not the people the best poet laureate and their shouts the truest song?' *AT Letters*, III, p. 26.
73 Matthew Rowlinson, 'The Ideological Moment of Tennyson's "Ulysses"', in *Tennyson*, ed. Rebecca Stott (London: Longman, 1996), pp. 148–60 (p. 152).
74 Isobel Armstrong, *Victorian Poetry: Poetry, Poetics and Politics*, 2nd edn (London: Routledge, 1996), p. 56.
75 *Memoir*, 1897, I, p. 477.
76 Jerome Buckley, for example, comments that 'none . . . now greatly attracts our attention'. 'The Persistence of Tennyson', in *The Victorian Experience: The Poets*, ed. Richard A. Levine (Athens: Ohio University Press, 1982), pp. 1–22 (p. 14).
77 *AT Letters*, II, p. 323 (11 March 1863).
78 For example, referring to 'The blind hysterics of the Celt' (*In Memoriam*, 1850, CIX, 16).
79 Robin L. Inboden, 'The "Valour of Delicate Women": The Domestication of Political Relations in Tennyson's Laureate Poetry', *Victorian Poetry*, 36 (1998), 205–21 (p. 211).
80 Dyson and Tennyson, p. 116. Italics in the original. Matthew Dennison, *The Last Princess: The Devoted Life of Queen Victoria's Youngest Daughter*, 2nd edn (New York: St Martin's Griffin, 2009) examines the bereaved Victoria's obsessive dependence on Princess Beatrice.
81 Girouard, p. 127.
82 Robert Bernard Martin, p. 577.
83 Tennyson quoted in the headnote to 'Princess Alice', *The Poems of Tennyson*, ed. Christopher Ricks, 2nd edn, 3 vols (London: Longman, 1987), III, p. 35. Hereafter *Poems*. Princess Alice died on 14 December 1878, the seventeenth anniversary of the Prince Consort's death.
84 Richard Williams, p. 57.
85 The *Saturday Review*, cited in Richard Williams, p. 172.
86 Richard Williams, pp. 54–6.

87 Richard Williams, p. 212.
88 Richard Williams, pp. 123–5.
89 Richard Williams, p. 215.
90 Headnote to the 'Jubilee Ode', *Poems*, III, pp. 159–60.
91 Headnote to the 'Jubilee Ode', *Poems*, III, p. 160.
92 Dyson and Tennyson, p. 128.
93 Alfred Tennyson, *Idylls of the King*, ed. J.M. Gray, 2nd edn (London: Penguin, 1996), p. 355.
94 Langland, p. 14.
95 Lucas, p. 64.
96 Richard Williams discusses 'the persistence of radical criticism of the monarchy' between 1887 and 1901, pp. 58–73.

5 'To Serve as Model for the Mighty World': Tennyson and Medievalism

1 Alice Chandler, 'Order and Disorder in the Medieval Revival', *Browning Institute Studies*, 8 (1980), 1–9 (p. 1).
2 Charles Dellheim, 'Interpreting Victorian Medievalism', in *History and Community: Essays in Victorian Medievalism*, ed. Florence S. Boos (New York: Garland, 1992), pp. 39–58 (pp. 39–40).
3 Hilary Fraser, 'Victorian Poetry and Historicism', in *The Cambridge Companion to Victorian Poetry*, ed. Joseph Bristow (Cambridge: Cambridge University Press, 2000), pp. 114–36 (p. 115).
4 Robin Gilmour, *The Victorian Period: The Intellectual and Cultural Context of English Literature 1830–1890* (London: Longman, 1993), pp. 45–50; David Newsome, *The Victorian World Picture*, 2nd edn (London: Fontana, 1998), pp. 177–90.
5 Eighteenth-century medievalism is examined in Elizabeth Fay, *Romantic Medievalism: History and the Romantic Literary Ideal* (Basingstoke: Palgrave Macmillan, 2002).
6 Gilmour, 1993, pp. 48–50.
7 Newsome, p. 189.
8 Clare Broome Saunders, *Women Writers and Nineteenth-Century Medievalism* (New York: Palgrave Macmillan, 2009).
9 *Medievalism and the Quest for the 'Real' Middle Ages*, ed. Clare A. Simmons (London: Frank Cass, 2001), pp. 1–2 and 26, n. 1 and n. 2.
10 Chandler, 1980, pp. 1–2.
11 Extensively examined in Alice Chandler, *A Dream of Order: The Medieval Ideal in Nineteenth-Century English Literature* (London: Routledge & Kegan Paul, 1971) which, despite its publication date, is still regarded as a 'seminal' work by later critics such as Simmons (p. 2) and Saunders (p. 4).
12 Chandler, 1980, pp. 1–2.
13 Dellheim, p. 39.
14 *Young England: The New Generation*, ed. John Morrow (London: Leicester University Press, 1999) includes a selection of primary texts detailing Young England's history and beliefs.
15 Dellheim, pp. 44–6.

16 Dellheim, p. 53.
17 Inga Bryden, 'Reinventing Origins: the Victorian Arthur and Racial Myth', in *The Victorians and Race*, ed. Shearer West (Aldershot: Scolar, 1996), pp. 141–55 (p. 141). See also Inga Bryden, *Reinventing King Arthur: The Arthurian Legends in Victorian Culture* (Aldershot: Ashgate, 2005).
18 Hugh A. MacDougall, *Racial Myth in English History: Trojans, Teutons, and Anglo-Saxons* (Montreal: Harvest House, 1982), pp. 1–2.
19 Reginald Horsman, *Race and Manifest Destiny: The Origins of American Racial Anglo-Saxonism* (Cambridge, MA: Harvard University Press, 1981), p. 9.
20 Reginald Horsman, 'Origins of Racial Anglo-Saxonism in Great Britain before 1850', in *Race, Gender, and Rank: Early Modern Ideas of Humanity*, ed. Maryanne Cline Horowitz (Rochester, NY: University of Rochester Press, 1992), pp. 77–100 (p. 77).
21 Rosemary Jann, 'Democratic Myths in Victorian Medievalism', *Browning Institute Studies*, 8 (1980), 129–49 (p. 147).
22 Peter Mandler, '"In the Olden Time": Romantic History and English National Identity, 1820–50', in *A Union of Multiple Identities: The British Isles, c.1750–c.1850*, ed. Laurence Brockliss and David Eastwood (Manchester: Manchester University Press, 1997), pp. 78–92 (p. 82).
23 Stephanie L. Barczewski, *Myth and National Identity in Nineteenth-Century Britain: The Legends of King Arthur and Robin Hood* (Oxford: Oxford University Press, 2000), pp. v and vii.
24 *A History of Arthurian Scholarship*, ed. Norris J. Lacy (Cambridge: Brewer, 2006), p. vii.
25 Christopher Baswell and William Sharpe, 'Introduction: *Rex Quondam Rexque Futurus*', in *The Passing of Arthur: New Essays in Arthurian Tradition*, ed. Christopher Baswell and William Sharpe (New York: Garland, 1988), pp. xi–xix (p. xv).
26 Inga Bryden, *Reinventing King Arthur: The Arthurian Legends in Victorian Culture* (Aldershot: Ashgate, 2005). Roger Simpson, *Camelot Regained: The Arthurian Revival and Tennyson* (Cambridge: Brewer, 1990).
27 Bryden, 1996, p. 141.
28 Stephen Ahern, 'Listening to Guinevere: Female Agency and the Politics of Chivalry in Tennyson's *Idylls*', *Studies in Philology*, 101 (2004), 88–112 (p. 89).
29 *Tennyson: A Selected Edition*, ed. Christopher Ricks, 2nd edn (London: Longman, 1989), pp. 18–19. Hereafter *Selected Edition*.
30 Roger Simpson, 'Costello's "The Funeral Boat": An Analogue of Tennyson's "The Lady of Shalott"', *Tennyson Research Bulletin*, 4 (1984), 129–31 (p. 129).
31 Simpson, 1990, p. 196.
32 Richard Barber, *The Reign of Chivalry*, 2nd edn (Woodbridge: Boydell & Brewer, 2005), p. 169. Barber adds that the only historian Scott used was Froissart, who 'also idealised his sources' and put a 'romantic gloss on reality'.
33 Mark Girouard, *The Return to Camelot: Chivalry and the English Gentleman* (New Haven, CT: Yale University Press, 1981), pp. 112 and 180.
34 Leonée Ormond, 'Victorian Romance: Tennyson', in *A Companion to Romance: From Classical to Contemporary*, ed. Corinne Saunders (Malden, MA: Blackwell, 2004), pp. 321–40 (p. 332).
35 Britta Martens, '"Knight, Bard, Gallant": The Troubadour as a Critique of Romanticism in Browning's *Sordello*', in *Beyond Arthurian Romances: The*

Reach of Victorian Medievalism, ed. Lorretta M. Holloway and Jennifer A. Palmgren (New York: Palgrave Macmillan, 2005), p. 45.

36 Joseph Chadwick, 'A Blessing and a Curse: The Poetics of Privacy in Tennyson's "The Lady of Shalott"', *Victorian Poetry*, 24 (1986), 13–30. Carl Plasa, '"Cracked from Side to Side": Sexual Politics in "The Lady of Shalott"', *Victorian Poetry*, 30 (1992), 247–63.

37 Chadwick, pp. 13–15.

38 *Selected Edition*, p. 24.

39 Plasa, p. 254.

40 Edgar F. Shannon, Jr., 'Poetry as Vision: Sight and Insight in "The Lady of Shalott"', *Victorian Poetry*, 19 (1981), 207–23 (p. 208).

41 Chadwick, p. 25.

42 Kathy Alexis Psomiades, '"The Lady of Shalott" and the Critical Fortunes of Victorian Poetry', in *The Cambridge Companion to Victorian Poetry*, ed. Joseph Bristow (Cambridge: Cambridge University Press, 2000), pp. 25–45 (p. 29).

43 Shannon, 1981, p. 222

44 Shannon, 1981, pp. 214–15.

45 Newsome, pp. 57–8.

46 John Mitchell Kemble cited in headnote to 'Sir Launcelot and Queen Guinevere', *Selected Edition*, p. 97.

47 Hallam Tennyson, *Alfred Lord Tennyson: A Memoir By His Son* (London: Macmillan, 1897), II, p. 130. Hereafter *Memoir*, 1897.

48 Cited in the headnote to 'Sir Launcelot and Queen Guinevere', *Selected Edition*, p. 97.

49 Girouard, p. 200.

50 Quoted in Girouard, pp. 180–1.

51 *Selected Edition*, p. 97.

52 *The Letters of Alfred Lord Tennyson*, ed. Cecil Y. Lang and Edgar F. Shannon, Jr, 3 vols (Oxford: Clarendon Press, 1982–90), I, p. 125 ([Early October 1834]). Hereafter *AT Letters*.

53 Girouard, p. 180.

54 Girouard, p. 143.

55 Thomas Hughes, *Tom Brown at Oxford*, 2nd edn, 3 vols (Cambridge: Macmillan, 1861), I, p. 199.

56 Charles Kingsley, *David: Four Sermons* (Cambridge: Macmillan, 1865), p. 10.

57 Thomas Hughes, II, p. 97.

58 Marcia C. Culver, 'The Death and Birth of an Epic: Tennyson's "Morte d'Arthur"', *Victorian Poetry*, 20 (1982), 51–61 (p. 55).

59 Simpson, 1990, p. 216.

60 Barczewski, p. 155. See also pp. 111–17.

61 Dafydd Moore, 'Tennyson, Malory and the Ossianic Mode: *The Poems of Ossian* and "The Death of Arthur"', *The Review of English Studies*, 57 (2006), 374–91 (p. 388).

62 Cited in Simpson, 1990, p. 231.

63 [Richard Monckton Milnes], 'Poems', *Westminster Review*, 38 (1842), 371–90 (p. 373).

64 Richard D. Mallen, 'The "Crowned Republic" of Tennyson's *Idylls of the King*', *Victorian Poetry*, 37 (1999), 275–89 (p. 275).

65 Cited in *Memoir*, 1897, I, p. 194.

66 [John Sterling], *'Poems'*, *Quarterly Review*, 70 (1842), 385–416 (p. 401).
67 Elizabeth Barrett Browning, *Aurora Leigh and Other Poems*, ed. Cora Kaplan, 5th edn (London: Women's Press, 1993), p. 201.
68 *Memoir*, 1897, II, p. 127.
69 Robert Bernard Martin, *Tennyson: The Unquiet Heart*, 2nd edn (London: Faber and Faber, 1983), p. 263.
70 'Wherefore, in these dark ages of the Press' (1839), Christopher Ricks, *Tennyson*, 2nd edn (Basingstoke: Macmillan – now Palgrave Macmillan, 1989), pp. 148–9.
71 Cited in *Tennyson: The Critical Heritage*, ed. John D. Jump (London: Routledge & Kegan Paul, 1967), p. 127.
72 Cited in Edgar F. Shannon, Jr, *Tennyson and the Reviewers* (Cambridge, MA: Harvard University Press, 1952), p. 62.
73 Simpson, 1990, p. 192.
74 Although the Movement was founded in August 1840, founder-members described themselves as 'Young Englanders' from 1837, Morrow , p. 3.
75 Morrow, p. 14. Manners also expounded neo-feudalist ideas in his poem 'England's Trust (1841), which included the lines: 'Each knew his place – king, peasant, peer, or priest – | The greatest owned connexion with the least; | From rank to rank the generous feeling ran, | And linked society as man to man' Morrow, p. 116.
76 *Brewer's Dictionary of Phrase and Fable*, ed. Ivor H. Evans, 9th edn (London: Cassell, 1981), pp. 489–90.
77 Quoted in note to 'Godiva' line 79, *The Poems of Tennyson*, ed. Christopher Ricks, 2nd edn, 3 vols (London: Longman, 1987), II, p. 176. Hereafter *Poems*.
78 Dorothy Mermin, *Godiva's Ride: Women of Letters in England, 1830–1880* (Bloomington: Indiana University Press, 1993), p. 21.
79 Marion Shaw, 'The Contours of Manliness and the Nature of Woman', in *Critical Essays on Alfred Lord Tennyson*, ed. Herbert F. Tucker (New York: Hall, 1993), pp. 219–33 (pp. 219–20).
80 John Tosh, *Manliness and Masculinities in Nineteenth-Century Britain: Essays on Gender, Family and Empire* (Harlow: Pearson, 2005), pp. 1–5.
81 Robin Gilmour, *The Idea of the Gentleman in the Victorian Novel* (London: Allen & Unwin, 1981), p. 2.
82 P.J. Cain and A.G. Hopkins, *British Imperialism: Innovation and Expansion 1688–1914*, 2nd edn (London: Longman, 2003), p. 34.
83 Gilmour, 1981, p. 87.
84 J.H. Newman, *The Idea of a University, Defined and Illustrated*, ed. I.T. Ker (Oxford: Clarendon Press, 1976), pp. 179–81.
85 J.A. Mangan and James Walvin, 'Introduction', in *Manliness and Morality: Middle-Class Masculinity in Britain and America, 1800–1940*, ed. J.A. Mangan and James Walvin (Manchester: Manchester University Press, 1987), pp. 1–6 (p. 1).
86 Norman Vance, *The Sinews of the Spirit: The Ideal of Christian Manliness in Victorian Literature and Religious Thought* (Cambridge: Cambridge University Press, 1985), pp. 1–2.
87 *AT Letters*, II, p. 50 (16 November [1852]).
88 Edgar F. Shannon, Jr, 'The History of a Poem: Tennyson's *Ode on the Death of the Duke of Wellington*', *Studies in Bibliography*, 13 (1960), 149–77; Edgar F. Shannon,

Jr and Christopher Ricks, 'A Further History of Tennyson's *Ode on the Death of the Duke of Wellington'*, *Studies in Bibliography*, 32 (1979), 125–57.

89   Lytton Strachey (1921) cited in Elizabeth Langland, 'Nation and Nationality: Queen Victoria in the Developing Narrative of Englishness', in *Remaking Queen Victoria*, ed. Margaret Homans and Adrienne Munich (Cambridge: Cambridge University Press, 1997), pp. 13–32 (pp. 26–7).

90   Cited in John Lucas, *England and Englishness: Ideas of Nationhood in English Poetry 1688–1900* (London: Hogarth, 1990), p. 189.

91   The Prime Minister, Lord Derby, cited in headnote to the 'Ode on the Death of the Duke of Wellington', *Selected Edition*, p. 488.

92   Cited in Debra N. Mancoff, *The Return of King Arthur: The Legend Through Victorian Eyes* (London: Pavilion, 1995), p. 37.

93   On the sudden death of George Canning, in January 1828 Wellington was asked by George IV 'to form a government and try to restore Tory unity', T.A. Jenkins, 'Wellington, Toryism and the Nation', *History Today* (November 2002), 26–33 (p. 28).

94   Cited in Jenkins, p. 28.

95   Ricks, *Tennyson*, p. 309.

96   *Memoir*, 1897, I, p. 386.

97   See Edgar F. Shannon, Jr and Christopher Ricks, '"The Charge of the Light Brigade": The Creation of a Poem', *Studies in Bibliography*, 38 (1985), 1–44, for a full textual history and critical discussion of the poem's relation to *The Times* editorial of 13 November 1854.

98   Jerome J. McGann, *The Beauty of Inflections: Literary Investigations in Historical Method and Theory*, 2nd edn (Oxford: Clarendon Press, 2001), pp. 197–200.

99   Kathryn Ledbetter, *Tennyson and Victorian Periodicals: Commodities in Context* (Aldershot: Ashgate, 2007), pp. 121 and 127.

100 Byron Farwell, *Queen Victoria's Little Wars*, 2nd edn (Ware: Wordsworth, 1999), pp. 69–70.

101 *Memoir*, 1897, I, p. 342.

102 Peter Burroughs, 'Defence and Imperial Disunity', in *The Nineteenth Century*, ed. Andrew Porter, The Oxford History of the British Empire, III (Oxford: Oxford University Press, 1999), pp. 320–45 (p. 324).

103 Samuel Smiles, *Self-Help: With Illustrations of Conduct & Perseverance*, 7th edn (London: Murray, 1950), p. 338.

104 Headnote to 'The Revenge', *Poems*, III, p. 25. An additional influence was J.A. Froude, 'England's Forgotten Worthies' (1852), reprinted in 1867.

105 *The Last Fight of the Revenge at Sea*, ed. Edward Arber, English Reprint 29 (London, 1871), p. 7.

106 G.I. Wolseley, 'England as a Military Power in 1854 and in 1878', *Nineteenth Century*, 13 (1878), 433–56 (p. 456).

107 Headnote to 'The Fleet', *Poems*, III, p. 131.

108 Smiles, p. 332.

109 *AT Letters*, III, p. 220, n. 1.

110 J. Timothy Lovelace, *The Artistry and Tradition of Tennyson's Battle Poetry* (New York: Routledge, 2003), p. 109.

111 Ledbetter, p. 136.

112 *Memoir*, 1897, II, pp. 319–20.

113 Ann Thwaite, *Emily Tennyson: The Poet's Wife*, 2nd edn (London: Faber and Faber, 1997), p. 524.

114 The dialogue mirrors the conversation between Irenaeus and Tlepolemus in 'Peace and War: A Dialogue', *Blackwood's Edinburgh Magazine*, 76 (1854), 589–99, which Tennyson also used for Part I of *Maud* (1855).

115 *Memoir*, 1897, I, p. 194.

116 *Memoir*, 1897, II, p. 128.

117 Linda K. Hughes, 'Tennyson's Urban Arthurians: Victorian Audiences and the "City Built to Music"', in *King Arthur Through the Ages*, ed. Valerie M. Lagorio and Mildred Leak Day, 2 vols (New York: Garland, 1990), II, pp. 39–61 (p. 40).

118 Walter Bagehot, *The English Constitution*, ed. Miles Taylor (Oxford: Oxford University Press, 2001), p. 193.

119 As Cammy Thomas notes, Tennyson 'has softened the rape in Malory', 'The Two Arthurs', *Tennyson Research Bulletin*, 6 (1993), 99–111 (p. 100).

120 [W.E. Gladstone], '*Idylls of the King* [1859] and Earlier Works', *Quarterly Review*, 106 (1859), 454–85 (p. 465).

121 Morrow, p. 14.

122 *Memoir*, 1897, I, p. 326, n. 4.

123 As James Eli Adams observes, the scene 'strikingly embodies' *Past and Present*, Augustus Egg's 'well-known representation of an adulterous wife . . . exhibited at the Royal Academy in 1858'; 'Harlots and Base Interpreters: Scandal and Slander in *Idylls of the King*', *Victorian Poetry*, 30 (1992), 421–39 (p. 433).

124 Saunders, p. 136.

125 *Memoir*, 1897, I, p. 189.

126 *Memoir*, 1897, I, p. 81.

127 Cited in Kaplan, ed., p. 201 (see Browning, Elizabeth Barrett).

6 'Ever-broadening England': Tennyson and Empire

1 Andrew Porter, 'Preface', in *The Nineteenth Century*, ed. Andrew Porter, The Oxford History of the British Empire, III (Oxford: Oxford University Press, 1999), pp. ix–xi (p. ix).

2 Robert H. MacDonald, *The Language of Empire: Myths and Metaphors of Popular Imperialism, 1880–1918* (Manchester: Manchester University Press, 1994), p. 6.

3 Hallam Tennyson, *Alfred Lord Tennyson: A Memoir, By His Son* (London: Macmillan, 1899), p. 837. Hereafter *Memoir*, 1899.

4 Richard A. Sylvia, 'Reading Tennyson's *Ballads and Other Poems* in Context', *Journal of the Midwest Modern Language Association*, 23 (1990), 27–44 (p. 27).

5 Catherine Hall, 'The egalitarian instinct', *Guardian Review*, 20 April 2002, p. 3.

6 Don Randall, 'Autumn 1857: The Making of the Indian "Mutiny"', *Victorian Literature and Culture*, 31 (2003), 3–17 (p. 15, n. 1). In this chapter I follow Randall's example and 'retain this naming in my text as it is, throughout the Victorian era . . . , the most common and recognizable way of referring to the 1857 uprisings in India'.

7 Catherine Hall, *Civilising Subjects: Metropole and Colony in the English Imagination, 1830–1867* (Cambridge: Polity, 2002), p. 12.

8 Douglas A. Lorimer, 'Race, Science and Culture: Historical Continuities and Discontinuities, 1850–1914', in *The Victorians and Race*, ed. Shearer West (Aldershot: Scolar, 1997), pp. 12–33 (p. 14).

9 Andrew Porter, 'Introduction: Britain and the Empire in the Nineteenth Century', in Porter, ed., pp. 1–28 (pp. 1–4). A more recent study of 'new imperial history' similarly 'begin[s] from the premise that historians and critics should address metropole and colonies as interrelated analytic fields', Kathleen Wilson, 'Introduction: Histories, Empires, Modernities', in *A New Imperial History: Culture, Identity, and Modernity in Britain and the Empire, 1660–1840*, ed. Kathleen Wilson (Cambridge: Cambridge University Press, 2004), pp. 1–26 (pp. 18–19).

10 Colin Graham, *Ideologies of Epic: Nation, Empire and Victorian Epic Poetry* (Manchester: Manchester University Press, 1998), p. 17.

11 Patrick Brantlinger, *Rule of Darkness: British Literature and Imperialism, 1830–1914* (Ithaca, NY: Cornell University Press, 1988), p. 8.

12 Lynne B. O'Brien, 'Male Heroism: Tennyson's Divided View', *Victorian Poetry*, 32 (1994), 171–82 (p. 171).

13 Robin L. Inboden, 'The "Valour of Delicate Women": The Domestication of Political Relations in Tennyson's Laureate Poetry', *Victorian Poetry*, 36 (1998), 205–21 (p. 205).

14 Marion Shaw, 'Tennyson's Dark Continent', *Victorian Poetry*, 32 (1994), 157–69 (p. 161).

15 Wm. Roger Louis, 'Foreword', in Porter, ed., pp. vi–viii (p. vii).

16 'Introduction', in Porter, ed., p. 19.

17 Elleke Boehmer, 'Introduction', in *Empire Writing: An Anthology of Colonial Literature 1870–1918*, ed. Elleke Boehmer (Oxford: Oxford University Press, 1998), pp. xv–xxxvi (p. xvii).

18 Ansgar Nünning, 'On the Discursive Construction of an Empire of the Mind: Metaphorical Re-Membering as a Means of Narrativizing and Naturalizing Cultural Transformations', *Yearbook of Research in English and American Literature*, 20 (2004), 59–93 (pp. 87, 88, 89, 91); on page 91 and elsewhere Nünning refers to 'the British empire'.

19 Hall, *Civilising Subjects*, p. 22.

20 Hall, 'The egalitarian instinct', p. 3. The history of Haiti, which became an independent republic in 1804, is discussed in C.L.R. James, *The Black Jacobins: Toussaint L'Ouverture and the San Domingo Rebellion*, 4th edn (London: Penguin, 2001).

21 Headnote to 'Anacaona', *The Poems of Tennyson*, ed. Christopher Ricks, 2nd edn, 3 vols (London: Longman, 1987), I, p. 308. Hereafter *Poems*.

22 *Tennyson in Lincoln: A Catalogue of the Collections in the Research Centre*, ed. Nancie Campbell, 2 vols (Lincoln: Tennyson Society, 1971), I, p. 22. Headnote to 'Anacaona', *Poems*, I, pp. 308–9.

23 David G. Riede, 'Tennyson's Poetics of Melancholy and the Imperial Imagination', *Studies in English Literature*, 40 (2000), 659–78 (pp. 670–1).

24 Alexander Lyon Macfie, 'Introduction', *Orientalism: A Reader*, ed. Alexander Lyon Macfie (New York: New York University Press, 2000), pp. 1–8 (pp. 1–4).

25 Edward W. Said, *Orientalism: Western Conceptions of the Orient*, 4th edn (London: Penguin, 1995), p. 3.

26 Colin Graham, p. 17.

27 Julie F. Codell and Dianne Sachko Macleod, 'Introduction: Orientalism Transposed: the "Easternization" of Britain and Interventions to Colonial Discourse', in *Orientalism Transposed: The Impact of the Colonies on British Culture*, ed. Julie F. Codell and Dianne Sachko Macleod (Aldershot: Ashgate, 1998), pp. 1–10 (p. 1).

28 Mary Louise Pratt, *Imperial Eyes: Travel Writing and Transculturation*, 2nd edn (New York: Routledge, 2008), p. 7.

29 Riede, pp. 671–2.

30 [William Johnson Fox], '*Poems, Chiefly Lyrical*', *Westminster Review*, 14 (1831), 210–24 (p. 216).

31 Riede, p. 660.

32 Robert Johnson, *British Imperialism* (Basingstoke: Palgrave Macmillan, 2003), p. 2. Succeeding references to Johnson in this paragraph are from pp. 2–3.

33 Said, p. 3.

34 'Introduction', in Porter, ed., p. 5.

35 Washington Irving, *A History of the Life and Voyages of Christopher Columbus*, 4 vols (London: Murray, 1828), II, pp. 420 and 425.

36 Susan Shatto, 'The Strange Charm of "Far, Far Away": Tennyson, the Continent, and the Empire', in *Creditable Warriors: 1830–1876*, ed. Michael Cotsell, English Literature and the Wider World, III (London: Ashfield, 1990), pp. 113–29 (p. 123).

37 Irving, II, p. 123.

38 Emily A. Haddad, 'Tennyson, Arnold, and the Wealth of the East', *Victorian Literature and Culture*, 32 (2004), 373–91 (p. 373). Succeeding references to Haddad in this paragraph are taken from pp. 376 and 381.

39 Alan Sinfield, *Alfred Tennyson* (Oxford: Blackwell, 1986), p. 43.

40 Hallam Tennyson, *Alfred Lord Tennyson: A Memoir, By His Son*, 3rd edn, 2 vols (London: Macmillan, 1897), I, p. 56. Hereafter *Memoir*, 1897.

41 *The Letters of Alfred Lord Tennyson*, 3 vols (Oxford: Clarendon Press, 1982–90), ed. Cecil Y. Lang and Edgar F. Shannon, Jr, I, p. 149 ([8 or 9 January 1837]). Hereafter *AT Letters*. In the original letter, held in the Wren Library of Trinity College, Cambridge, Tennyson censored the offensive term, which consists of a lower case 'b' followed by a dash.

42 Edgar F. Shannon, Jr., *Tennyson and the Reviewers* (Cambridge, MA: Harvard University Press, 1952), p. 28. Although 'nominally' edited by Lord Northampton, *The Tribute* was 'actually' edited by Richard Monckton Milnes; Roger Evans, 'Charles Tennyson Turner and his Audience', *Tennyson Research Bulletin*, 9 (2008), 188–200 (p. 193).

43 Haddad, p. 381.

44 Brantlinger, 1988, p. 9.

45 *Poems*, I, p. 523, note to lines 11–12.

46 D.A. Washbrook, 'India, 1818–1860: The Two Faces of Colonialism', in Porter, ed., pp. 395–421 (p. 400).

47 Johnson, p. 4.

48 Hall, 'The egalitarian instinct', p. 3.

49 Headnote to 'O mother Britain', *Poems*, II, p. 46.

50 David Thomson, *England in the Nineteenth Century: 1815–1914*, 3rd edn, The Pelican History of England, 8 (London: Penguin, 1991), pp. 88–9.

51 *Guardian*, 2 August 1834, cited in *Guardian*, 5 November 2007, p. 5.

52 Gad Heuman, 'The British West Indies', in Porter, ed., pp. 470–93 (p. 470).
53 Hall, *Civilising Subjects*, p. 70.
54 Said, pp. 12 and 3.
55 'Introduction', in Porter, ed., p. 21.
56 Catherine Hall, '"From Greenland's Icy Mountains . . . to Afric's Golden Sand": Ethnicity, Race and Nation in Mid-Nineteenth-Century England', *Gender & History*, 5 (1993), 212–30 (pp. 217–18).
57 Nünning, p. 61.
58 Shaw, 1994, p. 161.
59 *Tennyson: A Selected Edition*, ed. Christopher Ricks, 2nd edn (Harlow: Longman, 1989), pp. 70–1. Hereafter *Selected Edition*.
60 Isobel Armstrong, *Victorian Poetry: Poetry, Poetics and Politics*, 2nd edn (London: Routledge, 1996), p. 87.
61 *Memoir*, 1897, I, p. 196.
62 Sinfield, p. 53.
63 Matthew Rowlinson, 'The Ideological Moment of Tennyson's "Ulysses"', in *Tennyson*, ed. Rebecca Stott (Harlow: Longman, 1996), pp. 148–60 (p. 151).
64 *Memoir*, 1897, II, p. 133, n. 1.
65 Shannon, 1952, p. 82.
66 Rowlinson, pp. 149–50.
67 Gauri Viswanathan, 'Currying Favor: The Politics of British Educational and Cultural Policy in India, 1813–54', in *Dangerous Liaisons: Gender, Nation, and Postcolonial Perspectives*, ed. Anne McClintock, Aamir Mufti and Ella Shohat (Minneapolis: University of Minnesota Press, 1997), pp. 113–29 (p. 119).
68 Chris Baldick, *The Social Mission of English Criticism 1848–1932* (Oxford: Clarendon Press, 1983), pp. 70–1.
69 *The Golden Treasury*, ed. Francis Turner Palgrave, 5th edn (London: Oxford University Press, 1964), p. xii.
70 Rowlinson, pp. 152–3.
71 C.C. Eldridge, *The Imperial Experience: From Carlyle to Forster* (Basingstoke: Macmillan – now Palgrave Macmillan, 1996), p. 14. Rowlinson (p. 152) notes that 'imperialism' was first recorded in English in 1851.
72 Cited in Rowlinson, p. 152.
73 *The Times*, 17 March 1876, cited in Eldridge, p. 14.
74 John O. Waller, *A Circle of Friends: The Tennysons and the Lushingtons of Park House* (Columbus: Ohio State University Press, 1986), p. 183.
75 Henry George, Earl Grey, *The Colonial Policy of Lord John Russell's Administration*, 2nd edn, 2 vols (London: Bentley, 1853), I, p. 13.
76 Shatto, p. 124.
77 O'Brien, p. 179.
78 Riede, p. 667.
79 Armstrong, 1996, p. 96.
80 Seamus Perry, *Alfred Tennyson* (Tavistock: Northcote House, 2005), p. 86.
81 Lorimer, p. 29
82 Thomas Carlyle, *Past and Present*, ed. Richard D. Altick (New York: New York University Press, 1965), p. 7.
83 Reginald Horsman, 'Origins of Racial Anglo-Saxonism in Great Britain before 1850', in *Race, Gender, and Rank: Early Modern Ideas of Humanity*, ed.

Maryanne Cline Horowitz (Rochester, NY: University of Rochester Press, 1992), pp. 77–100 (p. 77).

84 Reginald Horsman, *Race and Manifest Destiny: The Origins of American Racial Anglo-Saxonism* (Cambridge, MA: Harvard University Press, 1981), pp. 9–10. Succeeding references to Horsman, 1981, in this paragraph are taken from pp. 14–15.

85 Horsman, 1992, p. 80. Succeeding references to Horsman, 1992, in this paragraph are taken from pp. 85 and 89.

86 Nancy Stepan, *The Idea of Race in Science: Great Britain 1800–1960* (London: Macmillan, 1982), p. ix.

87 Lorimer, p. 16.

88 The volume was republished in 1862 as *The Races of Men: A Philosophical Enquiry into the Influence of Race over the Destinies of Nations* with several 'supplementary chapters'.

89 Stepan, pp. 41 and 44.

90 Lorimer, p. 15. *An Essay on the Inequality of the Human Races*, by Joseph Arthur Comte de Gobineau, was published 1853–55; however, Nancy Stepan notes (p. 41) that the book's 'influence was negligible on science until much later'.

91 Robert Knox, *The Races of Men: A Philosophical Enquiry into the Influence of Race over the Destinies of Nations*, 2nd edn (London: Renshaw, 1862), pp. 1–2.

92 Horsman, 1992, p. 95.

93 Knox, 1862, pp. 12–13. Further quotations from Knox in this paragraph are followed by the relevant page numbers in parentheses. Italics in the original.

94 *Cultures of Empire: Colonizers in Britain and the Empire in the Nineteenth and Twentieth Centuries: A Reader*, ed. Catherine Hall (Manchester: Manchester University Press, 2000), p. 7.

95 'Introduction', in Porter, ed., p. 9.

96 Brantlinger, 1988, particularly Chapter 7 'The Well at Cawnpore: Literary Representations of the Indian Mutiny of 1857', pp. 199–224. Randall, p. 3.

97 Laura Callanan, '"So Help Me God, the Truth and Not the Truth": Hyper-Realism and the Taxonomy of Truth-Seeking in the Royal Commission's Inquiry into the 1865 Jamaica Rebellion', in *Victorians Institute Journal*, 30 (2002), 7–37.

98 *Memoir*, 1897, I, pp. 423–4.

99 Randall, p. 4.

100 Brantlinger, p. 205.

101 *The White Man's Burdens: An Anthology of British Poetry of the Empire*, ed. Chris Brooks and Peter Faulkner (Exeter: University of Exeter Press, 1996), p. 193. Simon Dentith points out that in its original volume 'Havelock's March' was accompanied by poems praising Garibaldi and 'an alternative and more democratic national anthem', *Epic and Empire in Nineteenth-Century Britain* (Cambridge: Cambridge University Press, 2006), p. 141.

102 *Memoir*, 1897, I, p. 435.

103 *Memoir*, 1897, I, p. 432.

104 Headnote to 'Dedicatory Poem to the Princess Alice', *Poems*, III, p. 35. When her children were ill with diphtheria, Princess Alice nursed them herself; she and her four-year-old daughter died, the other children recovered.

105   *AT Letters*, III, p. 173 ([5 June 1879]).
106   Dorothy Jones, 'Fabricating Texts of Empire', *Kunapipi*, 16 (1994), 1–16 (p. 5).
107   Gautam Chakravarty, *The Indian Mutiny and the British Imagination* (Cambridge: Cambridge University Press, 2005), p. 107.
108   *Memoir*, 1897, I, pp. 479–80.
109   Inboden, p. 213.
110   'The sand was killing in their souls; the wind a fiery flood; | Oh, for one waft of heather-breath from off a Scottish wold! | One shower that makes our English leaves smile greener for its gold!', quoted in Brooks and Faulkner (p. 195) without line numbers.
111   Sylvia, p. 36.
112   Inboden, p. 213.
113   Inboden, p. 214.
114   Callanan, p. 8.
115   *The Times*, 18 November 1865, p. 8; *Times Digital Archive, 1785–1985* [accessed 28 March 2010].
116   *Memoir*, 1897, II, pp. 40–1.
117   Robert Bernard Martin, *Tennyson: The Unquiet Heart*, 2nd edn (London: Faber and Faber, 1983), pp. 458–9.
118   Mary R. Baine and Rodney M. Baine, 'Blake's Other Tigers, and "The Tyger"', *Studies in English Literature, 1500–1900*, 15 (1975), 563–78 (p. 565).
119   *Memoir*, 1897, II, p. 41.
120   Byron Farwell, *Queen Victoria's Little Wars*, 2nd edn (Ware: Wordsworth, 1999), p. 1.
121   Calculating that 'Her colonial empire . . . costs England 1,000,000*l* per annum, or about 9*d* yearly per head of the population of the United Kingdom', James Spedding concluded that 'The colonies are worth keeping on account of the trade we do with them and they with us.' [James Spedding], 'The Future of the British Empire', *Westminster Review*, 38 (1870), 47–74 (pp. 59 and 63).
122   *Memoir*, 1897, II, p. 101.
123   Robert Inglesfield, 'Tennyson and the Imperial Federation League', *Tennyson Research Bulletin*, 7 (1998), 83–6 (p. 85).
124   *The Times*, 30 October, 1872, p. 9; *Times Digital Archive, 1785–1985* [accessed 29 March 2010].
125   *AT Letters*, III, p. 41 (8 November 1872).
126   *AT Letters*, III, p. 55 (18 March 1873).
127   Hall, *Cultures of Empire*, p. 1.
128   J.R. Seeley, *The Expansion of England: Two Courses of Lectures* (London: Macmillan, 1883), p. 184.
129   Hall, *Cultures of Empire*, p. 2.
130   Brantlinger, p. 19.
131   *Memoir*, 1897, II, p. 255.
132   *Memoir*, 1897, II, p. 343.
133   Cecily Devereux, 'Tennyson, W.T. Stead, and "The Imperialism of Responsibility": "Vastness" and "The Maiden Tribute"', *Victorian Newsletter*, 93 (1998), 13–17 (p. 14).
134   J.W. Robertson Scott, *The Life and Death of a Newspaper* (London: Methuen, 1952), p. 176.

135 Cited in Devereux, p. 16.
136 *Memoir*, 1897, II, p. 372.
137 Headnote to 'Akbar's Dream', *Poems*, III, p. 235. The books sent by Jowett are listed in *Memoir*, 1897, II, p. 388.
138 Paul Stevens and Rahul Sapra, 'Akbar's Dream: Moghul Toleration and English/British Orientalism', *Modern Philology*, 104 (2007), 379–411 (p. 389).
139 John McBratney, 'Rebuilding Akbar's "Fane": Tennyson's Reclamation of the East', *Victorian Poetry*, 31 (1993), 411–17 (p. 413).
140 The historic Akbar's 'son and successor' was 'Jahangir'; Stevens and Sapra, pp. 399–400.
141 Tennyson's headnote to 'Akbar's Dream', *Poems*, III, p. 236.
142 *Memoir*, 1897, II, p. 388.
143 Visiting Tennyson at Farringford in January 1892, the composer Hubert Parry found the poet 'much exercised about eternal punishment'; Robert Bernard Martin, p. 577.
144 Said, p. 12.
145 Francis Palgrave, cited in *Memoir*, 1899, p. 837.
146 Brantlinger, p. 8.
147 O'Brien, p. 171; Inboden, p. 205.
148 Sylvia, p. 27.

Conclusion: Fabricating Englishness

1 Krishan Kumar, *The Making of English National Identity* (Cambridge: Cambridge University Press, 2003), p. xii.
2 Elizabeth Helsinger, *Rural Scenes and National Representation: Britain, 1815–1850* (Princeton, NJ: Princeton University Press, 1997), p. 7.
3 Helsinger, p. 241, n. 18.
4 Catherine Hall, 'The Rule of Difference: Gender, Class and Empire in the Making of the 1832 Reform Act', in *Gendered Nations: Nationalisms and Gender Order in the Long Nineteenth Century*, ed. Ida Blom, Karen Hagemann and Catherine Hall (Oxford: Berg, 2000), p. 108.
5 Francis Palgrave cited in Hallam Tennyson, *Alfred Lord Tennyson: A Memoir, By His Son* (London: Macmillan, 1899), p. 837.

Works Cited

Abrams, M.H., ed., *The Norton Anthology of English Literature*, 5th edn, 2 vols (New York: Norton, 1962)

Ackroyd, Peter, *Albion: The Origins of the English Imagination* (London: Chatto & Windus, 2002)

Ackroyd, Peter, *The History of England: Volume 1, Foundation* (London: Macmillan, 2011)

Adams, Charles Hansford, ed., *The Narrative of Robert Adams, A Barbary Captive: A Critical Edition* (Cambridge: Cambridge University Press, 2005)

Adams, James Eli, 'Harlots and Base Interpreters: Scandal and Slander in *Idylls of the King*', *Victorian Poetry*, 30 (1992), 421–39

Adams, James Eli, *Dandies and Desert Saints: Styles of Victorian Masculinity* (Ithaca, NY: Cornell University Press, 1995)

Ahern, Stephen, 'Listening to Guinevere: Female Agency and the Politics of Chivalry in Tennyson's *Idylls*', *Studies in Philology*, 101 (2004), 88–112

Ahmad, Aijaz, *In Theory: Classes, Nations, Literatures* (London: Verso, 1992)

Allen, Peter, *The Cambridge Apostles: The Early Years* (Cambridge: Cambridge University Press, 1978)

Allingham, H. and D. Radford, eds, *William Allingham: A Diary, 1824–1889*, 3rd edn (Harmondsworth: Penguin, 1985)

Altick, Richard D., *The English Common Reader*, 2nd edn (Columbus: Ohio State University Press, 1968)

Altick, Richard D., 'Signs of the Times, 1837–1887', *Victorian Poetry*, 25 (1987), 89–105

Anderson, Benedict, *Imagined Communities: Reflections on the Origin and Spread of Nationalism*, 3rd edn (London: Verso, 2006)

Anstruther, Ian, *Coventry Patmore's Angel* (London: Haggerston, 1992)

Arber, Edward, ed., *The Last Fight of the Revenge at Sea*, English Reprint 29 (London, 1871)

Armstrong, Isobel, *Victorian Scrutinies: Reviews of Poetry 1830–1870* (London: Athlone Press, 1972)

Armstrong, Isobel, *Victorian Poetry: Poetry, Poetics and Politics*, 2nd edn (London: Routledge, 1996)

Ash, Timothy Garton, 'No cant, please, we're British: But we do need a better sense of citizenship', *Guardian*, 13 March 2008, p. 23

Bagehot, Walter, *The English Constitution*, ed. Miles Taylor (Oxford: Oxford University Press, 2001)

Baine, Mary R. and Rodney M. Baine, 'Blake's Other Tigers, and "The Tyger"', *Studies in English Literature, 1500–1900*, 15 (1975), 563–78

Baldick, Chris, *The Social Mission of English Criticism 1848–1932* (Oxford: Clarendon Press, 1983)

Barber, Richard, *The Holy Grail: Imagination and Belief* (London: Allen Lane, 2004)

Barber, Richard, *The Reign of Chivalry*, 2nd edn (Woodbridge: Boydell & Brewer, 2005)

Barczewski, Stephanie L., *Myth and National Identity in Nineteenth-Century Britain: The Legends of King Arthur and Robin Hood* (Oxford: Oxford University Press, 2000)

Barrell, John, *The Dark Side of the Landscape: The Rural Poor in English Painting 1739–1840* (Cambridge: Cambridge University Press, 1980)

Barton, Anna, *Tennyson's Name: Identity and Responsibility in the Poetry of Alfred Lord Tennyson* (Aldershot: Ashgate, 2008)

Baswell, Christopher and William Sharpe, eds, *The Passing of Arthur: New Essays in Arthurian Tradition* (New York: Garland, 1988)

Batchelor, John, *Tennyson: To Strive, To Seek, To Find* (London: Chatto & Windus, 2012)

[Bell, Robert?], 'Poems', *Atlas*, 16 December 1832, p. 842

Berberich, Christine, '"I was Meditating about England": The Importance of Rural England for the Construction of "Englishness"', in *History, Nationhood and the Question of Britain*, ed. Helen Brocklehurst and Robert Phillips (Basingstoke: Palgrave Macmillan, 2004), pp. 375–85

Berberich, Christine, 'This Green and Pleasant Land: Cultural Constructions of Englishness', in *Landscape and Englishness*, ed. Robert Burden and Stephan Kohl (Amsterdam: Rodopi, 2006), pp. 207–24

Biddiss, Michael D., *Father of Racist Ideology: The Social and Political Thought of Count Gobineau* (London: Weidenfeld & Nicolson, 1970)

Boehmer, Elleke, ed., *Empire Writing: An Anthology of Colonial Literature 1870–1918* (Oxford: Oxford University Press, 1998)

Bowden, Marjorie, *Tennyson in France* (Manchester: Manchester University Press, 1930)

Boyd, David L., 'Tennyson's Camelot Revisited: An Augustinian Approach to the *Idylls*', in *The Arthurian Tradition: Essays in Convergence*, ed. Mary Flowers Braswell and John Bugge (Tuscaloosa: University of Alabama Press, 1988), pp. 163–74

Brantlinger, Patrick, *Rule of Darkness: British Literature and Imperialism, 1830–1914* (Ithaca, NY: Cornell University Press, 1988)

Brantlinger, Patrick, *Victorian Literature and Postcolonial Studies* (Edinburgh: Edinburgh University Press, 2009)

Brett-Smith, H.F.B., ed., *Peacock's Four Ages of Poetry, Shelley's Defence of Poetry, Browning's Essay on Poetry* (Oxford: Blackwell, 1921)

Brightfield, Myron F., *John Wilson Croker* (Berkeley, CA: University of California Press, 1940)

Bristow, Joseph, ed., *The Victorian Poet: Poets and Persona* (London: Croom Helm, 1987)

Brooks, Chris and Peter Faulkner, eds, *The White Man's Burdens: An Anthology of British Poetry of the Empire* (Exeter: University of Exeter Press, 1996)

Browning, Elizabeth Barrett, *Aurora Leigh and Other Poems*, ed. Cora Kaplan, 5th edn (London: Women's Press, 1993)

Bryant, Hallman B., 'The African Genesis of Tennyson's "Timbuctoo"', *Tennyson Research Bulletin*, 3 (1981), 196–202

Bryden, Inga, 'Reinventing Origins: the Victorian Arthur and Racial Myth', in *The Victorians and Race*, ed. Shearer West (Aldershot: Scolar, 1996), pp. 141–55

Bryden, Inga, *Reinventing King Arthur: The Arthurian Legends in Victorian Culture* (Aldershot: Ashgate, 2005)

Buckley, Jerome H., 'The Persistence of Tennyson', in *The Victorian Experience: The Poets*, ed. Richard A. Levine (Athens: Ohio University Press, 1982), pp. 1–22

Buckley, Jerome H., 'Tennyson's Landscapes', *Tennyson Research Bulletin*, 6 (1996), 278–88

Bulwer-Lytton, Edward, *England and the English*, 2nd edn, 2 vols (London: Bentley, 1833)

Burden, Robert and Stephan Kohl, eds, *Landscape and Englishness* (Amsterdam: Rodopi, 2006)

Burroughs, Peter, 'Defence and Imperial Disunity', in *The Nineteenth Century*, ed. Andrew Porter, The Oxford History of the British Empire, III (Oxford: Oxford University Press, 1999), pp. 320–45

Cain, P.J. and A.G. Hopkins, *British Imperialism: Innovation and Expansion 1688–1914*, 2nd edn (London: Longman, 2003)

Callanan, Laura, '"So Help Me God, the Truth and Not the Truth": Hyper-Realism and the Taxonomy of Truth-Seeking in the Royal Commission's Inquiry into the 1865 Jamaica Rebellion', *Victorians Institute Journal*, 30 (2002), 7–37

Cambridge Prize Poems 1828–1835 (Cambridge: Smith, 1835)

Campbell, Nancie, ed., *Tennyson in Lincoln: A Catalogue of the Collections in the Research Centre*, 2 vols (Lincoln: Tennyson Society, 1971)

Cannadine, David, *Ornamentalism: How the British Saw Their Empire*, 2nd edn (London: Penguin, 2002)

[Carlyle, Thomas], 'Signs of the Times', *Edinburgh Review*, 49 (1829), 439–59

[Carlyle, Thomas], *Occasional Discourse on the Negro Question* (London: Bosworth, 1853)

Carlyle, Thomas, *Past and Present*, ed. Richard D. Altick (New York: New York University Press, 1965)

Carlyle, Thomas, *On Heroes, Hero-Worship, and the Heroic in History*, ed. Michael K. Goldberg (Berkeley, CA: University of California Press, 1993)

Chadwick, Joseph, 'A Blessing and a Curse: The Poetics of Privacy in Tennyson's "The Lady of Shalott"', *Victorian Poetry*, 24 (1986), 13–30

Chakravarty, Gautam, *The Indian Mutiny and the British Imagination* (Cambridge: Cambridge University Press, 2005)

Chandler, Alice, *A Dream of Order: The Medieval Ideal in Nineteenth-Century English Literature* (London: Routledge & Kegan Paul, 1971)

Chandler, Alice, 'Order and Disorder in the Medieval Revival', *Browning Institute Studies*, 8 (1980), 1–9

Chase, Malcolm, *Chartism: A New History* (Manchester: Manchester University Press, 2007)

Chater, Kathy and Simon Fowler, 'A Storehouse of Knowledge', *Ancestors* (September 2005), 58–9

Christ, Carol T., 'T.S. Eliot and the Victorians', *Modern Philology*, 79 (1981), 157–65

Christ, Carol T., *Victorian and Modern Poetics* (Chicago: University of Chicago Press, 1984)

Christ, Carol T. and John O. Jordan, eds, *Victorian Literature and the Victorian Visual Imagination* (Berkeley, CA: University of California Press, 1995)

Cobbett, William, *Rural Rides*, ed. Ian Dyck (London: Penguin, 2001)

Cochran, Rebecca, 'Tennyson's Hierarchy of Women in *Idylls of the King*', in *History and Community: Essays on Victorian Medievalism*, ed. Florence S. Boos (New York: Garland, 1992), pp. 81–107

Codell, Julie F. and Dianne Sachko Macleod, eds, *Orientalism Transposed: The Impact of the Colonies on British Culture* (Aldershot: Ashgate, 1998)

Colley, Linda, *Britons: Forging the Nation 1707–1837*, 3rd edn (New Haven, CT: Yale University Press, 2005)

Colls, Robert, *Identity of England* (Oxford: Oxford University Press, 2002)

[Croker, John Wilson], 'Poems', *Quarterly Review*, 49 (1833), 81–96

Cronin, Richard, 'Victorian Romance: Medievalism', in *A Companion to Romance: From Classical to Contemporary*, ed. Corinne Saunders (Malden, MA: Blackwell, 2004), pp. 341–59

Culler, Dwight A., 'The English Idyls', in *Tennyson: A Collection of Critical Essays*, ed. Elizabeth A. Francis (Eaglewood Cliffs, NJ: Prentice-Hall, 1980), pp. 70–94

Culver, Marcia C., 'The Death and Birth of an Epic: Tennyson's "Morte d'Arthur"', *Victorian Poetry*, 20 (1982), 51–61

Darby, Wendy Joy, *Landscape and Identity: Geographies of Nation and Class in England* (Oxford: Berg, 2000)

Davies, Norman, *The Isles: A History*, 2nd edn (Basingstoke: Macmillan – now Palgrave Macmillan, 2000)

Day, Aidan, 'The Spirit of Fable: Arthur Hallam and Romantic Values in Tennyson's "Timbuctoo"', *Tennyson Research Bulletin*, 4 (1983), 59–71

Day, Aidan, *Tennyson's Scepticism* (Basingstoke: Palgrave Macmillan, 2005)

Day, Aidan and P.G. Scott, 'Tennyson's *Ode on the Death of the Duke of Wellington:* Addenda to Shannon and Ricks', *Studies in Bibliography*, 35 (1982), 320–3

Dellheim, Charles, 'Interpreting Victorian Medievalism', in *History and Community: Essays in Victorian Medievalism*, ed. Florence S. Boos (New York: Garland 1992), pp. 39–58

Dennison, Matthew, *The Last Princess: The Devoted Life of Queen Victoria's Youngest Daughter*, 2nd edn (New York: St Martin's Griffin, 2009)

Dentith, Simon, *Epic and Empire in Nineteenth-Century Britain* (Cambridge: Cambridge University Press, 2006)

Devereux, Cecily, 'Canada and the Epilogue to the *Idylls*: "The Imperial Connection" in 1873', *Victorian Poetry*, 36 (1998), 223–41

Devereux, Cecily, 'Tennyson, W.T. Stead, and "The Imperialism of Responsibility": "Vastness" and "The Maiden Tribute"', *Victorian Newsletter*, 93 (1998), 13–17

Dixon, John, *A Schooling in English: Critical Episodes in the Struggle to Shape Literary and Cultural Studies* (Buckingham: Open University Press, 1991)

Douglas-Fairhurst, Robert and Seamus Perry, eds, *Tennyson Among the Poets* (Oxford: Oxford University Press, 2009)

Drabble, Margaret, ed., *The Oxford Companion to English Literature* (Oxford: Oxford University Press, 1985)

Dyson, Hope and Charles Tennyson, eds, *Dear and Honoured Lady: The Correspondence between Queen Victoria and Alfred Lord Tennyson* (London: Macmillan, 1969)

Eagleton, Terry, *Literary Theory: An Introduction*, Anniversary Edition (Maldon, MA: Blackwell, 2008)

Ebbatson, Roger, 'Enoch Arden's Other Island', *Tennyson Research Bulletin*, 6 (1995), 240–53

Ebbatson, Roger, *Tennyson's English Idylls*, Tennyson Society Occasional Paper 12 (Lincoln: Tennyson Society, 2003)

Ebbatson, Roger, *An Imaginary England: Nation, Landscape and Literature, 1840–1920* (Aldershot: Ashgate, 2005)

Eidson, John Olin, *Tennyson in America: His Reputation and Influence from 1827 to 1858* (Athens, GA: University of Georgia Press, 1943)

Eldridge, C.C., *The Imperial Experience: From Carlyle to Forster* (Basingstoke: Macmillan – now Palgrave Macmillan, 1996)

Eliot, T.S., 'In Memoriam', *Essays Ancient and Modern* (London: Faber and Faber, 1936)

Ellis, Sarah Stickney, *The Women of England: Their Social Duties, and Domestic Habits* (London: Fisher, 1839)

Emerson, Ralph Waldo, *English Traits* (London: Routledge, 1856)

'Essay on Milton', in *Essays, by Lord Macaulay: Reprinted from the Edinburgh Review, Complete Edition* (London: Routledge, 1887), pp. 1–30

Evans, Ivor H., ed., *Brewer's Dictionary of Phrase and Fable*, 9th edn (London: Cassell, 1981)

Evans, Roger, 'Charles Tennyson Turner and his Audience', *Tennyson Research Bulletin*, 9 (2008), 188–200

Fara, Patricia, *Newton: The Making of Genius* (New York: Columbia University Press, 2002)

Farwell, Byron, *Queen Victoria's Little Wars*, 2nd edn (Ware: Wordsworth, 1999)

Fay, Elizabeth, *Romantic Medievalism: History and the Romantic Literary Ideal* (Basingstoke: Palgrave Macmillan, 2002)

Fisher, John H., *The Emergence of Standard English* (Lexington: University Press of Kentucky, 1996)

Fletcher, Pauline, *Gardens and Grim Ravines: The Language of Landscape in Victorian Poetry* (Princeton, NJ: Princeton University Press, 1983)

[Forster, John], '*Poems*', *True Sun*, 19 January 1833, p. 3

[Fox, William Johnson], '*Poems, Chiefly Lyrical*', *Westminster Review*, 14 (1831), 210–24

[Fox, William Johnson], '*Poems*', *Monthly Repository*, 73 (1833), 30–41

Fraser, Hilary, 'Victorian Poetry and Historicism', in *The Cambridge Companion to Victorian Poetry*, ed. Joseph Bristow (Cambridge: Cambridge University Press, 2000), pp. 114–36

Fredeman, William E., '"The Sphere of Common Duties": The Domestic Solution in Tennyson's Poetry', *Bulletin of the John Rylands Library*, 54 (1972), 357–83

Fredeman, William E., 'A Charivari for Queen Butterfly: *Punch* on Queen Victoria', *Victorian Poetry*, 25 (1987), 47–74

Fredeman, William E., 'The Last Idyll: Dozing in Avalon', in *The Passing of Arthur: New Essays in Arthurian Tradition*, ed. Christopher Baswell and William Sharpe (New York: Garland, 1988), pp. 264–76

Freedman, Jonathan, 'Ideological Battleground: Tennyson, Morris, and the Pastness of the Past', in *The Passing of Arthur: New Essays in Arthurian Tradition*, ed. Christopher Baswell and William Sharpe (New York: Garland, 1988), pp. 235–48

[Froude, J.A.], 'England's Forgotten Worthies', *Westminster Review*, 58 (1852), 32–67

Froude, J.A., *Oceania, or England and her Colonies* (London: Longmans, Green, 1886)

Gardiner, Juliet, *Queen Victoria* (London: Collins & Brown, 1997)

Gervais, David, *Literary Englands: Versions of 'Englishness' in Modern Writing* (Cambridge: Cambridge University Press, 1993)

Gettmann, Royal A., *A Victorian Publisher: A Study of the Bentley Papers* (Cambridge: Cambridge University Press, 1960)

Gilbert, Elliot L., 'The Female King: Tennyson's Arthurian Apocalypse', in *King Arthur: A Casebook*, ed. Edward Donald Kennedy (New York: Garland, 1996), pp. 229–55

Gilmour, Robin, *The Idea of the Gentleman in the Victorian Novel* (London: Allen & Unwin, 1981)

Gilmour, Robin, *The Victorian Period: The Intellectual and Cultural Context of English Literature 1830–1890* (London: Longman, 1993)

Girouard, Mark, *The Return to Camelot: Chivalry and the English Gentleman*, 2nd edn (New Haven, CT: Yale University Press, 1981)

[Gladstone, W.E.], 'Idylls of the King [1859] and Earlier Works', *Quarterly Review*, 106 (1859), 454–85

Graham, Colin, *Ideologies of Epic: Nation, Empire and Victorian Epic Poetry* (Manchester: Manchester University Press, 1998)

Graham, Walter, *English Literary Periodicals* (New York: Nelson, 1930)

Gray, J.M., *Thro' the Vision of the Night: A Study of Source, Evolution and Structure in Tennyson's Idylls of the King* (Edinburgh: Edinburgh University Press, 1980)

Grey, Henry George, *The Colonial Policy of Lord John Russell's Administration*, 2nd edn, 2 vols (London: Bentley, 1853)

Guardian, 5 November 2007, p. 5

Haddad, Emily A., 'Tennyson, Arnold, and the Wealth of the East', *Victorian Literature and Culture*, 32 (2004), 373–91

Hagen, June Steffensen, *Tennyson and his Publishers* (London: Macmillan, 1979)

Hair, Donald S., *Domestic and Heroic in Tennyson's Poetry* (Toronto: University of Toronto Press, 1981)

Hall, Catherine, '"From Greenland's Icy Mountains . . . to Afric's Golden Sand": Ethnicity, Race and Nation in Mid-Nineteenth-Century England', *Gender and History*, 5 (1993), 212–30

Hall, Catherine, 'The Rule of Difference: Gender, Class and Empire in the Making of the 1832 Reform Act', in *Gendered Nations: Nationalism and Gender Order in the Long Nineteenth Century*, ed. Ida Blom, Karen Hagemann and Catherine Hall (Oxford: Berg, 2000), pp. 107–35

Hall, Catherine, 'The Nation Within and Without', in *Defining the Victorian Nation: Class, Race, Gender and the Reform Act of 1867*, ed. Catherine Hall, Keith McClelland and Jane Rendall (Cambridge: Cambridge University Press, 2000), pp. 179–233

Hall, Catherine, 'The egalitarian instinct', *Guardian Review*, 20 April 2002, p. 3

Hall, Catherine, *Civilising Subjects: Metropole and Colony in the English Imagination, 1830–1867* (Cambridge: Polity, 2002)

Hall, Catherine, ed., *Cultures of Empire: Colonizers in Britain and the Empire in the Nineteenth and Twentieth Centuries: A Reader* (Manchester: Manchester University Press, 2000)

Hall, James, ed., *Dictionary of Subjects and Symbols in Art*, 9th edn (London: Murray, 1987)

[Hallam, Arthur Henry], 'On some of the Characteristics of Modern Poetry, and on the Lyrical Poems of Alfred Tennyson', *Englishman's Magazine*, 1 (1831), 616–28

Halperin, David M., *Before Pastoral: Theocritus and the Ancient Tradition of Bucolic Poetry* (New Haven, CT: Yale University Press, 1983)

Hargrove, Nancy D., 'Landscape as Symbol in Tennyson and Eliot', *Victorians Institute Journal*, 3–6 (1974–77), 73–83

Harrison, Antony H., *Victorian Poets and the Politics of Culture: Discourse and Ideology* (Charlottesville, VA: University Press of Virginia, 1998)

Harrison, J.F.C., *Early Victorian Britain 1832–51*, 2nd edn (London: Fontana, 1979)

Hart, John, *A Methode . . . to read English* (London: Denham, 1570)

Helsinger, Elizabeth K., *Rural Scenes and National Representation: Britain, 1815–1850* (Princeton, NJ: Princeton University Press, 1997)

Heuman, Gad, 'The British West Indies', in *The Nineteenth Century*, ed. Andrew Porter, The Oxford History of the British Empire, III (Oxford: Oxford University Press, 1999), pp. 470–93

Hobsbawm, Eric and Terence Ranger, eds, *The Invention of Tradition* (Cambridge: Cambridge University Press, 1983)

Hobsbawm, Eric and George Rudé, *Captain Swing*, 2nd edn (London: Phoenix, 2001)

Hodder, Karen, 'The Lady of Shalott in Art and Literature', in *Sexuality and Subordination: Interdisciplinary Studies of Gender in the Nineteenth Century*, ed. Susan Mendus and Jane Rendall (London: Routledge, 1989), pp. 60–88

Holloway, Lorretta M. and Jennifer A. Palmgren, eds, *Beyond Arthurian Romances: The Reach of Victorian Medievalism* (New York: Palgrave Macmillan, 2005)

Homans, Margaret, *Royal Representations: Queen Victoria and British Culture, 1837–1876* (Chicago: Chicago University Press, 1998)

Hoppen, K. Theodore, *The Mid-Victorian Generation, 1846–1886* (Oxford: Clarendon Press, 1998)

Horsman, Reginald, *Race and Manifest Destiny: The Origins of American Racial Anglo-Saxonism* (Cambridge, MA: Harvard University Press, 1981)

Horsman, Reginald, 'Origins of Racial Anglo-Saxonism in Great Britain before 1850', in *Race, Gender, and Rank: Early Modern Ideas of Humanity*, ed. Maryanne Cline Horowitz (Rochester, NY: University of Rochester Press, 1992), pp. 77–100

Howkins, Alun, *Reshaping Rural England: A Social History 1850–1925* (London: HarperCollins, 1991)

Howkins, Alun, 'Deserters from the Plough', *History Today*, 43 (1993), 32–8

Hughes, Linda K., 'Tennyson's Urban Arthurians: Victorian Audiences and the "City Built to Music"', in *King Arthur through the Ages*, ed. Valerie M. Lagorio and Mildred Leak Day, 2 vols (New York: Garland, 1990), II, pp. 39–61

Hughes, Linda K., '"Come Again, and Thrice as Fair": Reading Tennyson's Beginning', in *King Arthur's Modern Return*, ed. Debra N. Mancoff (New York: Garland, 1998), pp. 51–64

Hughes, Thomas, *Tom Brown at Oxford*, 2nd edn, 3 vols (Cambridge: Macmillan, 1861)

Hutchinson, Thomas, ed., *The Complete Poetical Works of Percy Bysshe Shelley* (London: Oxford University Press, 1952)

Inboden, Robin L., 'The "Valour of Delicate Women": The Domestication of Political Relations in Tennyson's Laureate Poetry', *Victorian Poetry* , 36 (1998), 205–21

Inglesfield, Robert, 'Tennyson and the Imperial Federation League', *Tennyson Research Bulletin*, 7 (1998), 83–6

Irving, Washington, *A History of the Life and Voyages of Christopher Columbus*, 4 vols (London: Murray, 1828)

Irving, Washington, *The Sketch Book*, ed. T. Balston (London: Oxford University Press, 1912)

Irving, Washington, *The Sketch Book of Geoffrey Crayon, Gent.* (New York: Heritage, 1939)

Jackson, George, *Popular Errors in English Grammar, Particularly in Pronunciation* (London: Wilson, 1830)

Jackson, Jeffrey, E., 'The Once and Future Sword: Excalibur and the Poetics of Imperial Heroism in *Idylls of the King*', *Victorian Poetry*, 46 (2008), 207–29

James, C.L.R., *The Black Jacobins: Toussaint L'Ouverture and the San Domingo Rebellion*, 4th edn (London: Penguin, 2001)

Jameson, Fredric, *The Political Unconscious: Narrative as a Socially Symbolic Act*, 4th edn (London: Routledge, 1996)

Jann, Rosemary, 'Democratic Myths in Victorian Medievalism', *Browning Institute Studies*, 8 (1980), 129–49

Jenkins, Simon, *A Short History of England* (London: Profile, 2011)

Jenkins, T.A., 'Wellington, Toryism and the Nation', *History Today* (November 2002), 26–33

Johnson, Catharine B., ed., *William Bodham Donne and His Friends* (London: Methuen, 1905)

Johnson, Robert, *British Imperialism* (Basingstoke: Palgrave Macmillan, 2003)

Johnson, Samuel, *The Plan of a Dictionary of the English Language* (London: Knapton, 1747)

Jones, Dorothy, 'Fabricating Texts of Empire', *Kunapipi*, 16 (1994), 1–16

Jones, Edwin, *The English Nation: The Great Myth*, 2nd edn (Stroud: Sutton, 2000)

Jump, John D., ed., *Tennyson: The Critical Heritage* (London: Routledge & Kegan Paul, 1967)

Kiernan, V.G., 'Tennyson, King Arthur and Imperialism', in *Poets, Politics and the People*, ed. Harvey J. Kaye (London: Verso, 1989), pp. 129–51

[Kingsley, Charles], 'Tennyson', *Fraser's Magazine*, 42 (1850), 245–55

Kingsley, Charles, *David: Four Sermons* (Cambridge: Macmillan, 1865)

Knight, Stephen, *Arthurian Literature and Society*, 2nd edn (Basingstoke: Macmillan – now Palgrave Macmillan, 1985)

Knowles, James, 'Aspects of Tennyson: A Personal Reminiscence', *Nineteenth Century*, 33 (1893), 164–88

Knox, Robert, *The Races of Men: A Philosophical Enquiry into the Influence of Race over the Destinies of Nations*, 2nd edn (London: Renshaw, 1862)

Kolb, Jack, ed., *The Letters of Arthur Henry Hallam* (Columbus: Ohio State University Press, 1981)

Kuhn, William M., *Henry & Mary Ponsonby: Life at the Court of Queen Victoria*, 2nd edn (London: Duckbacks, 2003)

Kumar, Krishan, *The Making of English National Identity* (Cambridge: Cambridge University Press, 2003)

Lacy, Norris J., ed., *A History of Arthurian Scholarship* (Cambridge: Brewer, 2006)

Landon, Letitia, *Flowers of Loveliness: Twelve Groups of Female Figures, Emblematic of Flowers* (London: Ackermann, 1836)

Lang, Cecil Y. and Edgar F. Shannon, Jr, eds, *The Letters of Alfred Lord Tennyson*, 3 vols (Oxford: Clarendon Press, 1982–90)

Langford, Paul, *Englishness Identified: Manners and Character 1650–1850* (Oxford: Oxford University Press, 2000)

Langland, Elizabeth, 'Nation and Nationality: Queen Victoria in the Developing Narrative of Englishness', in *Remaking Queen Victoria*, ed. Margaret Homans and Adrienne Munich (Cambridge: Cambridge University Press, 1997), pp. 13–32

Ledbetter, Kathryn, *Tennyson and Victorian Periodicals: Commodities in Context* (Aldershot: Ashgate, 2007)

Levi, Peter, *Tennyson* (Basingstoke: Macmillan – now Palgrave Macmillan, 1993)

Lilly, W.S., 'British Monarchy and Modern Democracy', *Nineteenth Century*, 41 (1897), 853–64

Linley, Margaret, 'Sexuality and Nationality in Tennyson's "Idylls of the King"', *Victorian Poetry*, 30 (1992), 365–86

Linley, Margaret, 'Nationhood and Empire', in *A Companion to Victorian Poetry*, ed. R. Cronin, A. Chapman and A. Harrison (Malden, MA: Blackwell, 2002), pp. 421–37

Longford, Elizabeth, *Victoria R.I.*, 2nd edn (London: Weidenfeld & Nicolson, 1987)

Lootens, Tricia, 'Victorian Poetry and Patriotism', in *The Cambridge Companion to Victorian Poetry*, ed. Joseph Bristow (Cambridge: Cambridge University Press, 2000), pp. 255–79

Lorimer, Douglas A., 'Race, Science and Culture: Historical Continuities and Discontinuities, 1850–1914', in *The Victorians and Race*, ed. Shearer West (Aldershot: Scolar, 1997), pp. 12–33

Lovelace, J. Timothy, *The Artistry and Tradition of Tennyson's Battle Poetry* (New York: Routledge, 2003)

Lowenthal, David, 'The Island Garden: English Landscape and British Identity', in *History, Nationhood and the Question of Britain*, ed. Helen Brocklehurst and Robert Phillips (Basingstoke: Palgrave Macmillan, 2004), pp. 137–50

Lucas, John, 'Love of England: The Victorians and Patriotism', *Browning Society Notes*, 17 (1987–88), 63–76

Lucas, John, *England and Englishness: Ideas of Nationhood in English Poetry 1688–1900* (London: Hogarth, 1990)

Lucas, John, 'Voices of Authority, Voices of Subversion: Poetry in the Late Nineteenth Century', in *The Cambridge Companion to Victorian Poetry*, ed. Joseph Bristow (Cambridge: Cambridge University Press, 2000), pp. 280–301

MacDonald, Robert H., *The Language of Empire: Myths and Metaphors of Popular Imperialism, 1880–1918* (Manchester: Manchester University Press, 1994)

MacDougall, Hugh A., *Racial Myth in English History: Trojans, Teutons, and Anglo-Saxons* (Montreal: Harvest House, 1982)

Macfie, Alexander Lyon, ed., *Orientalism: A Reader* (New York: New York University Press, 2000)

Machann, Clinton, 'Tennyson's King Arthur and the Violence of Manliness', *Victorian Poetry*, 38 (2000), 199–226

MacPhee, Graham and Prem Poddar, eds, *Empire and After: Englishness in Postcolonial Perspective* (New York: Berghahn, 2007)

Mallen, Richard D., 'The "Crowned Republic" of Tennyson's *Idylls of the King*', *Victorian Poetry*, 37 (1999), 275–89

Mancoff, Debra N., *The Arthurian Revival in Victorian Art* (New York: Garland, 1990)

Mancoff, Debra N., *The Arthurian Revival: Essays on Form, Tradition, and Transformation* (New York: Garland, 1992)

Mancoff, Debra N., *The Return of King Arthur: The Legend Through Victorian Eyes* (London: Pavilion, 1995)

Mancoff, Debra N., 'To Take Excalibur: King Arthur and the Construction of Victorian Manhood', in *King Arthur: A Casebook*, ed. Edward Donald Kennedy (New York: Garland, 1996), pp. 257–80

Mandler, Peter, '"In the Olden Time": Romantic History and English National Identity, 1820–50', in *A Union of Multiple Identities: The British Isles, c.1750–c.1850*, ed. Laurence Brockliss and David Eastwood (Manchester: Manchester University Press, 1997), pp. 78–92

Mandler, Peter, *The English National Character: The History of an Idea from Edmund Burke to Tony Blair* (London: Yale University Press, 2006)

Mangan, J.A. and James Walvin, eds, *Manliness and Morality: Middle-Class Masculinity in Britain and America, 1800–1940* (Manchester: Manchester University Press, 1987)

Marshall, Dorothy, *The Life and Times of Victoria*, 2nd edn (London: Weidenfeld and Nicolson, 1992)

Martin, Kingsley, *The Crown and the Establishment* (London: Hutchinson, 1962)

Martin, Robert Bernard, *Tennyson: The Unquiet Heart*, 2nd edn (London: Faber and Faber, 1983)

McBratney, John, 'Rebuilding Akbar's "Fane": Tennyson's Reclamation of the East', *Victorian Poetry*, 31 (1993), 411–17

McGann, Jerome J., ed., *Lord Byron: The Complete Poetical Works*, 7 vols (Oxford: Clarendon Press, 1980–93), I (1983)

McGann, Jerome J., *The Beauty of Inflections: Literary Investigations in Historical Method and Theory*, 2nd edn (Oxford: Clarendon Press, 2001)

Mermin, Dorothy, *Godiva's Ride: Women of Letters in England, 1830–1880* (Bloomington: Indiana University Press, 1993)

Merriam, Harold G., *Edward Moxon: Publisher of Poets* (New York: Columbia University Press, 1939)

Miller, Karl, 'Star of the Borders', *Guardian Review*, 9 August 2003, pp. 4–6

[Milnes, Richard Monckton], '*Timbuctoo*', *Athenaeum*, 22 July 1829, p. 456

[Milnes, Richard Monckton], '*Poems*', *Westminster Review*, 38 (1842), 371–90

Mingay, G.E., *Rural Life in Victorian England*, 2nd edn (London: Futura, 1979)

Mingay, G.E., *A Social History of the English Countryside* (London: Routledge, 1990)

Mitchell, Charles, *The Newspaper Press Directory* (London, 1846)

Morgan, Thaïs E., 'The Poetry of Victorian Masculinities', in *The Cambridge Companion to Victorian Poetry*, ed. Joseph Bristow (Cambridge: Cambridge University Press, 2000), pp. 203–27

Moore, Dafydd, 'Tennyson, Malory and the Ossianic Mode: *The Poems of Ossian* and "The Death of Arthur"', *Review of English Studies*, 57 (2006), 374–91

Morrow, John, ed., *Young England: The New Generation* (London: Leicester University Press, 1999)

Morse, David, *High Victorian Culture* (Basingstoke: Macmillan – now Palgrave Macmillan, 1993)

Motter, T.H. Vail, ed., *The Writings of Arthur Hallam* (New York: Modern Language Association of America, 1943)

Mugglestone, Lynda, 'The Rise of Received Pronunciation', in *A Companion to The History of the English Language*, ed. Haruko Momma and Michael Matto (Malden, MA: Blackwell, 2008), pp. 243–50

Nash, David and Antony Taylor, eds, *Republicanism in Victorian Society* (Stroud: Sutton, 2000)

Newman, J.H., *The Idea of a University, Defined and Illustrated.*, ed. I.T. Ker (Oxford: Clarendon Press, 1976)

Newsome, David, *The Victorian World Picture* (London: Fontana, 1998)

Nicolson, Harold, *Tennyson: Aspects of his Life, Character and Poetry* (London: Constable, 1923)

Nünning, Ansgar, 'On the Discursive Construction of an Empire of the Mind: Metaphorical Re-Membering as a Means of Narrativizing and Naturalizing Cultural Transformations', *Yearbook of Research in English and American Literature*, 20 (2004), 59–93

O'Brien, Lynne B., 'Male Heroism: Tennyson's Divided View', *Victorian Poetry*, 32 (1994), 171–82

O'Donnell, Angela G., 'Tennyson's "English Idyls": Studies in Poetic Decorum', *Studies in Philology*, 85 (1988), 125–44

Ormond, Leonée, 'Tennyson and Pastoral: Love in a Landscape', *Browning Society Notes*, 15–17 (1985–88), 24–31

Ormond, Leonée, 'Victorian Romance: Tennyson', in *A Companion to Romance: From Classical to Contemporary*, ed. Corinne Saunders (Malden, MA: Blackwell, 2004), pp. 321–40

Orwell, George, *The Lion and the Unicorn: Socialism and the English Genius* (London: Secker & Warburg, 1941)

Orwell, George, *The English People* (London: Collins, 1947)

Osborne, Hugh, 'Hooked on Classics: Discourses of Allusion in the Mid-Victorian Novel', in *Translation and Nation: Towards a Cultural Politics of Englishness*, ed. Roger Ellis and Liz Oakley-Brown (Clevedon: Multilingual Matters, 2001), pp. 120–66

'Our Principles', *Englishman's Magazine*, 1 (1831), 1–4

'Our Weekly Gossip on Literature and Art', *Athenaeum*, 13 April 1833, p. 234

Oxford English Dictionary Online, http://dictionary.oed.com

Paden, W.D., *Tennyson in Egypt: A Study of the Imagery in his Earlier Works* (Lawrence: University of Kansas Publications, 1942)

Padley, Jonathan, 'No Idyl(l) Matter: The Orthographic and Titular History of Alfred Tennyson's *English Idyls*', *Tennyson Research Bulletin*, 9 (2007), 97–110

Page, Frederick, ed., *Byron: Poetical Works* (London: Oxford University Press, 1970)

Palgrave, Francis Turner, ed., *The Golden Treasury*, 5th edn (London: Oxford University Press, 1964)

Parrinder, Patrick, 'Character, Identity, and Nationality in the English Novel', in *Landscape and Englishness*, ed. Robert Burden and Stephan Kohl (Amsterdam: Rodopi, 2006), pp. 89–102

Pattison, Robert, *Tennyson and Tradition* (Cambridge, MA: Harvard University Press, 1979)

Paxman, Jeremy, *Empire: What Ruling the World Did to the British* (London: Viking, 2011)

'Peace and War: A Dialogue', *Blackwood's Edinburgh Magazine*, 76 (1854), 589–99

Peltason, Timothy, 'Learning How to See: *The Holy Grail*', *Victorian Poetry*, 30 (1992), 463–81

Perry, Seamus, *Alfred Tennyson* (Tavistock: Northcote House, 2005)

Phillips, Catherine, '"Charades from the Middle Ages"? Tennyson's *Idylls of the King* and the Chivalric Code', *Victorian Poetry*, 40 (2002), 241–53

Phillips, Jerry, 'Educating the Savages: Melville, Bloom, and the Rhetoric of Imperialist Instruction', in *Recasting the World: Writing After Colonialism*, ed. Jonathan White (Baltimore, MA: Johns Hopkins University Press, 1993), pp. 25–44

Pinion, F.B., *A Tennyson Chronology* (Basingstoke: Macmillan – now Palgrave Macmillan, 1990)

Plasa, Carl, '"Cracked from Side to Side": Sexual Politics in "The Lady of Shalott"', *Victorian Poetry*, 30 (1992), 247–63

Plowden, Alison, *The Young Victoria* (Stroud: Sutton, 2000)

Plunkett, John, *Queen Victoria: First Media Monarch* (Oxford: Oxford University Press, 2003)

Poon, Angelia, *Enacting Englishness in the Victorian Period: Colonialism and the Politics of Performance* (Aldershot: Ashgate, 2008)

Porter, Andrew, ed., *The Nineteenth Century*, The Oxford History of the British Empire, III (Oxford: Oxford University Press, 1999)

Porter, Bernard, *The Absent-Minded Imperialists: Empire, Society, and Culture in Britain* (Oxford: Oxford University Press, 2004)

Potter, Simon, J., ed., *Newspapers and Empire in Ireland and Britain: Reporting the British Empire, c.1857–1921* (Dublin: Four Courts Press, 2004)

Powell, David, *Nationhood and Identity: The British State since 1800* (London: Tauris, 2002)

Pratt, Mary Louise, *Imperial Eyes: Travel Writing and Transculturation*, 2nd edn (New York: Routledge, 2008)

Prince, Hugh, 'Victorian Rural Landscapes' in *The Victorian Countryside*, ed. G.E. Mingay, 2 vols (London: Routledge & Kegan Paul, 1981), pp. 17–29

Prochaska, Frank, *The Republic of Britain 1760–2000* (London: Allen Lane, 2000)

Psomiades, Kathy Alexis, '"The Lady of Shalott" and the Critical Fortunes of Victorian Poetry', in *The Cambridge Companion to Victorian Poetry*, ed. Joseph Bristow (Cambridge: Cambridge University Press, 2000), pp. 25–45

Randall, Don, 'Autumn 1857: The Making of the Indian "Mutiny"', *Victorian Literature and Culture*, 31 (2003), 3–17

Rappaport, Helen, *Magnificent Obsession: Victoria, Albert and the Death that Changed the Monarchy*, 2nd edn (Bath: Windsor-Paragon, 2012)

Raymond, J., ed., *Queen Victoria's Early Letters* (London: Batsford, 1963)

Reynolds, Matthew, *The Realms of Verse 1830–1870: English Poetry in a Time of Nation-Building* (Oxford: Oxford University Press, 2001)

Rich, Paul, 'The Quest for Englishness', in *Victorian Values: Personalities and Perspectives in Nineteenth-Century Society*, ed. Gordon Marsden, 2nd edn (London: Longman, 1998), pp. 255–69

Richards, Bernard, ed., *English Verse 1830–1890*, 5th edn (London: Longman, 1994)

Ricks, Christopher, 'Two Early Poems by Tennyson', *Victorian Poetry*, 3 (1965), 55–7

Ricks, Christopher, 'The Princess and the Queen', *Victorian Poetry*, 25 (1987), 133–9

Ricks, Christopher, ed., *The Poems of Tennyson*, 2nd edn, 3 vols (London: Longman, 1987)

Ricks, Christopher, *Tennyson*, 2nd edn (Basingstoke: Macmillan – now Palgrave Macmillan, 1989)

Ricks, Christopher, ed., *Tennyson: A Selected Edition*, 2nd edn (London: Longman, 1989)

Riede, David G., 'Tennyson's Poetics of Melancholy and the Imperial Imagination', *Studies in English Literature*, 20 (2000), 659–78

Robberds, J.W., ed., *A Memoir of the Life and Writings of the late William Taylor of Norwich*, 2 vols (London: Murray, 1843)

Robson, John M., ed., *John Stuart Mill: An Autobiography* (London: Penguin, 1989)

Robson, W.W., 'Tennyson and Victorian Balladry', in *Tennyson: Seven Essays*, ed. Philip Collins (Basingstoke: Macmillan – now Palgrave Macmillan, 1992), pp. 160–82

Rosenberg, John D., 'Tennyson and the Landscape of Consciousness', *Victorian Poetry*, 12 (1974), 303–10

Rosenberg, John D., 'Tennyson and the Passing of Arthur', in *The Passing of Arthur: New Essays in Arthurian Tradition*, ed. Christopher Baswell and William Sharpe (New York: Garland, 1988), pp. 221–34

Rowlinson, Matthew, 'The Ideological Moment of Tennyson's "Ulysses"', in *Tennyson*, ed. Rebecca Stott (Harlow: Longman, 1996), pp. 148–60

Royle, Edward, *Chartism* (London: Longman, 1980)

Ruskin, John, *Sesame and Lilies*, ed. Deborah Epstein Nord (New Haven, CT: Yale University Press, 2002)

Ryals, Clyde de L., '*Idylls of the King*: "Margins Scribbled, Crost, and Crammed with Comment"', *Tennyson Research Bulletin*, 5 (1989), 101–8

Said, Edward W., *Orientalism: Western Conceptions of the Orient*, 4th edn (London: Penguin, 1995)

Saunders, Clare Broome, *Women Writers and Nineteenth-Century Medievalism* (New York: Palgrave Macmillan, 2009)

Schur, Owen, *Victorian Pastoral: Tennyson, Hardy, and the Subversion of Forms* (Columbus: Ohio State University Press, 1989)

Scott, J.W. Robertson, *The Life and Death of a Newspaper* (London: Methuen, 1952)

Scruton, Roger, *England: An Elegy*, 2nd edn (London: Pimlico, 2001)

Seeley, J.R., *The Expansion of England: Two Courses of Lectures* (London: Macmillan, 1883)

[Senior, Nassau], 'France, America, and Britain', *Edinburgh Review*, 75 (1842), 1–48

Shannon, Edgar F., Jr, *Tennyson and the Reviewers* (Cambridge, MA: Harvard University Press, 1952)

Shannon, Edgar F., Jr, 'The History of a Poem: Tennyson's *Ode on the Death of the Duke of Wellington*', *Studies in Bibliography*, 13 (1960), 149–77

Shannon, Edgar F., Jr, 'Poetry as Vision: Sight and Insight in "The Lady of Shalott"', *Victorian Poetry*, 19 (1981), 207–23

Shannon, Edgar F., Jr and Christopher Ricks, 'A Further History of Tennyson's *Ode on the Death of the Duke of Wellington*', *Studies in Bibliography*, 32 (1979), 125–57

Shannon, Edgar, F., Jr and Christopher Ricks, '"The Charge of the Light Brigade": The Creation of a Poem', *Studies in Bibliography*, 38 (1985), 1–44

Shatto, Susan, 'The Strange Charm of "Far, Far Away": Tennyson, the Continent, and the Empire', in *Creditable Warriors: 1830–1876*, ed. Michael Cotsell, English Literature and the Wider World, III (London: Ashfield, 1990), pp. 113–29

Shaw, Marion, 'Tennyson and his Public 1827–1859', in *Writers and their Background: Tennyson*, ed. D.J. Palmer (London: Bell, 1973), pp. 52–88

Shaw, Marion, *Alfred Lord Tennyson* (London: Harvester Wheatsheaf, 1988)

Shaw, Marion, 'The Contours of Manliness and the Nature of Woman', in *Critical Essays on Alfred Lord Tennyson*, ed. Herbert F. Tucker (New York: Hall, 1993), pp. 219–33

Shaw, Marion, 'Tennyson's Dark Continent', *Victorian Poetry*, 32 (1994), 157–69

Sheridan, Thomas, *A General Dictionary of the English Language* (London: Dodsley, 1780)

Shires, Linda M., 'Patriarchy, Dead Men, and Tennyson's *Idylls of the King*', *Victorian Poetry*, 30 (1992), 401–19

Simmons, Clare A., *Reversing the Conquest: History and Myth in Nineteenth-Century British Literature* (New Brunswick, NJ: Rutgers University Press, 1990)

Simmons, Clare A., ed., *Medievalism and the Quest for the 'Real' Middle Ages* (London: Frank Cass, 2001)

Simpson, Roger, 'Costello's "The Funeral Boat": An Analogue of Tennyson's "The Lady of Shalott"', *Tennyson Research Bulletin*, 4 (1984), 129–31

Simpson, Roger, *Camelot Regained: The Arthurian Revival and Tennyson 1800–1849* (Cambridge: Brewer, 1990)

Sinfield, Alan, *Alfred Tennyson* (Oxford: Blackwell, 1986)

Sinnema, Peter, *The Wake of Wellington: Englishness in 1852* (Athens: Ohio University Press, 2006)

Smiles, Samuel, *Self-Help: With Illustrations of Conduct and Perseverance*, 7th edn (London: Murray, 1950)

Sparer, J. Douglas, 'Arthur's Vast Design', *Victorian Poetry*, 21 (1983), 119–31

[Spedding, James], *'Poems'*, *Edinburgh Review*, 77 (1843), 373–91

[Spedding, James], 'The Future of the British Empire', *Westminster Review*, 38 (1870), 47–74

Staines, David, *Tennyson's Camelot: The Idylls of the King and its Medieval Sources* (Waterloo, Ontario: Wilfrid Laurier University Press, 1982)

Stedman, E.C., ed., *A Victorian Anthology, 1837–1895* (Boston: Houghton, Mifflin, 1896)

Stepan, Nancy, *The Idea of Race in Science: Great Britain 1800–1960* (London: Macmillan, 1982)

[Sterling, John], *'Poems'*, *Quarterly Review*, 70 (1842), 385–416

Stevens, Paul and Rahul Sapra, 'Akbar's Dream: Moghul Toleration and English/ British Orientalism', *Modern Philology*, 104 (2007), 379–411

Strachey, Lytton, *Queen Victoria*, 6th edn (London: Chatto & Windus, 1922)

Strong, Roy, *Visions of England* (London: Bodley Head, 2011)

Sylvia, Richard A., 'Sexual Politics and Narrative Method in Tennyson's "Guinevere"', *Victorian Newsletter*, 76 (1989), 23–8

Sylvia, Richard A., 'Reading Tennyson's *Ballads and Other Poems* in Context', *Journal of the Midwest Modern Language Association*, 23 (1990), 27–44

Tanner, Duncan, Chris Williams, Wil Griffith and Andrew Edwards, eds, *Debating Nationhood and Governance in Britain, 1885–1945: Perspectives from the 'Four Nations'* (Manchester: Manchester University Press, 2006)

Taylor, Antony, *'Down with the Crown': British Anti-Monarchism and Debates about Royalty since 1790* (London: Reaktion, 1999)

Taylor, Beverly and Elisabeth Brewer, *The Return of King Arthur: British and American Arthurian Literature since 1900* (Cambridge: Brewer, 1983)

Tennyson, Alfred, *Poems, Chiefly Lyrical* (London: Wilson, 1830)

Tennyson, Alfred, *Poems* (London: Moxon, 1832)

Tennyson, Alfred, *Poems*, 2 vols (London: Moxon, 1842)

Tennyson, Alfred, *Enid and Nimuë: The True and the False* (London: Moxon, 1857)

Tennyson, Alfred, *Idylls of the King* (London: Moxon, 1859)

Tennyson, Alfred, *Idylls of the King* (London: Strahan, 1869)

Tennyson, Alfred, *The Holy Grail and Other Poems* (London: Strahan, 1870)

Tennyson, Alfred, *Tiresias and Other Poems* (London: Macmillan, 1885)

Tennyson, Alfred, *Idylls of the King*, ed. J.M. Gray, 2nd edn (London: Penguin, 1996)

Tennyson, Alfred and Charles Tennyson, *Poems by Two Brothers* (London: Simpkin and Marshall, 1827)

Tennyson, Charles, *Alfred Tennyson* (London: Macmillan, 1949)

Tennyson, Hallam, ed., *Poems by Two Brothers* (London: Macmillan, 1893)

Tennyson, Hallam, *Alfred Lord Tennyson: A Memoir, By His Son*, 2 vols (London: Macmillan, 1897)

Tennyson, Hallam, *Alfred Lord Tennyson: A Memoir, By His Son* (London: Macmillan, 1899)

Tennyson, Hallam, ed., *Poems, Annotated by Alfred, Lord Tennyson*, 9 vols (London: Macmillan, 1907)

Terhune, Alfred McKinley and Annabelle Burdick Terhune, eds, *The Letters of Edward FitzGerald: Volume 1 1830–1850*, 4 vols (Princeton, NJ: Princeton University Press, 1980)

'The Decencies', *New Monthly Magazine and Humorist*, 53 (1838), 118–24

The National Archives Currency Converter, http://www.nationalarchives.gov.uk/currency

The Poetical Works of Elizabeth Barrett Browning, The Oxford Edition (London: Frowde, 1910)

The Poetical Works of Robert Browning (London: Oxford University Press, 1940)

The Times Digital Archive, 1785–1985

Thomas, Cammy, 'The Two Arthurs', *Tennyson Research Bulletin*, 6 (1993), 99–111

Thomas, Julia, *Pictorial Victorians: The Inscription of Values in Word and Image* (Athens: Ohio University Press, 2004)

Thomson, David, *England in the Nineteenth Century, 1815–1914*, 3rd edn, The Pelican History of England, 8 (London: Penguin, 1991)

Thwaite, Ann, *Emily Tennyson: The Poet's Wife*, 2nd edn (London: Faber and Faber, 1997)

Tillotson, Kathleen, 'Tennyson's Serial Poem', in Geoffrey and Kathleen Tillotson, *Mid-Victorian Studies* (London: Athlone Press, 1965), pp. 80–109

Timko, Michael, '"The Central Wish": Human Passion and Cosmic Love in Tennyson's Idyls', *Victorian Poetry*, 16 (1978), 1–15

Tosh, John, *Manliness and Masculinities in Nineteenth-Century Britain: Essays on Gender, Family and Empire* (Harlow: Pearson, 2005)

Tosh, John, *A Man's Place: Masculinity and the Middle-Class Home in Victorian England*, 2nd edn (New Haven, CT: Yale University Press, 2007)

Trench, Richard Chenevix, *On the Study of Words*, 2nd edn (London: Parker, 1852)

Trench, Richard Chenevix, *English: Past and Present: Five Lectures* (London: Parker, 1855)

Tucker, Herbert F., *Tennyson and the Doom of Romanticism* (Cambridge, MA: Harvard University Press, 1988)

Tucker, Herbert F., *Epic: Britain's Heroic Muse 1790–1910* (Oxford: Oxford University Press, 2008)

Turner, Paul, *Tennyson* (London: Routledge & Kegan Paul, 1976)

Ulloa, Antonio de, *Voyage to South America*, 2 vols (London, 1772)

Unsigned review, '*Poems by Two Brothers*', *Literary Chronicle and Weekly Review*, 19 May 1827, p. 308

Unsigned review, '*Poems by Two Brothers*', *Gentleman's Magazine and Historical Chronicle*, 97 (1827), p. 609

Unsigned review, '*Poems, Chiefly Lyrical*', *Atlas*, 27 June 1830, p. 411

Unsigned review, '*Journal d'un voyage à Temboctou et à Jenné, dans l'Afrique Centrale, &c., 1824–1828*', *Quarterly Review*, 42 (1830), 450–75

Unsigned review, '*Poems*', *Athenaeum*, 1 December 1832, pp. 770–2

Unsigned review, 'The Grosvenor Exhibition (Third Notice)', *Athenaeum*, 19 January 1884, p. 93

Vallone, Lynne, *Becoming Victoria* (New Haven, CT: Yale University Press, 2001)

Vance, Norman, *The Sinews of the Spirit: The Ideal of Christian Manliness in Victorian Literature and Religious Thought* (Cambridge: Cambridge University Press, 1985)

Varouxakis, Georgios, *Victorian Political Thought on France and the French* (Basingstoke: Palgrave Macmillan, 2002)

Viswanathan, Gauri, 'Currying Favor: The Politics of British Educational and Cultural Policy in India, 1813–54', in *Dangerous Liaisons: Gender, Nation, and Postcolonial Perspectives*, ed. Anne McClintock, Aamir Mufti and Ella Shohat (Minneapolis: University of Minnesota Press, 1997), pp. 113–29

Walker, John, *Critical Pronouncing Dictionary and Expositor of the English Language* (London: Robinson, 1791)

Waller, John O., *A Circle of Friends: The Tennysons and the Lushingtons of Park House* (Columbus: Ohio State University Press, 1986)

Wardroper, John, *Kings, Lords and Wicked Levellers: Satire and Protest 1760–1837* (London: Murray, 1973)

Washbrook, D.A., 'India, 1818–1860: The Two Faces of Colonialism', in *The Nineteenth Century*, ed. Andrew Porter, The Oxford History of the British Empire, III (Oxford: Oxford University Press, 1999), pp. 395–421

Watts, Bob, '"Slow Prudence": Tennyson's Taming of the Working Class', *Victorian Poetry*, 37 (1999), 493–505

Whyte, Frederic, *The Life of W.T. Stead*, 2 vols (London: Cape, 1925)

Williams, Raymond, *The Country and the City* (London: Hogarth, 1985)

Williams, Richard, *The Contentious Crown: Public Discussion of the British Monarchy in the Reign of Queen Victoria* (Aldershot: Ashgate, 1997)

Wilson, Effingham, 'The Moral and Political Evils of the Taxes on Knowledge', *Westminster Review*, 15 (1831), 238–67

[Wilson, John], 'Tennyson's Poems', *Blackwood's Edinburgh Magazine*, 31 (1832), 721–41

Wilson, Kathleen, ed., *A New Imperial History: Culture, Identity, and Modernity in Britain and the Empire, 1660–1840* (Cambridge: Cambridge University Press, 2004)

Wolffe, John, *Great Deaths: Grieving, Religion, and Nationhood in Victorian and Edwardian Britain* (Oxford: Oxford University Press, 2000)

Wolfson, Susan J., ed., *Felicia Hemans: Selected Poems, Letters, Reception Materials* (Princeton, NJ: Princeton University Press, 2000)

Wolseley, G.I., 'England as a Military Power in 1854 and in 1878', *Nineteenth Century*, 13 (1878), 433–56

Younge, Gary, *Who Are We – and Should it Matter in the 21st Century?* (London: Viking, 2010)

Zeepvat, Charlotte, *Queen Victoria's Family* (Stroud: Sutton, 2001)

Index

Monthly Repository, 39–40, 41, 42
Moore, Dafydd, 116
Moore, Thomas, 11, 13
More, Sir Thomas, 64
Morgan, Thaïs E., 70
Morning Post, 69
Morris, William, 52, 104, 105
Morrow, John, 194, 197
Motherwell, William, 41
Moultrie, John, 120
Moxon, Edward, 22, 30–1, 38, 42, 43, 48, 49, 50, 121, 184, 187
Murray, John, 41

Nash, David, 76
Newman, John Henry, 123
New Monthly Magazine and Humorist, 3, 4, 22, 36, 37, 42
Newsome, David, 104, 111, 192
Nichols, John, 180
Nicolson, Harold, 43
Nineteenth Century, 96, 128, 159
Noctes Ambrosianae, 25, 27, 183
'North, Christopher', *see* Wilson, John
Northampton, Lord, 144, 201
Nünning, Ansgar, 149, 200

O'Brien, Lynne, 139, 154, 173
O'Donnell, Angela, 56
Ormond, Leonée, 53, 108
Orwell, George, 5

Padley, Jonathan, 189
Palgrave, Francis, 137, 152
Pall Mall Gazette, 169
Palmerston, Lord, 75
Parry, Hubert, 96
Patmore, Coventry, 37, 59, 109, 149, 185
Pattison, Robert, 55–6, 58, 66
Paxman, Jeremy, 2
Peacock, Thomas Love, 15
Peel, Sir Robert, 191
Percy, Thomas, 64–5
Perrault, Charles, 53
Perry, Seamus, 155
Plasa, Carl, 108, 109
Plunkett, John, 78, 85–6
Porter, Andrew, 138

Pratt, Mary Louise, 16–17, 138–9, 141
Prichard, James Cowles, 157
Prince of Wales (Edward VII), 90, 94, 96, 98, 167, 193
Prochaska, Frank, 76, 86–7, 88
Prolusiones Academicae, 14, 181
Psomiades, Kathy Alexis, 110

Quarterly Review, 19, 41–3, 44, 51, 70, 120
Quincey, Thomas de, 33–4

Randall, Don, 138, 158–9, 199
Rappaport, Helen, 193
Rendall, Jane, 179
Reynolds, Matthew, 37
Reynold's Newspaper, 98
Richards, Bernard, 15
Ricks, Christopher, 53, 80, 84, 123, 186, 198
Riede, David G., 140, 141–2, 155
Rintoul, Robert Stephen, 19
Robson, W.W., 64–5, 183
Rogers, Samuel, 43
Rossetti, Christina, 162
Rowlinson, Matthew, 152, 202
Ruskin, John, 27, 53, 62, 104, 123, 175

Said, Edward, 140, 141, 142, 149
Sapra, Rahul, 171
Saunders, Clare Broome, 104, 134, 194
Scott, Sir Walter, 104, 108, 183, 195
Seeley, J.R., 166
Sellwood, Emily, *see* Tennyson, Emily
Senior, Nassau, 4
Seymour, Lord George, 3
Shah, Tahir, 182
Shakespeare, William, 23, 24, 25, 33, 54, 60, 66, 109, 150, 189
Shannon, Edgar F., 50, 109–10, 123, 152, 181, 187, 198
Shatto, Susan, 143, 154
Shaw, Marion, 122, 139, 182
Shelley, Percy Bysshe, 15, 20, 23, 36, 37–8, 41–2, 50, 69, 78, 110, 178
Sheridan, Thomas, 32
Simmons, Clare A., 104–5, 106, 194
Simpkin and Marshall, 9, 10